PROTEST AND CHANGE

PROTEST AND CHANGE
studies in social movements

T.K. OOMMEN

SAGE Publications
New Delhi/Newbury Park/London

Copyright © T.K. Oommen, 1990

First published in 1990 by

Sage Publications India Pvt Ltd
32, M-Block Market, Greater Kailash I
New Delhi 110 048

Sage Publications Inc **Sage Publications Ltd**
· 2111 West Hillcrest Drive 28 Banner Street
Newbury Park, California 91320 London EC1Y 8QE

Published by Tejeshwar Singh for Sage Publications India Pvt Ltd,
phototypeset by Jayigee Enterprises, Madras, and printed by
Chaman Offset Printers, Delhi.

ISBN 81-7036-198-2 (India)
0-8039-9652-7 (US)

To the students of Jawaharlal Nehru University,
who constantly remind me of the potentiality
of protest as an instrument
of change

Contents

Acknowledgements

Of the 10 chapters in the book, six were published between 1977 and 1987, although not exactly in the same form. Two chapters will be published elsewhere in the course of 1990 and three are being published for the first time in this volume.

Chapter 1 was published under the title 'Sociological Issues in the Analysis of Social Movements in Independent India' in *Sociological Bulletin*, vol. 26, no. 1, 1977, pp. 14-37. Chapter 2 was published with the title 'Social Movements' in *Survey of Research in Sociology and Social Anthropology*, vol. II, Indian Council of Social Science Research, 1985 pp. 81-149. Chapter 3 is an amalgam and a condensed version of two papers: 'Theoretical Framework and Empirical Research: Their Interactions in the Analysis of Two Social Movements' (*Sociological Bulletin*, vol. 36, no. 2, pp. 15-34) and 'On the Craft of Studying Social Movements: Two Illustrations' (*The Eastern Anthropologist*, vol. 40, no. 3, 1987, pp. 185-202).

Chapter 5 appeared in *Journal of Social and Economic Studies* (new series), vol. 3, no. 2, 1986, pp. 107-29; Chapter 8 in K.L. Sharma (ed.), *Social Stratification in India*, Manohar, 1986, pp. 161-90; and Chapter 9 in *Contributions to Indian Sociology* (new series), vol. 18, no. 1, 1984, pp. 45-61, with the same titles.

Chapters 4 and 6 will subsequently be published in, respectively, *International Sociology*, vol. 5, no. 2, 1990, and the Professor M.N. Srinivas Felicitation volume edited by A.M. Shah and B.S. Baviskar. I thank all the editors and publishers of the above journals and books for permitting me to use the papers for publication in this volume.

The Introduction, and Chapters 7 and 10 are being published here for the first time; while the Introduction has been written specially for this volume to highlight the interlinkages between the different chapters. Chapter 7 is the revised version of a paper presented at a seminar on Communication and Nation-building organized by Professor M.C. Sekhar of the Indian Institute of Mass Communication (New Delhi) in 1986. Chapter 10 grew out of a paper presented to the second India-Canadian Symposium on Institution, Communication and Social Interaction in 1988 in Mysore. I am thankful to the organizers of these seminars for giving me the opportunity to write and present these papers.

I am grateful to Dr. P.K. Jayaswal for preparing the index of the book, and to Dr. Lalita Chandrasekaran for reading the proofs.

T.K. OOMMEN

1 March 1990
New Delhi

Introduction

That social change is a ubiquitous phenomenon, and a static society is a conceptual nullity and an empirical impossibility are commonplace in contemporary social science. But the relative importance of the sources and direction of change are highly contentious matters. Even a cursory acquaintance with the sources of change clearly unfolds that at least until recently, the basic source of change has been taken to be the economy, irrespective of the variations in ideological orientations. Thus, the agrarian, industrial or information 'revolutions' were taken to be watersheds in human history. In contrast, the importance accorded to political revolutions is relatively less, although, of course, it has been increasingly recognized latterly. I suggest that this differential apperception is largely a matter of values, in that the quality of change brought about through these two types of revolutions are drastically different.

The general assumption in the case of changes brought about through economic revolutions has been that they result in the betterment of society in general. For example, it is argued that even as disparity between classes or categories increased because of capitalist development, the absolute position of the poor has improved. At any rate, the fact that pauperization and immiserization of a section of the population does take place even as economic growth proceeds at a rapid pace has convinced hardly a few so as to cry a halt to the on-going process of growth. Even though Mohandas Karamchand Gandhi did it, the idea scarcely caught on. The advocacy of limits of growth largely arose out of the realization that there are serious constraints put on growth due to the fast depleting natural resources. To put it pithily, the consensus is that economic development should go on and it would bring about desirable social changes.

As against the 'spread effect' of economic development, that of political revolution is one of 'displacement syndrome'. That is, all political revolutions, rebellions and revolts, by definition, imply the transfer of power from one category to another. Understandably, those who are likely to be deprived of power in the process would cognize these collective actions as undesirable. To complicate matters, the ruling elite would invariably project itself as *the* legitimate holder of power, although the sources of legitimacy may vary—divine or secular. And, there is a persistent tendency at least among a section of the population to support those who hold power. Therefore, any effort to question those who hold power, that is, to protest, is viewed with suspicion and disdain. As a result of this general disapproval of protest as a mechanism of change, the analysis of protest as a social phenomenon and its potentiality as a factor of change have been neglected. The present volume, by focusing on protest and change, hopes to correct this erroneous evaluation of protest, even if to a limited extent.

Traditions of the generation of knowledge are not only constricted by our cognition about values but also by the trajectory of disciplinary growth. While history and political science have for long been engaged in the study of organized protests and collective actions, that is, social movements and revolutions, sociology and social anthropology are relatively recent entrants to this terrain. Again, traditionally, social anthropology studied 'pre-modern' societies, and the types of protest analyzed were distinct, being variously described as millenarian, chiliastic or messianic movements. The sociologist who started studying movements invariably followed the familiar footsteps of historians, thereby ending up by studying terminated movements, resorting to post-factum analysis, based on records. This, in turn, meant that the tradition of studying movements is particularly weak in pre-modern societies and those in which the written tradition has emerged recently. Understandably, movement studies are recent in India in general and in Indian sociology and social anthropology in particular. The present volume should therefore be viewed against this background; it attempts to address itself to a relatively new and unchartered area.

When movement studies broke upon the Indian social science scene, they did so with force for two reasons. First, being virgin terrain, a large number of scholars were eager to sieze it; by the mid-1970s, social movements became a fashionable area of research (see Chapter 2). Second, movement studies gained currency in India in the context of the massive, long and protracted anti-colonial struggle. Understandably, an overwhelming majority of movement studies are but analyses of the anti-imperialist struggle and the mobilizations associated with it. Records relating to such movements invariably relate to the articulations and activities of the movement elite and its opponents. This necessarily meant that ordinary participants' perspectives on movements are not adequately reflected in them. To overcome this lacuna, 'oral history' and bottom-up perspective have been resorted to latterly in movement studies. In the bargain, what we get are two warring factions of scholars who articulate contradictory perspectives and champion mutually exclusive historiographies. They tend to present facts and ideas from two different perspectives. What are inclusive and complementary orientations are often transformed into exclusive and contradictory ones; the part is often conjured up as the whole. But students of on-going movements, as against terminated ones, have an advantage in that they can capture both the micro- and macro-dimensions, the view from above as well as the perspective from below, thereby capturing a relatively total picture. This book, largely although not exclusively, focuses on social movements in independent India, that is, on-going movements. Chapter 1 provides the poser in this context.

The ten chapters in the book, even as they discuss the same theme, protest and change, are grouped into three parts. Part 1, consisting of four essays, deals with theoretical, conceptual and methodological issues. Chapter 1 identifies the issues involved in the study of social movements in independent India. If one views collective actions as a mechanism which men create to move from the periphery of the system to its centre, one is not necessarily dismayed by the fact that a variety of movements emerge and survive in independent India. This is so because the very definition of the centre and the journey towards it are conditioned by the historicity of context. The central concern of the overarching anti-colonial struggle was to shake off subjecthood and to create an independent nation-state, to create a new centre. But in independent India wherein universal adult franchise is granted to all citizens, the concerns are radically different. The new question which is posed is: Why is it that some of the collectivities are treated as second-class citizens while some others define themselves as the upholders of the 'nation'?

The point of theoretical interest is that a theory of social movement implies a theory of social structure; system characteristics of a society mould the goals and means of social movements in that society. But social movements necessarily imply the projection of a desirable set of values; it is a project addressed to the future. The rise and fall of social movements indicate that human beings cannot be permanently imprisoned in the present social structure and no eternal moratorium can be imposed on their creativity. Thus viewed, social movement, and protest, which is a manifestation of it, is an effort to redefine or recapture the past, to restructure the present and reorient the future.

The immediate historical background of independent India, marked by external colonialism, largely determined the nature of Indian social reality. The resultant nation-state is a multi-national and multi-cultural entity. The first decade of free India witnessed a multiplicity of 'national' movements against the threat of internal colonialism and the Indian state responded by reorganizing the administrative units of India on a linguistic basis by mid-1950s. Understandably, the initial attempt did not adequately attend to the aspirations of all, and protests, particularly of the subaltern nationalities, persisted and continue to this very day.

But deprivations are rooted in a wide variety of factors and state response varies in regard to each of them. Thus, the enunciation of the policy of protective discrimination was intended to squarely deal with those collectivities which had experienced cumulative deprivation for centuries. Notwithstanding this admirable measure, protests and mobilizations of these categories also continue today. The point to be noted here is that while India has its share of protests and mobilizations based on class and gender, they are not specific to India. And, protests based on gender and class do not always assume the expected saliency precisely because primordial identitites—linguistic, regional, caste, tribal—are strong, deep and persisting.

The above proposition is clearly upheld if one looks at the types of social movements prevailing in independent India. It is no accident then that the majority of movements were and are those relating to the interests of religious, caste, regional, tribal and agrarian categories as is evident from Chapter 2. In fact, protests by agrarian categories are substantial precisely because of the large congruence between caste and class. And, by and large, they are confined to specific regions and language areas. Given the multiple identity of the collectivities involved, most movements pursue a variety of goals simultaneously. Thus, the very labelling of a movement based on 'who' is involved is problematic. Not only because the collective actors have multiple identities but also because 'what is at stake' is of supreme importance. This brings one to the methodological issues in the study of on-going movements which figure in all the four chapters in Part 1, although Chapter 3 specifically deals with this theme.

Methodological issues are of two types. Those relating to the selection of one's research theme, the process of evolving one's conceptual-theoretical framework, the relationship between empirical research, concept formation and theory construction, the relationship between micro- and macro-dimensions, and, the processual linkage between different aspects such as leadership, ideology, and organization constitute one set. While Chapter 3 mainly focuses on these issues, Chapters 1 and 2 also discuss some of them. Thus, issues relating to the boundary demarcation of movements, the differing levels of involvement in movements by a wide variety of participants, the tendency to mistake the part (one event in the long chain of a movement) for the whole, the factors which determine the scale of a movement, etc., all of which pose genuine problems to the students of on-going movements, are identified and discussed.

An important methodological issue in social science research is the problem of value. The student of social movements faces several peculiar problems in this context. First, the very perception about a 'movement' may vary drastically across people and time. To recall a familiar example, what was the Sepoy Mutiny in colonial historiography became the First War of Independence in nationalist historiography. While the first defined it in terms of who was involved, the second defined it in terms of what was involved. But both mistook the part for the whole in that the events c 1857 constituted just one link in the long chain of the colonial struggle.

Second, the importance accorded to a movement may be based on the perceived direct threat it poses to the establishment. Thus, the violent Naxalite movement evinced much more interest among the intelligentsia than did the non-violent Bhoodan-Gramdan movement, although the agrarian poor perhaps benefited much more from the latter. Third, the researcher involved with movements faces the problem of ideology-linked insider-outsider identity which takes on peculiar characteristics often irrelevant in the context of other studies. Admittedly, the enterprise of movement research is much more vexatious.

What is referred to as methodology in the book has another dimension: the issues relate to selecting the unit of study, isolating the impact of the movement (on participants, on movement opponents, on society in general), the logistics of getting involved in the study (as movements trigger off without 'prior notice', may terminate after a short duration or persist for an inordinately long time), and the physical risks involved, particularly in studying an underground/violent movement.

Fourth, it is not easy to reconcile the information from the committed follower and the virulent critic of the movement. Finally, the position of the researcher who undertakes the study of on-going movements is not enviable. His attributes and identities are at once assets and liabilities, depending upon the context in which he operates.

One of the persistent theoretical issues relating to studies of movements is the presumed dichotomy between mobilization and institutionalization. The problem is posed in Chapter 1 and touched upon in Chapter 2, but Chapter 4 is exclusively devoted to its discussion. To begin with, it is important to remember that this dichotomy is very much a part of the presumed structural opposition between movements and institutions. There are two major sources of this confusion—theoretical and empirical. Theoretically, the dichotomy between movements and institutions is embedded in Western epistemological dualism and the displacement syndrome it entails. Empirically, it is the resultant of exclusive reliance on the extremely limited evidence drawn from capitalist democracies.

If one recognizes that there is a social state between the fluid state (movements) and solid state (institutions) and these are processually linked, one can steer clear of a lot of confusion. Second, it must be noted that movements are instruments to realize a future state, a vision, as noted earlier. And, the realization of the vision of a movement is possible through institutionalization of values, the vehicles of which are institutions. Instead of squarely recognizing this, institutions are invariably viewed as degenerate forms of movements. Third, change is generally viewed as the resultant of displacement, in Western conceptualization. But there is enormous evidence from India to suggest that change can be the resultant of gradual accretion. Thus, displacement and accretion may be viewed as two routes to social change, which can coexist. In the same vein, mobilization and institutionalization are two different dimensions of a movement and are not necessarily mutually exclusive. They do not displace one another but go hand in hand. Institutions are solidified forms of movements. Movements are de-frozen versions of institutions.

Given this perspective, it is necessary to understand the exact relationship between movements and institutions. Perhaps the best way to explicate this is to delineate the relationship between nation-state, the most encapsulating of all institutions, and movements. Chapter 5 deals with this theme. But nation-state is also the setting in which most institutions and movements operate in the contemporary world. How does the state as an institution respond to social movements which challenge its authority and question its legitimacy? Chapter 6 answers this question. Apart from these, another chapter in Part II is devoted to the discussion of patterns of communication with special reference to social movements.

I have noted in Chapter 1 that there is a persistent tendency to view movements as pathological aberrations and as anti-systemic enterprises. This view is held not only by particular brands of theorists but also by the political, economic and cultural mainstreams. Admittedly, the nature and quantum of threat posed by movements to each of these mainstreams would vary, although, of course, the mainstreams themselves may often overlap and coalesce. To the extent that there is absolute isomorphism between the three mainstreams—economic, political and cultural—challenges from movements may not arise, and even if they do, may not be effective. In a polity where there exists a disjuncture between the three mainstreams, there is a possiblity that a variety of movements would emerge. The Indian situation fits such a description.

The present concern being the threat posed to the Indian state by social movements, the political mainstream constituted by the Indian National Congress, the dominant political party and the economic mainstream composed of the all-India bourgeoisie are not significant collective actors. Political parties are contenders for power *within* the nation-states. Similarly, the nation-state provides a common market in which the national bourgeoisie compete. On the other hand, given the multi-cultural constituency of the Indian nation-state, one should expect that some of these elements would pose a threat. But whether or not a collectivity poses a threat to an institution would depend upon the nature of the adversary. In the case of multi-cultural nation-states only a primordial collectivity which hopes to establish its hegemonic rule or those primordial collectivities which intend to disengage themselves from the nation-state pose serious challenges. Other primordial collectivities may confront the state but only for their economic betterment, political autonomy or cultural identity *within* the existing framework of the nation-state. Under Indian conditions not only movements with a secessionist intent but also movements with an assimilationist thrust pose threats, given the stupendous cultural pluralism and commitment to preserve it.

I have indicated above that all movements do not pose threats to the Indian state. But to suggest that all such movements are legitimate is to ignore the injury that some movements are capable of inflicting on certain institutions, including the institution of the state. Similarly, to argue that all movements against the state are illegitimate enterprises is to attribute eternal legitimacy to the state as an institution. There are authoritarian and democratic states; but even the very labelling may not be consensual. Thus, opinion could be sharply divided about the legitimacy enjoyed by one-party systems. While those who support such a political arrangement may hail it as people's democracy, those who oppose it would invariably label it totalitarian. While multi-party democracy may be dismissed as bourgeois democracy by socialists, those who attest it would insist that it is the only authentic variety of democracy.

In spite of the above differences, it is safe to say that in some 'democracies' (one-party or multi-party) there is a greater amount of concentration of authority, while in others there is greater decentralization and devolution of power and authority. True, the instruments invoked for the dispersal of power, vertically and horizontally, may vary, but devolution of power itself would be a reality. Therefore, it is fairly safe to assume that those systems which permit decentralization of power would witness the emergence and crystallization of protests and movements. But should these protests exceed the permissible limits defined by the state, a crackdown may be safely predicted. The point I am making is this: depending upon the nature of the state and character of the movements, one can visualize different modes of response to social movements by the state. This is the central theme of chapter 6.

One may posit four conceptual possibilities in the context of state response to social movements: facilitation, toleration, discreditation and repression. I have argued that the emergence of socialist and welfare states necessitated the mobilization of huge chunks of population into collective actions, not simply to legitimize state initiated measures but also to institutionalize change. To the extent that there is congruence between the ideology of a state and that of a movement, and the means employed by the movement is legitimate, the state would facilitate the movement. On the other end of the continuum, a disjuncture in goals and means as pursued by the state and movement would lead to confrontation. The state may tolerate a movement with even a radical ideology if the means used are legitimate. On the other hand, the state may resort to discreditation of a movement if it takes to non-legitimate means. In sum, the most critical variable which moulds state response to social movements in a democratic polity is the nature of response to state action by the collectivity. Thus, even as the state is indulging in repression of a section of the population, if it is successful in projecting the impression that it is doing so for the common welfare, in the interest of the people, and with their tacit approval, the response of the populace in general would be favourable.

The legitimacy of a state, the success of an institution, or, for that matter, the survival of a movement, depends upon the manner in which it projects itself to the wider world. That is, the content and styles of communication are of critical importance. This fact has prompted me to devote Chapter 7 to the discussion of this theme, although attention is confined to movements. A wide variety of factors—the type of society ('primitive', peasant, industrial or post-industrial); the contexts (religious or secular); and the levels (micro, meso- or macro-) influence the styles of communication within and across movements. Communication patterns within a movement as a whole or among different types of participants (e.g., core and peripheral) are radically different from communication styles across movements. With movement allies, the communication is necessarily cooperative but with movement enemies it is invariably confrontational. This in turn means that through the instrumentality of communication, participants are sacralized and opponents are stigmatized, even demonized.

The styles of communication are often at the root of erupting violence, be it sudden or eventual. Here, who owns and/or controls the agencies of communication—press, radio, television—becomes crucial. These ideologial apparatuses, depending upon who owns and controls them, can legitimize or de-legitimize violence. That is, violence, irrespective of its source, can be projected as an inevitable evil, but mark it, only for a noble and promising future. Again, the nature of the collectivity involved is important insofar as expectations from and about them vary radically. For example, violence indulged in by the youth and the working class are often tolerated at least upto a point; it seems that there is even a tacit assumption that some amount of violence ought to be expected from them. In contrast, violence indulged in by senior citizens, professors or priests, shocks the collective conscience almost instantly. Needless to say, it is the image about different collectivities which defines expectations about them. All these point to the compelling argument that attitudes to violence generated by movements also drastically vary depending upon who is involved, for what purpose it is used as a resource, and whether it is avoidable or inevitable.

The life-cycle and career of a movement also determine its style of communication. In charismatic movements, movements initiated by *gurus*, prophets or men of exemplary conduct, communication is top-down, highly centralized, and yet the style is widely accepted. The very content of communication gradually evolves as the leader articulates his ideas. In contrast, ideological movements invariably formulate the content of their communication well in advance and it is communicated by a multiplicity of structured groups. But decentralized communication invariably results in different interpretations of its content. To avoid this, coordination would be attempted which results in centralization and bureaucratization.

The third possibility is that a movement begins with the formation of an association, that is, an organizational nucleus. Inevitably, communication is bound to be restricted and boundary demarcation in terms of ins and outs would be clear in such a movement. Over time, however, the organizational nucleus would have to spread both vertically and horizontally if a movement has to emerge. That is, associational proliferation and organizational elaboration are indicators of the spread of movements in such cases. Once this happens, coordination of communication becomes inevitable. Necessarily, movement entrepreneurs and ordinary participants get differentiated within movements, leading to greater centralization.

Finally, a precipitous event may give birth to a revolt or rebellion, the basic causes of which may be submerged in spite of persisting discontentment over a period. Inevitably, a spokesperson has to emerge almost instantly. An ad hoc group emerges first (which would eventually be formalized as a committee), to communicate the grievances and plan future action. Understandably, the need to have a coordinator becomes evident and concentration of power in his hands would follow automatically. The general point then is that even as styles of communication vary depending upon the nature of movements, there is a tendency towards centralization of communication.

Irrespective of the content or style of communication, its object in the context of social movements is mobilizing specific social categories into collective actions. The patterns of mobilization in turn would vary depending upon the contexts and categories involved. Thus, social movements within a nation-state are enterprises addressed to the mobilization of one or another category. The three chapters in Part III deal with micro-situations, in that they discuss mobilizations of specific categories.

Although intense, intermittent, isolated revolts by agrarian classes did occur for centuries in India, they were invariably localized. In contrast, for the first time, large-scale, continuous, systematic and coordinated mobilizations of and by agrarian classes occurred in India in the wake of the anti-colonial struggle. This observation is equally applicable to other categories—tribes, castes, religious collectivities, students, women, youth, industrial workers. Ignoring this vital difference, a large number of analysts have advanced long-winded arguments to establish the specificity of interests, motivations and consciousness of particular categories. Without denying these specificities, I wish to affirm that what is pertinent in the context of the anti-colonial struggle is the *shared* interests, motivations and conciousness of a wide variety of social categories.

I have repeatedly pointed out that one should squarely recognize the historicity of context as a critical factor (see Chapters 1 and 2) in order to understand the basic difference between mobilizations and protests during the colonial and post-colonial phases. However, two types of mobilizations should be distinguished. First, those mobilizations which had an independent origin to start with but were eventually linked with an all-India leader, organization or event. That is, they became macro-mobilizations having started as micro-phenomena. On the other hand, a large number of mobilizations were inspired and initiated by a common ideology (nationalism), organization (Indian National Congress), or leadership (MK Gandhi). That is, they were macro-mobilizations right from their inception.

Second, the theory of vanguard which pre-supposes differentiation of particular categories is largely redundant in a colonial context. Anti-colonial mobilizations are by their very nature multi-class and poly-cultural because the primary and immediate deprivation, political subjection, is commonly shared and the agent of oppression is a common external enemy. True, it is necessary to motivate specific classes and categories invoking their particular deprivations to join the struggle because their definitions of the situation vary. But this does not nullify the overarching purpose or the omnipresent enemy.

These considerations point to the fact that the much-debated middle peasant thesis is the resultant of the fallacy of misplaced concreteness. In fact, even the latterly floated notion of dominant peasantry does not sit well in the context under reference, namely, the intense nationalist phase (1917-47) in the anti-colonial struggle. Precisely because the cause was common and the enemy external, the whole peasantry, not one or another segment of it, had to be involved. The situation in independent India is dramatically different and yet most political parties until recently impetuously stuck to the same strategy of mobilizing the whole peasantry, although through different associations, often ignoring the basic variations in the nature of deprivation experienced by their clientele. This misconstrued strategy was a colossal mistake which largely explains why much of the agrarian mobilizations in independent India are not exactly class-based but party-inspired. Thus, not only are several political parties involved in intense competition to organize the same agrarian class, but the same political party organizes several agrarian classes with opposing interests!

In the first couple of decades, the main thrust of agrarian mobilizations in independent India was against the absentee, feudal and big landowners by the tenants in pursuance of translating the slogan 'land to the tiller' into practise. The confluence of these mobilizations and the series of land reforms facilitated the emergence of owner-cultivators. It was precisely at this juncture that the state came out with its massive subsidies for farmers to effectively stem the recurring food crises, resulting in the emergence of the Green Revolution. The traditional band of tied-labour became free-floating wage labour and the ensuing confrontations in the agrarian context are between the capitalist farmers and the agrarian poor.

Having got attuned to the advantages of the subsidies provided by the state, the newly emerged prosperous farmer was not in a mood to pay tax or even to return the loan he got from the government. In fact, he wanted not only the continuation of the subsidy but also the guarantee of remunerative prices for his products. On the other hand, he was unwilling to pay the agricultural worker an adequate wage, sometimes even a subsistence wage. Predictably, agrarian mobilizations took a new turn; the rich capitalist farmer confronts the state with newer demands and the agricultural labour mobilizes against their employers, the capitalist farmer, demanding better working conditions. It is important to recall here that although anti-state mobilizations are common to both the colonial and the national state, there are critical differences. If the mobilizations against the colonial state were essentially political and multi-class, the protests against the national state are essentially economic and ultimately class-based. To say that both are anti-state is to say nothing, to miss the vital point instanced by the change in the historicity of context.

If I have conveyed the impression that in independent India agrarian mobilizations are neat and tidy class confrontations, let me hasten to add that this is far from my intention. In fact, consistent with the poser I make in Chapter 1, it is demonstrated in Chapter 8 that mobilization of agrarian categories is an enormously complicated task because of the multiple identities in which they are enmeshed. The impossibility of all-India mobilizations of any agrarian class is clearly unfolded. Given the cross-cutting identities and loyalties only sectoral mobilizations are possible.

One can speak of three main collective actors in the context of agrarian mobilizations in India today. First, the agrarian proletariat drawn mainly from Dalits, Adivasis and backward castes organized by leftist political parties demanding better working conditions and higher wages. Second, owner-cultivators drawn predominantly from middle castes organized by centrist and leftist parties demanding subsidies and remunerative prices from the state. Third, rich capitalist farmers drawn mainly from middle and upper castes organized by certain independent organizations which pursue agrarian capitalism as an ideology, as a sequel to industrial capitalism. Given this scenario, the possiblity of a true all-India mobilization of any particular category is limited; caste categories, economic conditions and the strength of political parties and agrarian organizations vary substantially across cultural-linguistic regions. This is why I have characterized agrarian mobilizations as 'micro' in orientation.

One of the serious gaps in our knowledge about protest relates to its micro-dimension. The notion of micro-protests as used in this volume has two connotations. First, it relates to protests by particular categories which are circumscribed by their attributes and are constrained to function in specific contexts. Second, it refers to what happens within a specific locale, institution or movement.

Given the limitations of traditional historiography which invariably failed to capture the view from below, attempts have been made to fill this gap latterly. But most of these efforts relate to highlighting the role subaltern classes played in the anti-colonial struggle, or at best, to describing their conditions during the colonial era. To the extent that these discussions are confined to the colonial context, the question relating to the changes that occur in the consciousness of subaltern classes under a changed historical situation, that is, in a politically independent nation-state, cannot be answered.

In Chapter 8, I have referred to the category of Dalit-proletariat in the context of agrarian struggles. The hyphenation points not merely to the duality in status and identity but also to the concomitant multiplicity of sources of deprivation and the resultant multi-layered character of their consciousness. In the case of the Dalits, an utterly degrading ritual status, an acute sense of powerlessness and grinding poverty conjointly shaped their consciousness. This in turn moulded their perception of the enemy and even patterns of mobilization. Therefore, it is no accident that collectivities below the pollution line invariably thought that their greatest enemies during the colonial era were not the British but those Indians who upheld and practised conservative religious and caste values. However, this is not to suggest that the Dalits were not interested in political freedom or involved in the anti-colonial struggle, but to indicate that if a particluar deprivation is specific to a category and that in their perception is the most debilitating deprivation, they will, in all probability, protest against it first.

Even a quick look at the trajectory of Dalit protests unfolds an interesting pattern. The Dalits, notwithstanding their debilitating poverty, did not organize to improve their economic conditions; to start with they protested against slavery and untouchability. Theirs was not a class action to begin with, but their efforts were geared to wrest human dignity for themselves. This was followed by struggles for political enfranchisement and mobilization against economic exploitation surfaced last. I am not suggesting even for a moment that the course of struggles followed this neat succession always, nor am I hinting that the Dalit struggles were one-point programmes. But I am insisting that in terms of the initial surfacing of deprivations there was a certain sequence and at given phases of history a particular deprivation assumed saliency in the Dalit collective cognition. This is the resultant of the hierarchy of deprivation as experienced by the Dalits.

There is yet another plausible reason for this sequence of protests to surface. That ritual degradation is common to all Dalits irrespective of their economic conditions or political privilege is amply illustrated by vast empirical evidence. Similarly, although adult franchise is a great equalizer, its actual exercise is not always smooth, either because one does not have politeracy or because one is intimidated in its exercise. Economic betterment does not happen to all at once or simultaneously, it is a gradual process. And, when it happens it divides people, into haves and have-nots. Invariably, it is the political brokers from among the Dalits who would first acquire the requisite political skills and their kith and kin who would secure the economic advantages. This brings in class differentiation, often jeopardizing united collective action.

The emergence of the Harijan bourgeoisie and Dalit political broker has resulted in precisely this. Needless to say, the Dalit proletariat is alienated from its primordial base (fellow Dalits) due to class differentiation and from its civic base (fellow proletariat) due to primordial attachments. The only way out of this impasse is either united class action or caste mobilization. If, for the former, a cultural revolt is a prerequisite, for the latter, categorial solidarity ignoring class differences is required. If cultural revolt is yet a far cry in India, assertion of caste solidarity does not augur well for ushering in a democratic, secular and socialist India!

We discussed the relationship between social movements and their broad social environment in Chapters 5 and 6. The inner dynamics or internal milieu of social movements, a rarely analyzed aspect, is the theme of chapter 10. For example, how the leaders project themselves to their present and potential clients is of great importance for the success of a movement. And, if the people are drawn from different historical and socio-cultural backgrounds, the same set of ideas may have to be presented in different forms and ways. The style and content of communication, the theme of Chapter 7, assumes great importance in this context. Communication is also of great importance in defining and maintaining the boundaries of social movements.

Perhaps a challenging task faced by all movements is how to create new identities for their followers. A wide variety of mechanisms, ranging from making a new recruit sign a prescribed pledge to insisting on his wearing an assigned insignia, may be resorted to. While these external mechanisms to maintain identity may help to identify the followers of a movement, they do not guarantee the development of a sense of belonging to it. Not infrequently, the process of *sacralization* and *demonization* will have to be resorted to in order to achieve this end. While sacralization attempts to transform those who belong to a movement into charismatic objects, demonization of the enemy creates the required distance from the enemy. These processes are often at work to create a new self-definition among, and a new life-style for, the followers of a movement. However, there will always be a hierarchy among participants — the core constituted by the leaders, the ordinary composed of the rank and file, and those on the margin who are in a dilemma as to whether to be in it or out of it.

The internal milieu of a movement will be influenced by the ups and downs in its career. But the specific manifestations of these will depend on a wide variety of factors. For example, the sudden demise of an all-powerful leader or the erosion of his charisma might pose the crisis of succession. On the other hand, even when a leader is alive and entrenched, an ambitious associate may pose an effective challenge to his supremacy. Often the challenge is occasioned because the leader commits fatal errors in terms of his personal life-style, or compromises on the basic goals or means of the movement. In either event, the development of a faction within the movement, which might eventuate in its split, cannot be ruled out. On the other hand, it is likely that two or more collective actors sharing the same ideals may combine to meet the challenge they face from a common and powerful enemy. In this process, they may fuse together to make a unified move-

ment. That is, fission and fusion are strategies which surface in the
career of movements to maintain their original purity and to augment their striking power. But movements need to maintain their
stability and for this they should inculcate appropriate values in
the involved individuals. Through adequate socialization, movements constantly endeavour to produce a band of committed participants who usually would identify themselves with them. Eventually,
the participants would also develop a new self-definition of themselves and may become martyrs of the movements, if need be.

The function of this rather long introduction is to affirm two
points. First, the chapters of this volume, even as they are distinct
and have been written over a period of time, are closely inter-
linked and often interpenetrating. Consequently, as a totality,
these essays make for coherence and unity. Second, most of the
chapters deal with neglected themes and unexplored areas in the
analyses of social movements. This provides a commonality and
hence a unity to these essays. This alone is adequate justification
to publish them in a single volume.

THEORY, CONCEPTS AND METHOD

1
Issues in the Analysis of Social Movements

The tradition of analyzing social movements in sociology is enveloped in the study of the processes of social change. For example,
the structural-functional approach, for which role is the basic unit
of analysis, views change in terms of three basic processes—structural differentiation, reintegration and adaptation. According to
this sequential model of change, a movement may appear in any
one of the stages depending upon certain system conditions. Thus,
emergence of specialized and autonomous units, elaboration of
division of labour and intensification of role specialization may
release considerable stresses and strains in the system, rendering
one or another social category socially deprived, which in turn may
inspire movements. But these movements are viewed as temporary
aberrations, essentially pathological, indeed indicative of transient
anomies. Movements are thus incapable of effecting long-term and
on-going processes of change because specialization permits maxi-
mum control over the environment by assuming more effective
roles and creating more efficient units. In this tradition, then,
movements are viewed as necessary accompaniments of the tension
released by structural differentiation and movement manipulation
as a tension-management mechanism by specialized role incumbents.
Since differentiation renders prevalent roles and norms obsolete,
it is necessary to develop new mechanisms of reintegration, which
follows a three-phase model. Due to dissatisfaction, men no longer
perform roles adequately; this is followed by protests by the deprived
who organize movements, and finally, new mechanisms of regulation
and coordination, such as unions, associations and welfare agencies,
are created to mobilize resources and commitments. A more flexible
and specialized system inevitably emerges. Thus, movements
are viewed essentially as adaptive mechanisms in a period of rapid

social change. With adaptation change is institutionalized (see Smelser 1962; Eisenstadt 1965).

The basic flaws of this approach, it seems to me, are three: it does not specify the source of deprivation; it considers human beings as mere creatures of societal determinism, sapping them of their creative vitality, and its unit of analysis is not appropriate for analyzing movements. One can locate a variety of sources of deprivation in all systems but ultimately what disturbs men is their distance from the centre of the system. Insofar as they occupy positions on the periphery of a system, they may be deprived in terms of wealth, power or privilege or all of them. In this sense, social movements are mechanisms through which men attempt to move from the periphery of a system to its centre. That is, movements are conscious efforts on the part of men to mitigate their deprivation and secure justice. Second, while movements are conditioned by social-structural factors, it implies voluntaristic action: men create movements to achieve the goals they hold dear. Third, movements are perhaps the chief mechanism through which the deprived categories demonstrate their power. United by an ideology, they create organizational devices to fight the evils and redress grievances. Once a social category develops commitment to a movement's ideology and organization, their mobilization may be relatively easy. Thus, movements emerge when men committed to a specified set of goals participate in protest-oriented, purposive collective actions. Therefore, its crucial aspects are mobilization and institutionalization. It seems then, that in order to analyze movements adequately, the researcher has to focus on these aspects and not on roles.

One of the vexing issues in movement analysis is how men come to develop commitment to a specified set of goals, to an ideology. It needs to be emphasized here that while structural similarity may be a necessary condition it may not be a sufficient one for the development of similar consciousness. At any rate, given the multi-dimensionality of structural positioning of individuals and groups, those with a similar position in one dimension may not share the same position in regard to other dimensions. Therefore, we need to recognize the importance of the divergence in structural positions of men and groups, the efforts needed to arouse their consciousness, the inevitability of conflict, in the process of their mobilization, and the desirability of institutionalization of collective efforts to provide them with purpose, while analyzing social movements.

Mobilization of people into collective actions implies the existence of a certain uniformity among participants based on their *interests* rooted in socio-economic background and *ideas* emanating from their political orientations and ideological commitments. Much of the problem in movement analysis stems from the presumed relationship or degree of correlation between these dimensions. While it is largely true that 'consciousness of kind' will not automatically follow the occupancy of similar structural positions, it seems to me that occupying certain structural positions facilitates the crystallization of consciousness relatively easily. Thus, membership in ascriptive groups invariably facilitates the development of primordial collectivism due to the heavy weight of tradition inculcated through the socialization process, the ascriptive and, therefore, the relatively fixed character of the position, the style of life associated with primordial collectivities, etc. In contrast, membership in civil collectivities (the assumption here is that mobility is possible and that it does occur) may not easily facilitate the development of consciousness among the members of these social categories unless individuals and groups are made aware of their structural similarity. That is, civil collectivism is the resultant of not only objective conditions but also subjective perceptions. The point to be emphasized here is that mobilization of men into collective actions is easier if certain of their structural attributes are invoked. Which of these attributes are of strategic significance in the mobilizational process is at least partly determined by the principles of social organization existing in that society, that is, its historicity.

The point here is: system characteristics of a society affect the ethos and style of social movements in that society. A 'primitive' or 'pre-political' society may mainly express its values in a religious vocabulary, its mobilizational efforts may be based on communal or primordial attachments. But with the emergence of 'nation-state' this vocabulary may be redefined to suit new conditions; it may be transformed into 'secular'. Similarly, mobilizational efforts may be increasingly anchored around civil collectivities. However, the movements will neither have the potentialities to root out the existing system completely nor will they succumb to the traditional structures entirely. Essentially then, social movements provide the stage for confluence between the old and new values and structures.

It is widely acknowledged that there are different routes to change and collective action is but one of them. While recognizing this, it is necessary to ask and answer the question, why does a collectivity resort to this particular route to change, that is, what are the factors which facilitate the emergence of social movements? One can certainly list a multiplicity of structural determinants which facilitate or block the emergence of social movements, but it seems to me that the most critical factor is the political values of a system as enshrined in its Constitution and reflected in the route it pursues to socio-economic development (including social policies) and the competing ideologies. This value package broadly projects the future vision of a society.

The foregoing discussion suggests that an adequate framework for the study of social movements should take into account the historicity, the elements of present social structure, and the future vision of the society in which they originate and operate. It is the dialectics between historicity (past experiences), social structure (present existential conditions) and the urge for a better future (human creativity) which provides the focal point for analysis of social movements. That is, a theory of social movements implies not only a theory of social structure but also a vision about the future of society. I must hasten to add that the interlocking of the past-present-future implies that social movements reflect the confluence between the persistent, changing and evolving elements of a system. Further, the framework also suggests that an analysis of social movements in India, a nation-state, can be our legitimate concern. At a deeper level the framework implies that men make history and constantly learn from their historicity. Movements are neither mere accidents nor entirely the resultants of manipulations by leaders and demagogues, but the consequence of conscious efforts of men to change systems in the light of their past experiences, avoiding pitfalls. Finally, the continuous occurrence of movements implies that man is not imprisoned by present structures and no moratorium on his creativity can be imposed.

II

In order to explicate the potentiality of our framework it is necessary to elaborate upon each of the dimensions involved. Traditional India was characterized by political fragmentation and linguistic-regional insulation, hierarchical social division and institutionalized inequality, cultural-ethnic diversity and social tolerance, primacy of group over individual, and transcendence of mundane concerns (cf.Y. Singh 1973). Each of these elements in the historicity of Indian society influenced the nature and types of social movements which originated and spread in India. First, most of the movements were pre-political and religious in orientation, variously described as millenerian, chiliastic, revivalistic, revitalization, nativist, messianic, etc., (see Fuchs 1965). Even when the objectives of these movements were political or economic, mobilization of participants was mainly achieved by invoking their primordial similarity and employing religious symbols. Given the severity of the caste system and deeply entrenched social inequality, these movements were mainly directed against the evils that emanated from the caste system (S. Natarajan 1959). Since there existed a rough correlation between the caste hierarchy and the possession of wealth and power, the movement participants were specific primordial categories even when their deprivation was economically rooted. Because of the tremendous importance of the collectivity over individuals, often movements which aimed to bring about mobility had to mobilize members of status groups into collective actions (Silverberg 1968). Finally, political fragmentation and regional-linguistic insulation invariably blocked the development of all-India movements. All these affected the 'scale' of social movements, the pattern of their mobilization, and the 'level' at which they operated. It was only with the emergence of nationalism as an ideology that the divergent social movements of autonomous origin have been gradually welded together into an overarching Indian National Liberation Movement (A.R. Desai 1954). Even those ostensibly non-political movements came to have a political (national) colouration (Heimsath 1964) during the freedom struggle.

Independent India is characterized by rapid urbanization and industrialization, planned economic development, a series of social legislations undermining several traditional values and extending protection to 'weaker sections', commitment to 'socialism', secularism and democracy, political pluralism as reflected in a multi-party parliamentary democracy. Each of these elements again influences the origin, the nature, the types, and the spread of social movements.

The process of economic development inaugurated through national planning had accepted the notion of balanced regional development. Although a region is not a political but an economic unit, as the benefits of development are to be shared by a population characterized by considerable disparity, understandable anxiety

arose as to the basis of distribution of the extremely limited developmental inputs. Notwithstanding the fact that the Communist Party
of India championed the cause of linguistically based states (nationalities) even before independence, the CPI itself was somewhat
ambivalent about its policy in this context and it cannot be said
categorically that there was consensus with regard to this principle
even within the party (see Overstreet and Windmiller 1959). However, regional disparities and the fear of exploitation by other
linguistic groups gave birth to the emergence of a series of sub-
national movements within independent India, leading to the reorganization of Indian states based on language in 1956.

The acceptance of the linguistic principle for state formation
gave birth to three distinct variants of 'national' movements in
independent India: (a) secessionist movements (e.g., the Dravida
Munnetra Kazhagam movement at the initial stage, the Naga and
the Mizo underground movements) which mobilize people who
speak the same language, share the same style of life and inhabit a
common territory for the formation of sovereign states. (b) Movements for the formation of linguistic states with relative autonomy
but within the framework of nation-state. A country with enormous
linguistic variations, India provides contexts for endemic demands
for state formation based on language. Further, once language is
accepted as the criterion for state formation or even distribution of
state resources, those contexts in which language and other factors
coexist, also provide the womb for movements. The identification,
although wrongly, of Punjabi language with Sikhs and Urdu with
Muslims are cases in point. The former case led to the crystallization
of a movement mainly led by Punjabi-speaking Sikhs, eventuating
in the formation of a communally-oriented political party, the
Akali Dal, presumably championing the cause of those who speak
Punjabi but actually catering to the aspirations of Sikhs as a religious
group, further culminating in the division of Punjab into two states
(Nayyar 1966). Additionally, once language is accepted as the
basis of state formation, other primordial ties may be used to articulate demands in this context. The re-invigoration of the demand
for a separate Jharkhand state uniting the tribal groups belonging
to the border districts common to Bihar, Orissa and West Bengal
illustrates this tendency (see K.L. Sharma 1976 : 37-43). The
tendency in such contexts will often be to rediscover traditional
identities which lie frozen at the moment or even to create new

identities when none exist. Finally, once the linguistic states are formed, movements demanding state formation within these states or at least for the recognition of special 'regional status' will emerge. The Telengana regional movement and the Vidarbha movement are cases in point. (c) Movements which emphasize the rights of the sons of soil and breed animosities to 'outsiders'. These movements are mainly led by urban middle classes, particularly in those cities where a substantial migrant population with differing linguistic backgrounds compete for employment, licenses for industry, establishing new economic enterprises, admission to elite educational institutions, etc. The specific manifestation of these movements is found in the proliferation of '*senas*' in Indian cities espousing the demands for protecting the rights of the sons of soil. The ideology which asserts the rights of sons of soil is the resultant of inter-regional migration, an inevitable accompaniment of industrial urbanization. The outsiders, that is the migrants from other linguistic regions, are not viewed so much as exploitors but as intruders, intruding in to another cultural region. This modality of perception is based on the principles of state formation prevalent in India. What I am suggesting is this: intrusion and exploitation are perceptual categories conditioned by the principles of socio-political organization based on cultural and structural factors, respectively. The acceptance of a specific socio-political measure would invariably lead to the redefinition of the structure of aspirations of people and it facilitates their mobilization into collective actions to realize their aspirations.

Another social policy measure which facilitates the emergence of new movements or the re-invigoration of earlier movements is the policy of protective discrimination pursued in India. The social categories to which protection is extended through a series of legal and social policy measures are referred to as 'weaker sections' in official parlance—religious minorities, Scheduled Castes, Scheduled Tribes and Backward Classes—all of which are primordial collectivities. Given such a policy thrust it is inevitable that the mobilization of these categories takes place either for the demand of new rights and privileges or for the speedy implementation of those rights and privileges guaranteed to them through legislation.

The emergence of India as a nation-state is coterminous with the formation of another sovereign Muslim state, Pakistan, which provides a continuous basis for the mobilization of Indian Muslims.

Although predominantly populated by Hindus, India is one of the largest Muslim nations of the world with 90 million Muslims. The history of the Muslim regime in medieval India, their substantial number and the commitment to secularism as a value in independent India, the prevalence of poverty and illiteracy among Indian Muslims and the widespread feeling of discrimination among them are factors which the leaders of this most numerous religious minority constantly invoke to mobilize them into collective actions of various types. This is facilitated by the fact that secularism in the Indian context meant, in practice, fostering the coexistence of different religious communities. Coupled with this, the adoption of democracy permitted the formation of religion-based interest groups in the political arena articulating communal demands. Thus, Muslims, Sikhs, Christians, etc., often invoke their constitutionally defined minority status to appropriate material benefits and for this their leaders consider it to be politically expedient to demonstrate to the powers-that-be their communal solidarity by mobilizing them into collective actions.

The policy of protective discrimination initiated by the British to safeguard the interests of the depressed classes is vigorously pursued in independent India. A multiplicity of movements for the betterment of these categories emerged over the years. Notwithstanding the regional variations depending upon their existential conditions and level of politicization, the movements involving these categories are found all over India. Broadly speaking, these movements demonstrate three strains, each of which is anchored in the specific types of deprivation they experience. Thus, movements leading to conversion to other religions, particularly Christianity and Buddhism, were perceived as capable of emancipating them from the ritual degradations they experienced through the atrocities of the caste system. But with the advent of planned socio-economic development, the anchorage of their mobilization widened so as to include movements to secure material benefits, leading to a large number of castes claiming inferior ritual status, which became a new resource for claiming state patronage. However, they soon realized that economic benefits extended by the state were being pocketed mainly by the dominant individuals and groups among them and the poorer among them began rallying around political parties. Although the legislative measures such as political representation have partly castrated them of their vitality for mobilization through the process of co-option, it is being increasingly realized by the poorer among the depressed classes that political mobilization is one of the most effective channels for improving their material conditions. Yet, even the most articulate among them do not view the problem as one of mere material deprivation (that is, their positioning in the class system), but essentially one of status deprivation. The emergence of the Dalit Panther movement, mainly located in urban Maharashtra, is symptomatic of this (see Oommen 1977 a:153-93). The point I want to emphasize is this: it is wrong to think that the poor perceive deprivation only or even mainly in terms of material conditions. The structure of deprivation is moulded both by the traditional structures and new values of a system.

The commitment to democracy necessitated the involvement of people at the grass-root level in the decision-making process. In India this is achieved mainly through two channels: mobilization by political parties and mobilization through official agencies. Mobilization through both these channels is different from the collective actions initiated by social movements. Yet we cannot ignore these channels of mobilization while analyzing social movements. While political parties are organized groups with a formal structure competing for formal power, operating within the boundaries of nation-states, social movements consist of unbounded and open-ended social collectivities. More specifically, the relationship between party and movement can be formulated as follows:

1. A party may be part of a broader social movement or might have emerged out of a movement.
2. A party may be independent of any particular social movement and embody in its membership all or parts of several social movements.
3. The same social movement may be represented in several political parties.
4. A social movement may reject affiliation with any political party. Admittedly, then, social movements are more amorphous social collectivities as compared with political parties and pressure groups (see Heberle 1951).

Political parties in India mobilize two types of categories into collective actions through the associations and unions they sponsor. These social categories can be grouped into (*a*) occupational/class categories (e.g., industrial workers, students, farmers) and (*b*) biological categories (e.g., youth, women). These associations and unions are intended to function more as movements than as mere organizations. In India these associations/movements operate more as appendages or tributaries of political parties than as autonomous entities. Consequently, as new political parties are formed or as existing ones split, new associations are formed or old ones split. This has two immediate consequences: (*i*) the division of mobilized categories resulting in the reduction of their bargaining capacity consequent upon the rivalry that develops among the competing factions or groups, and (*ii*) an increase in the absolute number of persons mobilized as each political party vies with the other for clientele. The point of interest for us here is to note that an adequate analysis of social movements in India should take into account the tactics and strategies of mobilization of political parties, which in turn are dependent upon their ideologies and organizations because most of the 'all-India' movements are but political mobilizations of political parties through their front-organizations. Typical examples of these are industrial and agricultural workers' movements, students' movements, women's movements, etc. It is important to keep in mind here that all these movements envelope within themselves a series of associations or unions functioning under the auspices of different political parties. When we refer to specific movements, we have in mind the conjoint activities of all the unions/associations of that social category. In this sense, a movement can be defined as a stream of associations in interaction and/or in confrontation.

Conventional wisdom in sociology views social movements as a united effort on the part of the deprived social categories to bring about social change. In this perspective, movements are defined as oppositional forces against the status quo. This perspective probably had greater validity at a time when the state operated as a mere police state, confining its attention to the protection of the citizens from external aggression and providing them with adequate internal security to facilitate the pursuit of their chosen economic activities. But with the emergence of the notion of welfare and socialist states, what has been hitherto defined as private worries have become public issues (Mills 1959). And, in the case of Third World countries, consequent upon their emergence as independent nation-states at a particular juncture in history, the state had to inspire and institutionalize far-reaching changes (see Worsely 1964; Rex 1974). In this process the state has had to mobilize its vast masses into collective actions; the state bureaucracy which was hitherto taken to be an agent of the status quo was gradually turned into, at least by definition, an instrument of change and development. This transformation in the functions of the state and the mode of its functioning has tremendous significance for the analysis of social movements in the contemporary world situation, particularly in developing countries. In all the socialist countries the state is the chief and often the only agent of mobilization of people, the most telling example of which is the Cultural Revolution in communist China. But the large-scale mobilization of people to bring about change is not altogether absent in other countries. Thus, India's massive rural reconstruction programme was intended to operate more as a movement than a bureaucratic venture. That is why one frequently comes across references to the community development, cooperative, Panchayati Raj or family planning 'movements'. It is not argued here that these and other governmental programmes can be easily equated with movements as is conventionally understood. However, what I am suggesting is that the change in the overall orientation and in the mode of functioning of the state is likely to bring about changes in the nature and types of developmental strategies and techniques of mobilization employed by it. If this is so, one must take into account this dimension while analyzing social movements. It may be that the state-inspired legislative measures accelerate the process of achieving movement goals initiated by the oppositional forces or that the thunder and storm of opposition-inspired movements are completely stolen, or at least partly reduced by state measures, thereby rendering social movements redundant in certain contexts (see Oommen 1975a: 1571-84).

Although India is often characterized as a rural country, its urban population is larger than the total population of many countries and cities have grown at such a rapid rate that we now encounter the problem of over-urbanization. This has led to the migration of a substantial population from rural areas, hitherto experiencing life in relatively fixed contexts with definite attachments. The emergence of a relatively mobile and free-floating urban-industrial population, coupled with certain distinctive characteristics of Hinduism, seem to be facilitating the emergence of a large number of urban-based sectarian movements centred around saints. Typical examples of these are the Radha Swamy movement, the Nirankari movement, the Brahma Kumari movement, the Divine Light Mission, the Satya Saibaba movement, the Ananda Margi movement, to mention a few. While all these 'movements' can be included under the rubric of religious movements, they also have a certain measure of autonomy as sectarian movements. The elements of traditional Hinduism which seem to be facilitating the emergence of these movements are polytheism and the absence of a Church. Hinduism has always had a multiplicity of gods. Therefore, the acceptance of a variety of saints of autonomous origin seems to be innate to Hinduism. Second, given the extremely amorphous character of Hinduism and the hierarchical division of the society through the caste system, internal differences, divisiveness, and lack of community seem to be all-pervading. In such a situation, characterized by flexibility and rigidity simultaneously, it seems to be natural for men to yearn for membership in communities and groups with relatively clear boundaries but with the possibilities of some options. And, these traditional aspects of a social structure are particularly problematic when men and groups are re-located in urban-industrial contexts. They tend to be alienated from the immediate surroundings and suffer from an identity crisis, devoid of specific and deep social attachments. Therefore, it is no accident that most of these saints emerge and operate in the urban milieu and their followers are mainly drawn from urban middle classes. These religious movements continue to operate successfully till such time as their leader-saints are condemned publicly for the criminal activities they allegedly indulge in (e.g., Ananda Margis) or till such time as internal schisms develop within them (e.g., Divine Light Mission) or, insofar as the saintly powers claimed by them are not demonstrated to be false. That is, insofar as their claim to saintliness is not challenged, their charisma stands validated, their legitimation is assured, and they are successful in mobilizing men into collective actions in the name of the belief system they stand for.

III

Thus far our discussion has concentrated on the relationship between historicity, social structure and value system of Indian society on the one hand, and the nature and types of social movements which originate and spread in India, on the other. Through this analysis we suggested that the overall features of any system mould the nature of its social movements. In order to fully appreciate our argument it is necessary to highlight some of the methodological issues in the study of social movements. The methodological problems faced by a student of social movements, as I see them, are basically two: (*a*) the problems related to the *scale* of the movement and (*b*) the issues related to the *units* and *levels* of observation.

The discussion on the scale of movements can be organized under three heads: (*a*) the number of participants, (*b*) the time-span of movements, and (*c*) the social composition of movement participants. Although the number of participants cannot be a definite criterion by which movements can be differentiated from non-movements, it cannot be ignored. Nobody is likely to designate the mobilization of a handful of individuals as a movement. Therefore, it is obvious that movement participants should be of a substantial number. The number of participants can be defined as substantial both in terms of the universe which forms the basis of mobilization as well as the absolute number mobilized into action. For instance, even if only a small percentage of a specific category, industrial workers or farmers, for instance, are mobilized into collective actions, we can legitimately label it a movement if they constitute thousands of persons. On the other hand, even when only a few hundreds of persons are activised insofar as they constitute a substantial proportion of the population which forms the universe of mobilization (as in the case of a small tribe), such a mobilization can also be designated a movement.

At this juncture, however, we are likely to be faced by new problems related to the definition of participants. It is well-known that it is extremely hazardous to demarcate the boundaries of movements in terms of the nature and types of activities of participants. All movements are likely to have a set of core participants, the leaders at different levels, who can be differentiated in terms of the functions they perform; those who propound the ideology of the movement (the theoreticians), and those who translate these into actual programmes through strategies and tactics (the men of action). Second, the rank and file who participate regularly in various kinds of mobilizational activities — picketing, *jathas*,

satyagrahas, *gheraoes*, strikes — and get arrested or killed and
become martyrs of the movement are the propelling force behind
any movement. Third, there will be a set of peripheral participants
who may identify themselves with movements, insofar as such
participation is not a risky venture perceived in terms of their life
chances and immediate material interests. Typically, they participate in one or more of the following activities: attend the mass
meetings organized under the auspices of the movement, read the
literature produced by the movement, make occasional financial
donations to the movement. While it is extremely difficult to demarcate the active from the less active participants, it is necessary to
recognize this gradation among them. The problem becomes particularly vexing when we note that several movements produce
counter-mobilization by oppositional forces. Often those who
indulge in counter-mobilization are much more active and an
adequate study of a movement should also take into account this
category of persons who are usually taken to be 'outside' the movement. Since much of the mobilizations are initiated by the organizational core of movements, unions and associations, it would be
legitimate to view a given movement as a stream of associations
operating parallely or in confrontation. In the final analysis, the
number of persons mobilized into collective actions either for or
against a movement becomes critical in understanding its scale.

   The time-span of movements is one of the most critical dimensions which defines the scale, yet it is one of the most neglected
aspects in studies of movements. Thus, uprisings, rebellions, civil
disturbances, revolts, insurrections, etc., are all indiscriminately
and interchangeably referred to as 'social movements' (see Gough
1974:1391-412; Dhanagare 1974:109-34, 1976:360-78); some of
these events existed for a short period (less than a year) and others
continued for a longer period. This confusion emanates from an
inadequate appreciation of the processual aspects of movements.
Movements are typically unstable and vascillating phenomena,
now calm, now active or violent, now moving methodically and
slowly, then plunging into action suddenly and erratically, and
then into relative lull or even utter despair. Therefore, rebellions,
revolts and uprisings are nothing but specific events in the relatively
long history of a movement. These events, which are often the more
visible aspects of movements, are usually sustained only for a short
period and should not be mistaken for the movement as a whole.

Further, it is also likely that in the history of some movements these types of events may not take place at all because of their non-violent orientation. But they should not be denied the label of movement. At any rate, whether or not a movement mobilizes men into violent collective actions would depend on the strategy and tactics that are perceived to be appropriate by the leadership at a given point in time. The history of the communist movement in India gives empirical support to such a proposition. The methodological implication of our analysis then is that it is confusing to designate specific revolts or rebellions (e.g., Tebhaga and Telengana peasant revolts or rebellions or the Champaran or Bardoli *satyagrahas)* as 'movements'; rather, we should perceive them as specific links in the long chain of agrarian or freedom movements in India, as the case may be. Further, not only are revolts or rebellions specific events in the history of a movement, but they may give birth to another movement of an entirely different nature as in the case of the Telengana peasant riot which provided the womb to the non-violent Bhoodan-Gramdan movement (Oommen 1972a). Alternatively, a violent revolt may ring the death-knell of a movement depending upon the intensity of violence involved and the attitude of the establishment and the collectivity at large towards violence, eventuating in the demise of the movement through repression or discreditation. Finally, certain movements suffer a natural demise as their goals are achieved, others would redefine their goals or add new goals so as to ensure continuity. Viewed from all these aspects, it is clear that the time-span of movements forms an important dimension of the scale of a movement and to designate specific events which occur in a limited range of time as movements is fallacious.

The third aspect of the scale of a movement refers to the social composition of the participants. The underlying assumption here is that the greater the social homogeneity of the participants the smaller is the scale, and the greater the heterogeneity, the greater the scale of the movement, provided the number involved is constant. By implication, this dimension is discerned in terms of the number of potential participants a movement can mobilize into action. Thus, if a movement is oriented towards the interests of a primordial collectivity such as caste, tribe, religion or language, its optimum scale will be smaller as compared with another movement which champions the interests of civil collectivities such as workers, students or farmers. That is, the dimension of the scale of a movement in the context of the social composition of participants is defined in terms of the heterogeneity/homogeneity of the population under reference. The problems bearing on the scale of movements is reflected in the very process of naming movements. An examination of the names of movements indicates that they are anchored around three factors: locality (e.g.,'movements' of Bardoli, Telengana, Bihar), issues (e.g., Tebhaga, anti-Cow Slaughter, regionalism) and social categories (e.g., peasants, workers, Scheduled Castes and Tribes, Muslims). It is clear from our foregoing discussion that in terms of our perspective some of these are clearly not movements: they are but specific events in the long history of movements. Further, if the locality anchorage is too narrow, discerned in terms of the category involved (that is, peasants in Bardoli), or if the issue involved is too narrowly defined (as in the case of Tebhaga or Cow Slaughter), then mobilization emanating out of these situations or issues cannot be meaningfully designated as movements. But if the locality anchorage is large enough, Bihar, for instance, or if it potentially involves the entire population of the region as in the case of the recent Telengana Separatist movement, or if it has the potentiality to mobilize a substantial size of the population as in the case of issue-centred movements (e.g., sub-national movements) or category-based mobilization (e.g., agricultural workers or Scheduled Tribes), the term movement can be meaningfully employed as the scale of the movement is likely to be of a viable size.

The labelling of a movement based on the social categories involved largely determines its scale. Thus, if the collectivities are primordial, the movements are likely to be localized, usually confining their activities to a specific regional-linguistic area. However, this is not to suggest that such movements will not spread to other regional-linguistic areas. Even as they do, they are likely to take a different shape as the social categories of exactly the same attributes may not be found in the new region into which it spreads. This is well illustrated by the Neo-Buddhist movement which had its anchorage among the Mahars of Maharashtra at the incipient stage but later spread among the Chamars of Uttar Pradesh (Lynch 1969). In contrast, if civil collectivities are the participants in a movement the theoretical possibility of its simultaneous spread at an all-India level exists if a centralized leadership provides the requisite ideology and organizational pattern to the movement. The cases of labour, agrarian or student movements are illustrative of this. It is not suggested that these movements will simultaneously articulate all over the country or that they will be of equal strength wherever they emerge, but such a possibility cannot be ignored. However, given the social diversity and regional-linguistic variations in India, even class/occupation-based movements are usually confined to certain pockets.

We must emphasize here the difficulty in labelling movements based on civil collectivism, a point I touched upon earlier. The problem here stems from two sources: *(a)* The hiatus between objective conditions of a collectivity and their subjective perceptions and *(b)* the tension between the differential emphases given to the varying dimensions of movements by researchers. Even when a collectivity, workers, students, etc., share the same objective conditions they may not perceive the deprivation they suffer or trace it to the same source. That is, crystallization of class or category consciousness will not automatically follow the occupancy of given positions. This may impede their mobilization and thwart the emergence of movements. Part of the problem here is rooted in the competing identities the constituents in each of these collectivities have. For example, since students are drawn from a multiplicity of primordial groups and insofar as primordial ties remain strong, their mobilization purely in terms of civil or ideological collectivism will not be very easy (Oommen 1975b: 10-38).

This brings us to the second point that we raised earlier, namely, the problem of the observer defining collectivities in objective terms and then attributing subjective qualities to them. For instance, Moore (1966) perceived primordial ties and hierarchical fracturing in Indian society as important factors which explain the relative absence of peasant movements. In contrast, Gough (1974) calls attention to the widespread occurrence of 'peasant movements' and argues that the caste system has not been a serious impediment to the emergence and spread of peasant movements. (In fact, Gough designates mobilizations of all varieties including transient rebellions as peasant movements and that is part of the reason why she perceives them to be widespread.) But it seems to me that both these perspectives have grains of truth and they could be profitably combined in analyzing peasant movements. Although Gough deals with an occupational category (peasantry), she does not deny that movement participants discern themselves in terms of primordial identities, a point which supports Moore's position. At the same time, she rightly points out that the goals of these movements are mainly instrumental; redressing their economic grievances. Thus, while Moore emphasizes the socio-cultural background of movement participants, Gough highlights their interests. It seems to me that most social movements in India are organized efforts of primordial collectivities pursuing instrumental collectivism. And, this is so because of the nature of our social structure which provides basic and deep primordial identities, and due to the content of social policies pursued by the state, defining social categories based on their primordial characteristics to extend the benefits of development. Thus, movement participants are not only Mahars, Muslims or Maharashtrians but also agricultural workers, slum dwellers or clerks, as well as Communists, Congressites, or Janathites. That is to say, the three identities basic to all movement participants are primordial/ascriptive, class/occupational and political/ideological. The frequent attempt on the part of analysts to ignore this three-in-one identity and emphasize only one or another of these has brought in very unsatisfactory research pay-offs. In contrast, our attempt should be to recognize the contextual importance of all these identities in mobilizing people into collective actions. This is possible if we recognize social heterogeneity and identity of movement participants as important aspects influencing movement scale as I have suggested.

The second basic methodological issue in the study of social movements relates to the units and levels of observation, as noted earlier. I have already referred to the problem of boundary demarcation of movements from the perspective of differential involvement of participants in movement activities. The unbounded and open-ended feature of social movements throws up a critical problem when we look for a viable unit of observation in an empirical analysis of social movements. Once again, part of the problem is rooted in the varying intensity of mobilization at different phases in the life-cycle of movements. Given this enigmatic processual dimension of movements, analysts of movements are constrained to focus their attention on the institutionalized segment, namely movement associations or organizations. The fact that many movements function as associational groups or grow into organized bodies have often meant that many studies of movements have also been analysis of associations (cf. K.P. Gupta 1974:25- 50). While people can join movement associations, hold and attend meetings, adopt definite programmes, what distinguishes the members of a movement is their *normative* commitment to it, which is qualitatively different from associational attachment or loyalty (Gusfield 1970). In spite of this difference between movements and associations, the confusion between the two persists due to the following reasons. First, the observable core of a movement is often its associational dimension and therefore movement activities are often studied, and perhaps rightly, through associational activities. Second, all crystallized movements will necessarily develop an organization to translate its ideology into programmes. Third, not infrequently, the emergence or change (growth) of a movement manifests in associational proliferation, each pursuing the same or different goals through different means, strategy or tactics. In the final analysis, movements are distinguished by conscious commitment to change, low degree of formalization of its organization, normative commitment and participation.

The basic problem that all social movements face is the inevitable tension between mobilization and institutionalization. Movements crystallize when men share beliefs and activities. But what distinguishes them from other similar kinds of social behaviour is institutionalization—the process of development of a network of relatively stable interactions, normative structure, gradation of participants. Without institutionalization no movement can attain its stability; yet the logical corollary of institutionalization may be the very demise of movements—they may become mere organizations or associations. Therefore, movements may be viewed as institutionalized collective actions, guided by an ideology and supported by an organizational structure. Without mobilization no movement can sustain itself, but if these mobilizations are uninformed by an ideology and an organizational basis, they cannot be distinguished from elementary forms of collective behaviour, like panic response. This intermediary stage between clearly formalized structures and vaguely articulated direction-less process is that which distinguishes movements from organizations on the one hand, and elementary forms of collective behaviour, on the other. Therefore, the focus of attention in movement studies should not only be mobilizational activities but also their institutionalized segment. Available studies on social movements in general and those in India in particular do not seem to appreciate this problem adequately. Consequently, movement studies either concentrate on mobilization or on institutionalization, implying a basic contradiction between these two processes. I have argued elsewhere that such an assumption cannot be sustained if we carefully analyze the life-cycle of social movements (Oommen 1977b: 286-304).

The recognition of the linkage between mobilization and institutionalization would help highlight the relationship between the ideology and programmes of movements. Movement ideology is usually formulated by the leadership and often in abstract terms, but it is a necessary input which provides the requisite passion to the rank and file to plunge into collective actions. But this ideological vision of the leadership needs to be translated into problem-oriented, issue-centred programmes, taking into account the existential conditions of the specific social category which is sought to be mobilized into collective actions. That is, the success of a movement depends largely on the perception by participants of the organic link between the ideology and programmes of the movement. Only then is effective, continuous and purposeful mobilization, which gets institutionalized overtime, possible. Mobilizations without purpose and uninformed by ideology remain mere rebellions and revolts. Similarly, mere ideological sensitization of people without their mobilization for concrete collective actions remains simple verbal articulation, it can rarely bring about any change.

The mobilized social category is invariably a deprived one and mobilization is always against an oppositional force—an enemy. Even when movement ideologies get crystallized it may not be very easy to understand the specific attributes of the enemy and there may be honest differences of opinion in this regard. Further, even when there exists consensus as to who is the enemy, the deprived social category may not perceive the attributes of their enemies due to their debilitating existential conditions—ignorance, illiteracy, poverty, powerlessness or affluence, false sense of power, etc. Even when the enemy is located and the deprived sections are aware of the same, there may be differences of opinion with regard to the manner in which the enemy is to be dealt with. Thus, those who attest the maxim, 'end justifies the means', invariably tend to destroy the enemy, while those who are wedded to the principle of maintaining the purity of means may attempt to convert the enemy. This difference in approach is inevitably reflected in the mobilizational techniques—violent and non-violent—employed by different movements. We have instances of both these types of movements in India in specific contexts (agrarian, the examples being the Naxalite and Bhoodan movements).

This value-orientational difference of movements is articulated in the perceptual vision of researchers, leading to varying emphases being given to different aspects of movements.

The significance of locating and sensitizing the deprived categories as a prerequisite to mobilization brings us back to the issue of the scale of movements. It is the critical nature of the resources possessed by the enemy which defines the nature of deprivation. Thus, those who perceive economic resources as central tend to identify the social categories involved in struggles as landlords and agricultural workers, owners of factories and industrial workers, money-lenders and bonded labourers. On the other hand, those who perceive status and power as the basic resource would tend to project caste Hindus and Scheduled Castes, the Hindus and Muslims, the Maharashtrians and south Indians, etc., as social categories in confrontation. The manner of perceiving and defining the basic resources of the enemy have far-reaching implications in determining the scale of movements. In the case of occupational/class categories, the enemy is all-pervasive and therefore mobilization could be universal, transcending many limitations. In the case of primordial categories the enemies are localized and circumscribed and therefore the mobilization would inevitably remain sectoral and confined to regional-linguistic contexts.

This brings us to the issue of the level of observation in movement studies. It seems to me that one of the fundamental methodological flaws of movement studies has been the exclusive emphasis on the macro-dimension, almost invariably ignoring the micro-dimension, thereby presenting a distorted picture. The usual tendency is to analyze movements in terms of their ideology, contained in the written or unwritten pronouncements of the top leadership; the central movement organization, the machinery through which the ideology is sought to be propagated and communicated; the strategies and tactics devised by leaders, the specific procedures adopted to put movement ideology into practice. This emphasis on the macro-dimension cannot give a picture of the actual operation and consequences at the grass-root level, wherein we observe the filtration or accretion process to which the ideology is subjected in order to meet the specific local conditions. Admittedly, there is a hiatus between the view from above and that from below. The ideological vision of the top leadership may not be meaningful to the grass-root participants unless it is translated into here and now problems as experienced by them. And, those who have attempted to view movements from below often perceive a different picture, and only discern the 'inside story' of movements as different from the 'formal picture' which emerges from a study of the macro-dimension alone (see, Pouchepadass 1974:67-88, Shah 1974: 80-109).

I must point out here why analysts of movement are constrained to concentrate on the macro-dimension. Rarely are on-going movements studied even by sociologists; typically, movement studies are undertaken after their demise, at least after the period of intense mobilization and this is so for several reasons. First, on-going movements continously reformulate their ideologies, restructure their organizational pattern and change their strategies and tactics to meet the challenges of the exigencies they face— movements live from moment to moment. This makes observation of movement processes hazardous. Second, the time-span of movements may be long enough that a particular researcher cannot often invest his entire time on the study of an on-going movement. Third, movements are often triggered off suddenly and researchers may not be prepared to plunge into studies immediately. Fourth, since movements are invariably controversial in their orientation, it will be difficult to avoid taking value positions if we study on-going movements. By the time a study is undertaken what is available to researchers is its documents, the articulations of movement leaders. Even when participants are identified and information is collected orally, those consulted are invariably leaders. If one resorts to analyzing records kept by law and order agencies about confrontations, the participants listed in these are likely to be those perceived as having a nuisance value by the local influentials as these records are often prepared on the basis of prompting by them. In the final analysis, an adequate understanding of the micro-dimension of movements is very difficult because of conventional research strategies and techniques in vogue. Therefore, unless a researcher makes deliberate attempts to view the movement he analyzes from below, he is not likely to capture the grass-root processes involved.

Ignoring the micro-dimension often gives birth to an inflated perception of the scale of a movement. Thus, movements which are often described as all-India movements are essentially regional-local ones confined to specific linguistic regions or even parts of it.

And, in the origin and spread of movements in India we can discern two patterns: (a) independent local origin (at the micro-level) either simultaneously or sequentially, followed by their coordination. In many of the movements in which the participants are identified in terms of their primordial identities, this seems to be the pattern; (b) simultaneous emergence in different regions through the inspiration of charismatic heroes or sponsored by all-India structures such as political parties. Most of the movements which mobilize class/occupational categories are of this type. While under both these patterns of movement crystallization, the ideology and organizational structure seem to be supplied by the top movement leadership in response to the prevalent political values and social policy measures, the tendency is to concentrate on specific and limited areas given the social diversity, cultural pluralism and differing political developments found in different parts of the country. It seems, then, that all-India movements can emerge only under two conditions: (*a*) when the country is faced by an external enemy, unifying all the socially diverse categories, or (*b*) under the magnetic spell of charismatic heroes who transcend all primordial attachments and who can mobilize the people against a commonly perceived enemy.

2
Movement Studies in India: The State of the Art

What impresses, in fact surprises, the student of social movements in India is the proliferation of movement studies in recent years. A quick perusal of the published works indicates that during the pre-Independence era, movement studies had hardly been attempted, in the first two decades after independence (1948–67) studies on movements had scarcely begun and by the third decade of independent India (1968–77) studies on movements came to be an important preoccupation of social scientists.[1] Even after making allowances for possible omissions of earlier publications (1900–47) due to their being out of print and inaccessible, one can safely assert that there has been an explosion of movement studies during the period 1968–77.[2] Therefore, it is particularly opportune to attempt a review

[1] While it will be an extremely interesting exercise in the sociology of knowledge to inquire into the reasons for the near absence of studies of movements until recently and their sudden proliferation at present, we would like to attempt only a tentative explanation here. First, studies of movements are typically an ex post facto enterprise and since India won freedom through one of the most unique and massive national liberation struggles, scholars could have attempted to study them only after its termination. Second, almost all movements during the freedom struggle in India were subsumed under the national liberation movement and therefore a meaningful analysis of any movement of the time could only be attempted in relation to that fact. For these reasons the national liberation movement and hence other movements (peasants, workers, students, caste movements, etc.) could not be studied. Third, universities and scholars were limited in number and the tradition of research was not very strong. Those who did research concentrated on analyzing structures rather than processes. For instance, in sociology the key areas of research until recently were caste, family and village. This resulted in the neglect of several crucial areas, social movements being one of them.

[2] A rough calculation was made ignoring those books which are out of print and journals which have ceased to be published and are hence not available for consultation. This indicates that only four books and less than ten articles were published on social movements during the period 1900-47. Nine books and ten articles were published during 1948-67 and 30 books and 80 articles during the period 1968-77. The

of the studies on movements in India at the present juncture.[3]

In undertaking this task we propose to discuss the conceptual frameworks enunciated, substantive themes covered and methodological issues involved. While most of the space is being devoted to the discussion on substantive areas—movements of specific social collectivities—we begin with a short discussion on the conceptual frameworks used and then go on to methodological issues.

CONCEPTUAL FRAMEWORKS

In spite of the fact that such terms as protest and dissent are invariably used to describe the nature of social movements, the very appropriateness of these terms to characterize Indian social movements has been raised by some (Badrinath 1977:42-46), not simply because these terms are Western in origin, but also because the nature of society in India rendered protest and dissent redundant due to the all-pervasive hierarchy and because authority was accepted not only as the arbiter of truth, but was also buttressed by elements of diversity. Further, through the very pluralism of thought, thought itself had been neutralized and made socially powerless. Thus, public check on the exercise of authority through responsible protest and dissent as expressed in the West was not tenable in India and hence the impossibility of social movements. In the same vein, Pratap Chandra (1977:85-101) argues that Indian culture and civilization can be understood only through a multilinear model and therefore terms such as 'protest' and 'dissent' which imply deviation from the mainstream are irrelevant in the Indian context. The reason why movements of dissent, protest or reform did not exist in ancient India was that uniformity in intellectual orientations, social structures, ideological preferences or even perceptions of truth did not exist. Notwithstanding these assertions, there are scholars who characterize social mobilizations in ancient India as protest or dissent (Devahuti 1977:131-41; Thapar 1977:115-30).

publications here refer only to (a) those appearing in English, (b) articles in professional journals, and (c) those written by persons who pursued a scholastic career.

[3] The fact that the Indian Council of Social Science Research did not commission a review of studies of movements in its first round of reviews which covered the period roughly up to 1969 testifies to (a) the paucity of studies of movements at that time, and (b) the low priority accorded to this area by the academics associated with decision-making at the time.

It is important to keep in mind here that the characteristics of a society shape the ethos and styles of its movements. Further, every social structure creates its own style of protests and modes of expressing these protests (Damle 1977:28-33). Therefore, an adequate framework for the study of social movements should take into account the historicity, the elements of social structure and the future vision of the society in which they originate and operate, and it is the dialectics between these which provides the focal point for the analysis of social movements (Oommen 1977c:37). Therefore, to argue that a movement as a social phenomenon is impossible in a given society is to ignore the intricate and complex relationships between social structure and social movements; what needs to be investigated is the nature and types of movements in a particular society and why they partake of these characteristics.

An inadequate perception of the importance of the *historical context* in shaping social movements has also given birth to misconceptions about the nature of movements (Desai 1954; Bipan Chandra 1979: 328-67). The predominant orientation of social movements in ancient and even in medieval India was religious and this for two reasons: the absence of a centralized political authority, and the nature of the authority challenged was invariably legitimized by religion (see Fuchs 1965; Parvathamma 1977:188-98; Saraswati 1977:167-87). However, this does not mean that the non-religious, that is, political or economic, content was absent in these movements. Often, religious symbols and styles of protest were invoked to achieve non-religious goals.[4] On the other hand, there are those who in their over-enthusiasm to discover 'class conflicts' everywhere characterize all these mobilizations as predominantly economic in orientation (Gough 1974:1391-1412).

During the period of the national liberation movement in India, most mobilizations were overtly against the forces of imperialism and colonialism, irrespective of the categories (students, peasants) or underlying motivations involved. But after freedom, the absence

[4] However, there are authors (K.P. Gupta 1974 : 25-50) who argue that religious movements in India are essentially independent of political involvements and did not pursue any structural reforms or political changes, invoking the case of the Ramakrishna Mission. But the motivation involved in preventing conversion from Hinduism to other religions or the 'political' activities of the Rashtriya Swayam Sevak Sangh do not support this position.

of an over-arching enemy and the differing perceptions about the 'evils' to be attacked necessarily led to (*a*) divergence in the targets of attack (political authority, economic exploitation, cultural domination) and (*b*) varying perceptions about the immediate targets of attack. This led to a diversification in the nature and proliferation of social movements in India. Lack of appreciation of this historical context of the movements has given birth to several sterile controversies.

The change in the historical context also leads to changes in perspectives of analyzing social movements; what were earlier perceived to be religious or reform movements (Farquhar 1924) later came to be viewed as socio-political in orientation (S. Natarajan 1959; Heimsath 1964). That is, the changing historical context shapes people's attitudes towards social movements and consequently the researcher's perception of them. This in turn influences the labelling of movements by scholars. Generally, the labelling of movements by scholars has been confusing rather than enlightening. Most of them do not follow any consistent set of criteria but simply designate movements based on a variety of factors. Movements are often labelled on the basis of a particular identity of participants even when the goals pursued are not innate to the interests of the specific identity. The movements are named after primordial collectivities such as religious, caste or linguistic groups, and civil collectivities such as peasants and students. Similarly, movement labelling is also done on the basis of the nature of collectivities against whom they are led; the anti-Brahmin movement, anti-leftist movement, etc., are examples of this.

This manner of labelling movements can be highly misleading for two reasons. First, the individuals and groups involved in these movements have several identities and the specific identity invoked may not have any relevance for the movement under discussion. Further, a particular identity may be invoked by the enemies of the movement to discredit it. Second, several social categories may be participating simultaneously in a movement, and to designate it after one of these categories would be misleading even if that category constitutes the bulk of the participants who have initiated it.

Yet another frequent tendency is to name movements based on their territorial anchorage, particularly the locality in which they originate and operate. Examples of these are the Bihar, Telengana,

Vidharbha and Naxalbari movements. Such designation of movements does not reveal the nature of these movements at all—the background of the participants, the goals pursued, the means employed, etc. Further, if the movement subsequently spreads to a wider territorial area, the initial labelling becomes obsolete, as illustrated by the case of the Naxalbari movement. Movements are also named after the issues they pursue, although not very frequently. Examples of these are the Tebhaga movement, and the anti-Hindi movement. The difficulties here are mainly two. First, since movements are likely to undergo goal transformations, the initial focus of the movement may change, making the name redundant. Second, these issues may be too narrow in their orientation and may be but one of the several issues pursued by the movement—hence there is the possibility of mistaking the part for the whole. Finally, movements are named after their initial or top leadership. The Ramakrishna Mission movement, the Gandhian movement, the J.P. movement are examples of this. Given the possibility of movements transcending the biological life-span of specific individuals, this mode of naming movements is inappropriate; the initial leaders are bound to disappear in course of time. Second, this mode of labelling movements smacks of the personality-centredness of movements, as against the systemic orientation; it relegates the role of the collectivity, which is so critical in any movement, to the background.

These reasons compel us to confine our discussion only to those authors who have made systematic attempts at classifying and evolving conceptual schemes for analyzing movements. However, in discussing the studies on substantive areas, we follow the widely-used practice of classifying movements based on the identity of participants because it is not only unrewarding to fit all the studies into any one conceptual scheme but also because we do not intend to impose our conceptual preferences on the authors of movement studies.

M.S.A. Rao (1978a:1-15) distinguishes between three levels of structural changes and pursuantly three types of social movements—reformist, transformative and revolutionary. Reform movements bring about partial changes in the value system, transformative movements aim at effecting middle-level structural changes, and the objective of revolutionary movements is to bring about radical changes in the totality of social and cultural systems. These movements also vary in terms of conflicts embedded in them: conflict is least in reform movements, it acquires a sharper focus in transformative movements, and in the case of revolutionary movements conflict is based on the Marxist ideology of class struggle. There are several conceptual ambiguities in Rao's classification of social movements and we shall refer here to only a few of them.

First, reform and revolutionary movements are distinguished in terms of the *quantum* of change, partial and total. Second, reform or transformative movements are distinguished in terms of *where the change occurs*; in the case of the former, change occurs in the value system and in the case of the latter it takes place at the middle level of the structure. The twin basic principles of any classification are exclusiveness and exhaustiveness. Rao violates the principle of exclusiveness by shifting the criteria of classification used in three types of movements. This shift in criteria brings in several problems. For instance, which type of social movement pursues either partial middle-level structural change or total middle-level structural change? How do we classify a movement which aims at partial as against total change in the value system? What of a movement which pursues revolutionary changes through non-violent means? How do we account for frequent intensely violent conflicts which occur in the course of movements that have primordial collectivities rather than class as their locus? These and several other equally important issues cannot be clarified within the classificatory schema proposed by Rao.

Partha Mukherji (1977 : 38-59 1978: 17-90) classifies movements based on the *quality* of change—accumulative, alternative and transformative. While accumulative changes are intra-systemic, the latter two are systemic changes. Alternative change is geared to create new structures (and by implication to destroy the existing ones); transformative change aims at replacing the existing structure and substituting it by another. This characterization is problematic in that unless one creates new structures one cannot replace and substitute the existing ones and, hence, the distinction between alternative and transformative change becomes pointless. Or is it that under conditions of transformative changes several competing structures already exist in the system and is it a matter of relocating legitimacy from one set of structures to another? If so, why is it that such a possibility does not obtain under conditions of alternative change? Mukherji distinguishes between three types of movements based on the nature of change they pursue: collective mobilization for action directed explicitly towards an alteration or transformation of the structures of a system is a social movement; collective mobilization aimed at wide-ranging and far-reaching changes in the major institutional system is a revolutionary movement; and collective mobilizations aimed at changes within the system are quasi-movements.

Mukherji's analysis implies that (*a*) revolutionary means suit only movements which pursue systemic changes, and (*b*) revolutionary movements should not only aim at far-reaching systemic changes but should necessarily pursue them through revolutionary means. Such a position is untenable because it cannot explain the lack of fit between means and ends in the case of several movements. For example, which is that type of movement which has intra-systemic change as its goal but adopts revolutionary means to achieve it? Again, if a movement pursues systemic changes through institutionalized and even non-violent means, how will we characterize it? To answer these questions we need to transcend the framework proposed by Mukherji.

I have elsewhere suggested (Oommen 1972a) that a situation of strain in a society may be met through one or another of the following response patterns depending upon the system characteristics: (*a*) emergence of a charismatic leader who promises to mitigate the evils at hand and lead the people to a future utopia (*b*) crystallization of a new ideology which champions the cause of the deprived, and (*c*) establishment of a new organization to deal with the problem at hand. It is argued that each of these developments may give rise to the emergence of three distinct types of movements—charismatic, ideological and organizational. The main focus of this typology is on the process of movement crystallization, the life-cycle and phases of social movements. Unlike other typologies it does not insist that movements are necessarily oriented to change; they may not only lead to system stability but in fact pursue it as a goal. It recognizes that even if all movements are change-oriented from the point of departure of the system state, some of the movements may be stability-oriented from the perspective of the point of destination. Finally, it recognizes the possibility of movements getting solidified as organizations over time.

The major limitations of this typology are two. First, it is based on a componential analysis of movements, in that it gives primacy to one or another component of the movement—leadership, ideology, organization—particularly at the formative stage of a movement. This tends to blur the relevance of other components which are equally important for the sustenance of movements. Second, organizational movements as a type would appear to be a contradiction in terms, insofar as movements usually refer to the processual rather than the structural aspects of social reality. However, it is important to note that organizations, in the context of organizational movements, emerge first as counter-structures or as parallel structures to meet the strains released by the institutionalized structures. To this extent, the newly emerging structure is endowed with an ideological base and it should be manned by a leadership different from that of the usual organizational leadership.

Apart from these attempts to evolve general typologies of movements, there have been a few efforts to categorize movements among one or another social collectivities—tribes, peasants, etc. We shall examine these attempts in the course of our discussion on movement studies relating to them. In concluding the present section we may add that the attempts hitherto made to evolve conceptual frameworks for analyzing social movements remain at best tentative, preliminary and bold beginnings. None of the attempts made so far is comprehensive enough to encapsulate all varieties of movements found in India. In order to evolve such a typology we should have many more studies of specific empirical cases unfolding their generalities as well as specificities, a task which is being attended to with increasing momentum in our country.

STUDIES ON SOCIAL MOVEMENTS

In this section we will discuss the studies on movements relating to specific social collectivities. Some of these are discussed separately—religious and caste, tribal and peasant movements—and others are clubbed together, taking into account the quantum of literature to be reviewed.

Religious and Caste Movements

A society like India with an ancient and plural religious tradition is bound to have a large number of movements anchored around religion. The ubiquitous Hindu caste system divides the population of India into countless jatis, based on an elaborate value system and an intricate normative pattern. We propose to discuss the religious and caste movements in the same section, although successively, as there is considerable overlapping and similarities between them. Many of the early religious movements were revolts against orthodox Brahminism and this characteristic is shared by contemporary caste movements also.

Religious movements in India can be divided broadly into three kinds in terms of their response to and consequences for Hinduism.

1. Movements which started essentially as protests against Hinduism and came to be established as independent religions such as Jainism and Buddhism.

2. *Bhakti* movements which attempted to purify Hinduism of its 'evils' and fought against the tyranny of the caste system but subsequently crystallized as sects such as Veerasaivism and Arya Samaj.

3. Movements oriented to opting out of the Hindu fold, conversion to other religions.

The emergence of Jainism and Buddhism in the 6th century BC, repudiating the authority of orthodox Brahminism, is reckoned to be the first major religious protest movement known in India. Jainism denied the authority of the vedas and revolted against vedic sacrifices. Buddhism, while accepting the essential teachings of the upanishads, joined hands with Jainism in denouncing Vedic sacrifices and Brahminic supremacy. While Buddhism may be viewed as a bridge between vedic Brahminism and non-vedic Jainism, in propagating religious ideas both Jainism and Buddhism followed the same path, orienting them to the cause of the common people, asserting the common spiritual right of all men, acknowledging compassion and love for all life, preaching in the language of the common people, and rejecting the authority of the arrogant Brahmin. The second major religious protest movement, Vaishnavism and Shaivism, sought to abolish the intermediary between man and God, the Brahmin. The movements initiated by Kabir, Chaitanya and Nanak represent this trend. A perusal of the available publications clearly indicates that hardly any sociological study focusing on the movement dimension has been undertaken in regard to Jainism and Buddhism and therefore we confine our attention to the remaining religious movements.

Among the sectarian movements,[5] Veerasaivism in Karnataka has been studied by several social scientists (McCormack 1963: 59-71; Parvathamma 1972, 1977: 188-98; Nandi 1975: 32-46; Venugopal 1977: 227-41; Bali 1979: 17- 51). The general tendency is to argue that (*a*) although it started as a movement against a rigid caste system, idol worship, untouchability and other such practices, Veerasaivism succumbed to the same evils it had decried, and (*b*) the movement underwent a process of institutionalization leading to the emergence of a codified ideology, hierarchical organization and religious bureaucracy which inevitably led to a compromising and reconciliatory rather than an opposing attitude towards Hindu orthodoxy, thereby eroding its vitality and ending up as a sect. However, Venugopal suggests that the Lingayats differ from a caste for two reasons : first, their explicit rejection of the notion of ritual pollution which is central to Hindu-caste ideology, and second, the sub-groups among Lingayats have a competitive relationship unlike the Hindu castes which are characterized by complementarity of relationships.

At any rate, it seems clear that Veerasaivism was not successful in restructuring the prevalent system; at best it led to an elaboration of the existing status hierarchy. Part of the reason for this may be located in the social and economic support base of the movement. The Lingayats were drawn from among priests, traders, peasants, craftsmen and low castes. Insofar as the entry of the priestly category was permitted it was inevitable that they would perpetuate their prestigious position. Further, the priestly group was dependent not only on temple lands but also on the monied traders and urban groups. This meant the accommodation of the latter groups which provided the material resources, with an appropriate status, within the system. Inevitably the lower-caste entrants had to be relegated to an inferior position.

Another sectarian movement was inspired and led by Kabir (1440-1518), a non-literate person who declared an open war against important religious forces of the time—orthodox Brahminism and

---

[5] It may be noted here that a large number of 'sectarian' or *guru*-centred movements in India await sociological attention. The more well-known among them are: the Divine Light Mission, the Brahmakumari movement, the Ananda Margi, the Nirankari, the Radha Swami movements etc. Almost all of them are centred around a *guru*, who is accepted as a charismatic hero by his followers or devotees.

Islam (Saraswati 1977: 167-87). Although disowned both by Hindu and Muslim orthodoxy, people, particularly of low-caste origin from both these religions, took to the teachings of Kabir, thereby rendering his movement and the sects emerging out of it, syncretic in character. The major elements in the ideology of the movement initiated by Kabir were: rejection of the caste system and the traditional priestly order; refusal to recognize the authority of the six Hindu schools of philosophy; denunciation of folklore; intellectualization of religion and using an exclusive language for religious purposes; disapproval of sectarian distinctions between Hindus and Muslims; condemnation of idolatry, polytheism, mythology, asceticism and similar religious notions.

Although Kabir denounced sectarianism and did not initiate disciples, over a dozen sects owe their origin to the ideas which Kabir propounded. Among these only the Satnamis[6] founded by Jagjivan Das and reorganized by Ghazi Das seem to have been studied by social scientists (Parganika 1967: 1-16; Babb 1972: 143-51). Notwithstanding the variations in details, all these sects trace their inspiration to a specific *guru*, denounce idolatry and use the vernacular for religious purposes. Kabir denounced myths but his followers mythologized him; he rejected the caste system but his followers adhere to the caste system and the notions of purity and pollution as is evident in their social interactions. Although he explicitly opposed the priestly order, the Brahmins gained importance in the Panth; in fact, seven Kabir Panth maths are headed by Brahmins. In short, the movement became institutionalized into different sects over a period of time.

The same tendency is found in the case of the Arya Samaj which originated in the Punjab (Jones 1968: 39-54; Bhatt 1973: 69-98; Jordens 1977: 145-62; Suri 1977: 214-26; Vashishta 1977: 227-37) as a Hindu renaissance movement largely to counter the proselytization attempts of Christians and Muslims. Punjab and its adjacent areas were particularly fertile for the spread of the Arya Samaj for two reasons. First, it was not a stronghold of Hindu orthodoxy; the Brahmin dominance was not marked. Second, Christian missionary work had not had any spectacular success here. Born in such a social environment, it was possible for it to characterize true Hinduism,

---

[6] For names of the other sects which were influenced by Kabir partially or fully see Saraswati (1977: 180).

that is Vedism, as far superior to the proselytizing religions and to argue that the Hindu priestly class was dispensable as they were perceived as an exploiting group by the laity.

However, the greatest challenge that the Arya Samaj faced was the iniquitous caste structure and the abhorrent practice of untouchability. The ideology of equality and the apparent absence of social discrimination in Christianity and Islam provided an important attraction to the lower castes. While conversion provided a ready-made mechanism to these religions for enlisting new adult members, the absence of such a mechanism and the difficulties in placing the newly enrolled members into the caste hierarchy were genuine challenges faced by Hinduism. *Shuddhi* (purification), the mechanism of reconversion introduced by the Arya Samaj, was an innovative response to meet the challenge posed by the threat of conversion. Although originally a mechanism of reconverting individuals, *shuddhi* was soon extended to Untouchable caste groups, up-grading them to a touchable status. *Shuddhi* bestowed on the Untouchables full religious status—access to vedic rites and the right to mix socially with caste Hindus. However, given the severity of the caste system and its oppressive character, the social rights of Untouchables who had undergone the *shuddhi* ceremony soon came to be restricted and they were treated as a source of pollution by the Arya Samajists with caste Hindu antecedents. The status within the caste framework, of those who took *shuddhi*, and were of Christian or Muslim origin, loomed large. The attempt to solve this problem through the creation of a new organization, Arya Bharati Sabha, to integrate the adherents of the Arya Samaj into a new *biradari* (brotherhood) irrespective of their origin, was stoutly opposed by most Arya Samajists, as it was against the teachings of Dayanand. The only practical solution was to allow each group to be *socially absorbed* into their groups of origin, which inevitably weakened the unity and force of the movement.

Apart from these internal contradictions, the movement also faced hostility from other religions. Although the Hindus and Sikhs presented a common front against Muslim and Christian conversion initially, this unity was shortlived as low-caste Sikhs were accepted into the Arya Samaj fold through *shuddhi*. The antagonism between Hindus and Muslims was also aggravated because of the reconversion into the Arya Samaj of the 'forcibly' converted Muslims. In the final analysis, the Arya Samaj seems to not only have reinforced the traditional caste system but aggravated inter-religious hostility.

Through an analysis of the Ramakrishna Mission (K.P. Gupta 1974 : 23-50) it has been suggested that the prevalent perspective of viewing modern religious movements in India as a response to the Western challenge is erroneous. Movements such as the Ramakrishna Mission clearly point to the innovative potentiality of Hinduism. Vivekananda realized the central significance of hierarchy not only as a social fact but also as a mental construct for Hindus. In such a society change can occur only from the top down and the medium of change can only be religious; social reform and politics can become relevant to a Hindu only if it comes through his religion, which is all-encompassing. Further, change occurs through the individual's realization of his divine potential; collective endorsement of any structural reform or political change is irrelevant.

While pointing out, on the one hand, the importance of hierarchy, religious ethos and the vertical transmission of change in Hindu society, Gupta suggests, on the other, that change is possible only through the individual realizing his divine potential. The relevant question is whether it is possible for an individual to realize his potential—divine or secular—in such a society. Further, implied in Gupta's argument is a synergetic model of the change process and therefore collective involvement and hence social movements are either impossible or irrelevant in such a society!

Conversion to a religion is essentially an individual act. However, in India it was inevitable that it should become a group phenomenon largely because of the fact that the social location and interaction of individuals independent of their present and antecedent caste status was impossible. Therefore, it was collectivities—tribes, castes, kingroups—rather than individuals which converted and this often meant mobilization of these groups for conversion. Hence, several social scientists tend to describe group conversion from Hinduism to other religions such as Islam (Rizvi 1977: 13-33), Buddhism (Zelliott 1977 : 119-44), the Bahai faith (Garlington 1977: 101-18), and Christianity (Forrester 1977: 35-66; Oddie 1975: 61-80. 1977a: 67-99) as movements.

The points emerging out of the studies of conversion movements are as follows :

1. It has been frequently argued that conversion, particularly to

Islam and Christianity, at particular historical periods, was motivated by economic and political gains. This argument has been contested by pointing out that (a) it ignored the importance of status identity and mobility, especially for converts from Untouchable castes, (b) conversion to religions like Buddhism, Sikhism and the Bahai faith also took place, none of which could have offered material induce-ments, and (c) to converts from well-off sections material incentives could not have been a motivating factor.

2. Conversion being a group phenomenon, one or more of the following resulted, particularly in conversions to Christianity : (a) if two or more castes of identical status with traditional animosity existed in a region only one got converted; (b) if both or all were converted they invariably embraced different denominations; (c) if two or more of these castes embraced the same denomination, cleavages continued within the fold of the church; (d) irrespective of denominational variations the social stigma continued and further fissions took place, as illustrated by the case of neo-Christians.

3. Individual or family conversions, as against mass conversions, were usually confined to upper or intermediate castes. This indicates that a certain level of ritual status, social rank and economic inde-pendence were prerequisites to withstand probable local opposi-tion to conversion. However, the lower castes, particularly those who were dependent on the converts from clean castes, followed the example of their masters, and the clean-caste converts would invariably assume leadership positions in the new context (Church), thereby perpetuating their dominance.

4. If, in a region, the lower castes were converted first and experi-enced distinct socio-economic improvement and gained definite political advantage, this 'demonstration effect' often prompted non-Brahmin clean castes to get converted as well. If upper-caste converts were already entrenched in leadership positions in a region, the new converts from low castes found little material gratification and experienced limited social integration, both of which would infuse a sense of alienation among them. In contrast, if a caste of low ritual and economic status was the first to get converted in a region, it might monopolize the benefits accruing from conversion and experience upward mobility.

5. If only a section of a caste was converted, there was a possi-bility that a dual social control system—the new religion and the

old *biradari*—regulating their conduct and shaping their style of life emerged, often generating tensions.

6. The strategy of conversions followed by different religious groups differed: Muslims tended to convert the elite first, attesting to a downward filtration theory; the Catholics usually attempted mass conversions which also meant converting the lower castes, and the Protestants concentrated on individuals and families.

7. If the proselytization technique adopted resembled the Hindu ethos, for instance, presenting the prophet as an *avatar* as the Bahai faith did, the distinctiveness of the new religion might be lost and the adherents might come to perceive it as an extension of the old one. On the other hand, if in the cognitive map of the people the values and norms of the new religion produce a cultural estrangement, its attraction for the potential converts might also erode as in the Bahai case.

8. If a religion hopes to draw lower castes into its fold and retain them it should have (*a*) absolute social equality, (*b*) a rational outlook, (*c*) intellectual creativity, (*d*) the possibility of converts continuing to draw their special privileges from the government as depressed classes, and (*e*) militancy in offering protection but allowing them to retain their own leadership and respectability.

9. Socio-political separatism of the lower-caste converts from others, both fellow castemen who continue in the Hindu fold and the Hindus as a whole, seems to be an inevitable consequence of conversion. This in turn facilitates the development of a distinct social identity and culture which may lead to the psychological emancipation of the converts if the appropriate climate is created in the new religion.

10. Over a period of time the intensity of conversion movements declined due to (*a*) the proselytization efforts of Islam and revivalism being discontinued in terms of rigid religious practices as manifested in the emergence of the Tabligh or Ahmadiya movement among the Muslims (Rizvi 1965; Spencer 1974; Marwah 1979), (*b*) the emergence of the Arya Samaj and reconversion to Hinduism through *shuddhi* (Y.B. Mathur 1972), (*c*) the denunciation of the practice of Untouchability by social reformers from among the caste Hindus, (*d*) the introduction of the policy of protective discrimination and the denial of caste-based privileges to converts, (*e*) the initiation of movements which sought self-respect for the backward castes within the Hindu fold, and (*f*) the extension of concessions, such as

allowing Untouchables entry into temples, initiated by a responsive political elite drawn from the caste Hindus.

Protests against Brahminical supremacy and the tendency to opt out of the mainstream of Hinduism either through the formation of new religions or through conversion to other religions were known in India since early times as we have already seen in the review of studies relating to religious movements. However, by the turn of the 19th century, with the origin and spread of the national movement, a qualitatively different type of movement, the Backward Classes movement, emerged in different parts of India among the various depressed caste groups. The critical difference between the current caste movements and the erstwhile religious movements is that while the latter attacked or opposed Hinduism and wanted its adherents to opt out of the Hindu fold, the former beckons its followers to adapt to Hinduism and seek solutions to problems within its framework, at any rate without rejecting their religion.

We can differentiate between three types of caste movements based on their goal orientations. They may be designated as: (*a*) status mobility movements, (*b*) caste unity movements, and (*c*) caste welfare movements. However, a particular movement may shift its goal orientation over a period of time either because the critical goal is achieved or because it has become redundant or because it cannot be achieved. We come across three sub-types of caste mobility movements viewed against the background of the style they pursue: (*a*) adaptive movements, (*b*) movements oriented to cultural revolts, and (*c*) counter-cultural movements. We shall discuss each of these in succession.

The oppressive as well as elastic character of the caste system and the failure of earlier attempts to escape caste-based discriminations by opting out of Hinduism, seem to have prompted many caste groups with low ritual status to improve their position by adopting the style of life of the norm-setting groups in their respective regions. This process is usually referred to as Sanskritization[7] and several empirical studies of this process have been attempted (Harper 1968: 56-65; Rowe 1968: 66-77; Bhat 1978: 169-89). It is important to note here that while the initial tendency was to view

---

[7] It was Srinivas who first conceptualized this process as Sanskritization. He reckoned it to be mainly a source of mobility for lower castes through the adoption of the culture and styles of life of the upper castes.

Sanskritization as an imitative process, protest orientation and counter-mobilization are necessary attributes of Sanskritizing movements (Ahmad 1971:164-91; Rao 1977:60) because the Sanskritizing low castes often did it in a spirit of recalcitrance and the upper castes invariably opposed such attempts. Further, the mechanism of caste mobility movements was not confined to Sanskritization. The introduction of the Census by the British and arrangement of castes in terms of presumed or established social and ritual superiority also gave birth to mobilization for higher status, usually by Untouchables, Shudras and some Muslim groups, through the Census authorities. Although not very significant in the beginning, this mechanism gained momentum by 1901 and became significant by 1931. If the administrative authorities were to be convinced and forced to make decisions, the articulation of collective interests through pressure groups, which involved mobilization and protest, was often necessary. Viewed against this background, it seems no accident that by the 1930s almost all backward castes formed their associations (sabhas) and started claiming higher status.

The formation of caste associations provided an instantaneous technique for mobilization of caste collectivities. Unlike the traditional caste *panchayat*, the catchment area and the scope of these associations have been much wider. The backward castes were the first to form these associations for the twin purposes of claiming higher ritual status and pursuing socio-economic advancement. In many cases the thrust ceased to be Sanskritization, in that they refused to accept the caste Hindus as their reference group but yet attempted to gain status and self-respect by remaining within the Hindu fold, often taking an overt anti-Brahmin stand, as illustrated by the Ezhavas of Kerala (see Jeffrey 1974:39-59, 1976:3-27; Rao 1978b) who often resorted to mass mobilization and protest to acquire their rights. In other cases, they piloted a cultural revolt (Omvedt 1976) as in the case of the Malis of Maharashtra, or tried to achieve their goal by influencing the political process (Hardgrave 1969) as did the Nadars of Tamil Nadu.

It is significant to note that in all these cases the castes involved were not economically depressed and at least a section among them were well-off by local standards. Ritually, too, they were not at the bottom and most importantly, their numerical strength was substantial, all of which were crucial factors in their revolt against the traditional elite and their culture. It is also likely that some of them could afford to be rebellious because they were supported by rulers of particular regions, as in the case of support extended by the Maharaja of Kolhapur to the non-Brahmin movement in Maharashtra (Copland 1973:209-25; Omvedt 1976). If indeed a caste with a very low ritual and socio-economic status but with substantial numerical strength mustered sufficient courage to revolt against the traditional elite they should have had a long tradition of urbanization, occupational diversification, exposure to modern education, and should have been led by an outstanding leader, accepted as a charismatic hero by them, as exemplified in the case of the Mahars of Maharashtra (Zelliot 1970:397-415). But in all probability, due to their very low ritual status they may not succeed in achieving their goal of status mobility within the Hindu fold and may be prompted to opt out of Hinduism as Ambedkar and his followers did by embracing Buddhism.

The third sub-type of caste mobility movement we have referred to above is geared to develop a counter-culture against caste Hindus, particularly Brahminical supremacy, but remaining firmly within the Hindu fold. There are two variants of this: (*a*) that which builds up a new myth, folklore and culture countering the dominant and mainstream culture, the Aryan culture based on 'racial', cultural and regional-linguistic differences (the archetype of this variety of movement is the Dravidian movement of Tamil Nadu), and (*b*) that which attempts to build a parallel culture, rather than trying to get absorbed in the 'mainstream' culture or merely protesting against it (the incipient Dalit Panther movement of Maharashtra exemplifies this trend). In terms of goal orientations the Dravidian movement may be divided into two phases: the caste (anti-Brahmin) phase and regional (anti-north) phase. While some of the authors (e.g., Irschik 1969; Devanandan 1970) confine their analysis to the first phase, others tend to deal with both the phases (e.g., Hardgrave 1965). However, we are here concerned only with the anti-Brahmin phase of the Dravidian movement (the regional phase will be taken up for discussion later).

As we have indicated above, this movement is different from others which attacked Brahminical supremacy in that it not only focused attention on the economic, political and cultural domination of Brahmins but it identified them as aliens (Aryans) and intruders into Dravidnad. It not only rejected and ridiculed the

Brahmin-created puranas as imaginary and the Brahmin-prescribed *varnashram dharma* as irrational and immoral, but attempted to create a counter-culture which is non-Brahminic and Dravidian in orientation. As a corollary to this, the norms set by Brahmins—child marriage, enforced widowhood, idol worship—too were denounced and in its place the movement sought to introduce and institutionalize rational norms of behaviour. Once the Brahmin dominance in Tamil Nadu declined,[8] it became imperative for the movement to shift its goal from anti-Brahminism if it were to survive. Thus, after a short period during which the movement pursued the goal of establishing a sovereign Dravidian state, it settled for the objective of moderating north Indian domination—economic and linguistic—and for greater authority for states within the federal set-up and promotion of Tamil nationalism and culture within the framework of the Indian Union, thereby becoming a regional movement.

In contrast to the Dravidian movement which was confined to Tamil Nadu, the Dalit Panther movement, although presently concentrated in urban Maharashtra and gradually spreading both within and outside the state, does not operate on a specific territorial basis. Its main thrust is the intellectual awakening and the creation of revolutionary consciousness among the oppressed through the publication of literature (Bhoite and Bhoite 1977:60-75) and occasional collective mobilizations (Oommen 1977a:153-93). However, they do not as yet have a sustained action programme, an important attribute of any movement.

The central tendency in social behaviour in India has been that the caste Hindus take to certain innovative behaviour and others follow suit. But it seems that for once the backward castes have offered a model of action to the forward castes, in forming the caste associations which constituted the beginning and provided the core of their mobilizational activities. But the problems of the latter were different and most of the associations formed by the

[8] It is extremely difficult to empirically verify whether or not the Brahmin dominance has declined, yet there are clear indications that it did in specific contexts. For instance, in the 1972 Tamil Nadu Assembly elections (of the 176 members) not a single Brahmin was elected. Of the 126 unreserved seats (50 were reserved for Scheduled Castes and Scheduled Tribes), 120 went to backward castes and only six to Mudaliars and Chettiars, non-Brahmin forward castes. In contrast, in the 1920s Brahmins with 5 per cent of the population occupied 90 per cent of white collar jobs.

forward castes were oriented towards social reforms—opposing child marriage, approving widow remarriage, encouraging women's education, promoting occupational diversification and modern education, breaking the social barriers between numerous *jatis*. That is, caste unity or consolidation for political or social purposes was the objective of the associations formed by the upper castes.

Several social scientists have called attention to these movements of caste fusions among the upper castes. (Rudolph and Rudolph 1960: 5-22; Kothari and Maru 1965: 35-50; Khare 1970; Conlon 1974: 351-65; Shah 1977a). Starting as efforts at fusion of sub-castes, several of the upper caste movements ended up by establishing a series of voluntary associations for the welfare of their clients or were united into caste federations which provided them with a platform for political consolidation or acted as bridges between tradition and modernity. It seems that most of these caste associations could provide their clientele with instrumental pay-offs but emotional or expressive unity has scarcely been achieved through them.

The introduction of the policy of protective discrimination for the welfare of backward castes, which recognized ritual inferiority as the criterion for extending economic and political benefits to them, changed the character and the strategy of mobilization among them. Instead of Census appeals and Sanskritization along with cultural revolts and the building of counter-cultures, they are organizing themselves politically in order to (*a*) get enlisted as Scheduled Castes/Backward Classes, (*b*) to wrest as much benefits from the state as possible, and (*c*) to insist that the constitutional guarantees are extended for a longer period and implemented faithfully. Although a number of social scientists have called attention to the dilemmas involved in the competing demands of status and power and the contradictions involved in such a socio-political process, hardly any analysis of the process of mobilization, styles of protest and the process of differentiation which emerged among the backward castes exists. The rare beginnings made in this direction only offer general statements (Oommen 1972b: 139-46; 1977a: 153-93). We need to undertake specific empirical studies of particular caste movements oriented to welfare in order to understand this process against the background of the regional cultural variations in India.

Apart from the studies of particular religious and caste movements, several authors (Heimsath 1964; S. Natarajan 1959; Metcalf
1965; Ghose 1969) attempt to relate the social reform movements,
which fought against several social evils (rooted in religious customs
and caste practices), with the wider current of nationalism. It has
been suggested that individual outrage against particular social
customs and religious beliefs has *always* been a feature of Indian
society; despite the high value placed on continuity, order, and the
wisdom of the social precedent. The rebel either became a *sanyasi*,
thus opting out of the system, or he came to be revered if he caught
the popular imagination. However, it is important to recall here
that (*a*) even when a person became a *sanyasi* he opted out of the
system only in regard to his personal life; his interaction with the
system, if he preferred to be a change agent, would have to continue,
and (*b*) at least some *sanyasis* came to enthuse people as innovators,
that is, as change agents. What is critical, however, is the process
of *social legitimation*, in which case only the rebels who acquired it
came to be hailed as innovators, failing which they were dismissed
as quixotic. But for the ideas put forward by the social innovators
to spread to a wider population many social barriers would have to
be broken.

Prior to the emergence of an all-India nationalism in the late
19th century, which was articulated through the Indian National
Congress, India experienced several 'nationalisms'—linguistic,
religious, caste. Therefore, it was necessary to transcend these
traditional primordial boundaries and the general social reform
associations drew their membership mainly from those whose
common interest was social reform, not religious communion or
caste identity. But the rigid hierarchical structure and the deep
institutionalization of the value of inequality was bound to be
reflected in the emergence and spread of reform movements.
Thus, for example, by the time of the First World War there were
three dominant streams of reform movements in Maharashtra,
namely, Brahmin-led urban-centred movements such as the Parthana
Samaj and National Social Conference; non-Brahmin or anti-
Brahmin movements of the kind led by the Phule, whose main
purpose was to gain social and religious recognition for the middle-
ranking castes; and the movement of the Mahars, the most oppressed
section of Maharashtrian society. Each of these movements pursued
the differing needs and interests of their respective constituency;

the latter two although mainly concerned with raising their respective position *vis-à-vis* the higher castes, did incorporate emancipation of women, breakdown of barriers between sub-castes, temperance, and the need to widen educational opportunities as their goals.

In contrast, the main themes of the upper-caste reform movement were widow remarriage and improvement of their condition, abolition of infant marriages and *purdah,* ending restrictions on overseas travel and abolition of locally respected high-caste customs, such as *kulinata* and female infanticide. This differential orientation of different caste groups clearly points to the relevance of the existential conditions and the level of consciousness of the people in the emergence and spread of social movements.

The original nationalists of the Congress were able to combine political struggle and social reform in their thinking and action because the standards for both were derived from the West (Heimsath 1964). The new nationalists had to repudiate not only the political ideas and methods of the Congress but also the social inspiration and methods of reform pursued by the National Social Conference, because both were alien in orientation. This indigenous orientation in nationalism then seemed to be running parallel to caste-based social reforms. Thus, although the pre-national primordial orientation was overshadowed by an all-India orientation, in retrospect it appears that it was a transitional phase and the subsequent emergence of indigenously inspired nationalism brought back the parochial orientation, which at least partly rendered the national movement militant (cf. S. Natarajan 1959; Ghose 1969). By the 1920s the rift between the two national reform movements ended and social reform became a part of the political programme for national advancement.

Heimsath (1964) suggests that India is an over-organized society and what can be achieved in the West through impersonal organizations is accomplished in India by the personal magnetism of a *guru*-like leader. *Guru* worship replaces organization as a means of mass persuasion; the ideas and traits enunciated and embodied by the *guru* come to be venerated and followed. Having understood this, Gandhi thought that the exemplary personal behaviour of the leader was the most important instrumentality in bringing about desirable social change in India. He broke from the style of earlier social reformers who had mainly confined their attention to the

ideational realm, and plunged into direct social action—*satyagraha,*
public demonstration, etc. Further, he involved the dispossessed in
social movements as participants and viewed the government as an
opponent. His success in massive mobilization of the populace can
be attributed largely to his charismatic appeal, the techniques
employed for mobilization, his recognition of the role of the deprived
in movements, and the characterization of the British government
as an enemy (cf. Oommen 1967: 85-89).

With the emergence of the secular welfare state, those at the
helm of affairs who were led by Nehru were of the view that the
state should regulate individual lives at least in matters affecting
social order and progress and they supported the government's right
to interfere with social customs.[9] Thus, social legislation sponsored
by the state came to be substituted for social reform movements.
However, available evidence indicates that legislation and movements operating independently cannot bring about social change
in a desired direction; it is only when a responsive political elite responds to the aspirations of the people, as articulated through
social movements, by passing and vigorously implementing radical
legislation which reinforces the ideals of the movement, that desirable social change can be institutionalized (see Oommen 1975a :
1571-84).

Tribal Movements

Tribal movements in India have two main geographical and
political anchorages. Movements among the encysted tribes of
central and eastern India have mainly been oriented to their betterment within the Indian Union and movements among the tribes of
the north-eastern frontier have often shown secessionist tendencies,
which cast doubt on the very possibility of their improvement
within the national framework and question the legitimacy of the
nation-state to encapsulate them. The empirical investigations of
tribal movements among the encysted tribes may be broadly divided
into two types: those which emphasize the religious/revivalistic or

[9] However, this assertion is contrary to the prevailing experience in India. This is
evident in governmental inability to legislate a uniform civil code, to take over
educational institutions run by religious minorities, etc. Further, even when legislation
exists (e.g., laws against Untouchability, child marriage, excessive dowry) the
government fails almost totally to implement the laws because of deep-rooted customs.

reformist/developmental orientation (Jay 1962: 282-315; Fuchs 1965; K.S. Singh 1966; Ekka 1972: 424-31; Bhadra 1977: 131-37; I.P. Desai 1977: 32-137; Troisi 1979: 123-48), and those which focus on the political-separatist orientation (J. Sen 1972 : 432-37; K.L. Sharma 1976:37-43; Dhan 1977:194-204; Bharadwaj 1977: 161-86; K.S. Singh 1977:317-43).

One of the earlier attempts to study tribal movements was that of Stephen Fuchs (1965) and perhaps the only book to date which deals with a large number of tribal movements. He characterizes these movements as messianic or millennial movements led by rebellious prophets, who are either individuals gifted with abilities to assume the role of a messiah, or they are allocated the role by the community when it faces economic distress, social strain or political oppression. Fuchs suggests that the success of such a movement would depend on the individual ability of charismatic leaders, thereby ignoring the relevance of system characteristics in determining the origin and success of movements and the relationship between the type of leadership and social structure. Not only does Fuchs not attempt any systematic categorization or rigorous conceptualization of movements, but even the empirical details presented are of a touch-and-go variety (as many as 50 movements are described in less than 300 pages!)

To crown it all, Fuchs often makes logically contradictory statements. While on the one hand, he argues that most movements arose due to acute economic deprivation and political oppression, he suggests, on the other, that social and spiritual values are much more potent motives for the initiation of reforms. Similarly, while on the one hand he argues for an understanding of the specificity of tribal cultures, on the other he recommends a policy of acculturation to assimilate completely the 'backward' communities into the national culture to 'avoid' 'dangerous future messianic movements'. It is clear, then, that Fuch's study of tribal movements is a poor example of an anthropological enquiry.

The other studies on tribal messianic movements deal with one or another of these movements and are invariably descriptive accounts. The general trend is to suggest that local tribal leaders initiate movements for revitalization, reform or status mobility, and a host of factors are listed for the success or failure of these movements. However, none of them utilize or propose a theoretical framework to analyze the empirical data.

Most of the movement studies of encysted tribes which focus on the political-separatist dimension refer to movements in the Chotanagpur region with particular reference to the Jharkhand movement. Chotanagpur is inhabited by some of the most populous tribal communities consisting of settled agriculturists and which were sensitized to Vaishnavism even prior to the advent of the British. Led by local tribal saints (Bhagats) steeped in the *bhakti* tradition, it was fairly easy for these tribes to understand and empathize with Gandhi's leadership, the Indian National Congress, and the national liberation movement. Further, Chotanagpur was the most advanced of the tribal regions in terms of literacy, political consciousness and industrial progress. Major tribal communities inhabited a geographically distinct and contiguous region. The Christian missions influenced the lives of tribes here substantially. Christianity provided them with a history and a myth. It planted the notion of private rights in land, promoted education and health care and emphasized a sense of separateness from the rest. Finally, the Chotanagpur tribal history is characterized by a tradition of militant and organized struggles.

K.S. Singh (1977: 317-43) describes the shift in orientation of tribal movements in Chotanagpur from 1900 to 1975 with the phrase, 'from ethnicity to regionalism' and identifies six phases in this transformation:

1. The pre-1920 phase characterized by the introduction of developmental programmes and initiation of reform movements along Christian denominational and inter-denominational (Catholic, Lutheran and Anglican) lines by missionaries.

2. The period 1920-38, marked by the activities of the Chotanagpur Unnati Samaj, dominated by an emerging tribal urban middle class drawn mainly from Lutherans and Anglicans.

3. The 1938-47 phase which saw the rise of a militant movement under the inspiration of the Adibasi Mahasabha, which brought together most Christian tribals, except Catholics and some non-Christian tribals. The Bengalis in Bihar and the Muslims in the region too supported the Mahasabha, and made common cause with the tribes, thereby widening the political base of the movement.

4. The period from 1949 to 1958 was crucial in that it saw the

emergence of the Jharkhand Party from the womb of the Adibasi Mahasabha. Although predominantly a tribal party, insofar as its orientation was regional, it was thrown open to all people from the region, thereby facilitating the transition from ethnicity to regionalism. The period from 1952-57 was the peak period of the Jharkhand movement and once the States Reorganisation Commission appointed by the Government of India refused the formation of a separate state based on ethnicity, much of its legitimacy was eroded.

5. The fifth phase was marked by the gradual decline of the Jharkhand Party (1959-62). The increasing impact of development programmes in the region and the growing involvement of tribals in them, the fission between the elite and the backward among the Christian tribals, the increasing possibility of tribal political interests being accommodated in the formal political structures, the inability of the party to provide a radical agrarian programme for the tribal masses, and the factionalization within the party are some of the reasons for its decline.

6. The last phase of tribal movements in Chotanagpur (1963-75) started after the fourth general election. This phase is characterized by the fragmentation of the Jharkhand Party[10], factionalization of tribal politics along ethnic lines, the rise of urban middle class pressure groups and political extremism, agrarian radicalism and cultural revivalism.

Notwithstanding the shift from ethnicity to regionalism, the Jharkhand movement could not develop into a full-fledged regional movement because *(a)* its appeal to the non-tribal sections was limited, given the movement's identification with and domination by tribals, *(b)* its past record of alliances with forces which worked against the national movement, *(c)* its internal structural contradictions, and *(d)* the exposure of the region to pan-Indian forces, the impact of development programmes, and the influence of the macro-political system. And perhaps partly because of this, the separatism in Chotanagpur did not develop into secessionism as in the north-east.

---

[10] At present there are several distinct Jharkhand parties with different social bases. For example, the Hul Jharkhand Party is almost entirely supported by Santhals, the All-India Jharkhand party by the Hos of Singhbhum, the other Jharkhand party by the Mundas, etc.

Although the political crisis in the north-east, particularly Naga-land, Mizoram, Manipur and Meghalaya where the demands for 'secession', 'autonomy', 'independence', etc., have been strong and persistent for quite some time, very few sociologically informed studies of this phenomenon have been attempted (Means and Means 1966-67; Dommen 1967:726-39; Chaube 1973; Misra 1978:618-24; Ramasubban 1978:393-412; Guha 1979:455-78). The prevalent explanations may be grouped under three heads : distinc-tiveness of the region and the people, internal-structural contradic-tions developed within the society of the north-east, and conflicts of interests between the local and the national bourgeoisie.

The main elements of the distinctiveness of the region and the people are: *(a)* the historical/physical isolation of the people till the British conquest, the official colonial policy of non-interference with the society and culture of the people, the ambivalent policy pursued by the Government of India in perpetuating a sense of isolation and autonomy among the people, along with the policy of drawing them into the mainstream of national life; *(b)* the location of the region on the international frontiers—Burma, former Pakistan and present Bangladesh, and China—which facilitates the supply of arms and ammunition, help in military training programmes, and protection to insurgents by permitting and encouraging the crossing of the national boundaries; *(c)* the nature of the physical terrain which facilitates guerrilla warfare; *(d)* the 'ethnic' difference between the people of the north-east and the plains people; and *(e)* the religious difference between people of the region and the rest of India. While several writers refer to one or more of these distinctive elements, none has attempted a comprehensive study of all these factors. In particular the geo-political dimension is always inadequately dealt with.

It has been frequently argued by some that the 'unrest' in the north-east is linked with Christian missionary activities and pros-elytization. But it is important to keep in mind that while the people of the north-east are of a distinctive physical strain as compared to the rest of the Indians, they vary drastically in terms of their religion; the Nagas and Mizos are mainly Christians, the Manipuris are predominantly Hindus, the Arunachalis belong to the Buddhist and Vaishnava sects, and the demands for autonomy or indepen-dence are not confined to Christian tribals although these pre-dominate among them. But it seems to be true that the missionary influence led to the rapid spread of education, contact with the outside world and the crystallization of political consciousness, all of which have led to the development of a sense of identity and self-hood among these tribals, which in turn has been instrumental in the emergence of 'nationalistic' movements among them. Therefore, while we cannot ignore the 'religious factor' in the emergence and spread of movements in the north-east, it is simplistic and misleading to attribute them to religion exclusively.

The internal-structural contradiction in the region gradually surfaced, consequent upon the demographic imbalance created due to the successive large-scale influx of refugees at the time of partition in 1947, in 1953 and 1964 from East Pakistan and in 1971 from Bangladesh. Apart from this, substantial internal migration, particularly of Bengalis in search of better opportunities, also took place. This demographic imbalance has had both political and economic consequences. The possibility of 'outsiders' becoming a decisive force in the context of electoral choices and capturing leadership positions within the region is being perceived increasingly by the local people. In economic terms the 'outsiders' have come to occupy not only a large proportion of jobs in prestigious occupations and professions but also have virtual monopoly of trade, commerce and industry. The domination of 'outsiders' ran parallel with the emergence of an educated and articulate indigenous middle class who are not only mere aspirants to the coveted positions occupied by the 'outsiders' but also believe that they have the first claim on these positions. Given the slow pace of economic development in the region, both the entrenched 'outsiders' and the ascendant 'insiders' cannot be accommodated by the system and hence the mobilization for the displacement of 'outsiders'. While much of the problem in the north-east can be explained in this vein, it cannot be reduced to that of the gap between the aspirations and fulfilment of the emerging urban white collar and professional occupational categories.

The third perspective put forward to explain movements like the ones in the north-east is couched in terms of an inevitable and growing conflict between the great and little nationalism. The great nationalism of India emerged in the colonial context as the ideology of the pan-Indian big bourgeoisie eager to capture an appropriate share of the growing market in India to the exclusion of, or in collaboration with, foreign capitalists. They perceived an

Indian state more conducive to meeting their aspirations and establishing the hegemony of Indian capitalism and hence they supported the independence struggle. On the other hand, the little nationalism emerged as the ideology of the regional small bourgeoisie, the local middle classes, who feared competition not only from the middle classes of other regions but also from the pan-Indian big bourgeoisie. Therefore, the ideology of the little nationalism is oriented to the exclusive control of regional markets by the respective middle classes. While this perspective highlights one of the dimensions—the economic—of the problem, it is not exhaustive enough to account for several other aspects; in fact it is unilinear in its thrust. Further, it implies questionable assumptions : the unity of interests and the unified character of the pan-Indian bourgeoisie, the absence of a regional base for them, the capacity of the regional bourgeoisie to replace the pan-Indian bourgeoisie, etc.

Although the empirical studies on tribal movements have been limited, considering the size and variety of tribal communities in India, several attempts have been made to systematize the available knowledge through evolving typologies of tribal movements. N.K. Bose (1941:188-94) refers to sub-national movements among tribes, which are typically characteristic of economically backward communities in new nations, initiated by the emerging elite to subserve their interests and aspirations. While it cannot be denied that some of these movements are spurious in that they may not have a genuine mass base, it is also true that in some others there is massive collective participation and they consciously pursue the goal of economic and political power for the masses. Therefore, it is wrong to dismiss all sub-national movements as mere manipulations of an emerging elite to suit its interests and meet its aspirations, as Bose seems to suggest.

B.K. Roy Burman (1971:25-33, 1979:101-22) distinguishes between proto-national and sub-national movements among tribes. Proto-national movements emerge when tribes experience a transformation from 'tribalism' to nationalism; it is a search for identity at a higher level of integration. In contrast, sub-national movements are a product of social disorganization pioneered by an acculturated elite engaged in the contraction of relationship and not the exclusion of it with the outside world. While proto-nationalism results from the expansion of the orbit of development, sub-nationalism is the resultant of the disparities of development. In sub-nationalism the ultimate sanction is the coercive power of the community; in contrast, in proto-nationalism it is primarily the moral consensus of the community. Roy Burman's dichotomous characterization of tribal movements implies that they are anchored in the problematic of identity; tribes either move towards a trans-tribal identity or reinforce a 'tribal' identity. Yet it is true that several tribal movements, while invoking primordial collectivism for mobilization, pursue instrumental goals, that is, socio-economic welfare. Further, there are instances of a cluster of tribes leading a joint movement, thereby transcending 'tribalism' but not necessarily moving towards nationalism. Admittedly then, this classification cannot satisfactorily account for the wide variety of tribal movements falling in this category.

L.K. Mahapatra (1968:46-93, 1972:399-409) attempts a descriptive typology of tribal movements based on a time sequence and the nature of the stimulus in existence during different periods of time. The tribal movements during the pre-British period were mainly religious in origin and content and reformative in orientation, pursuing the goal of status mobility or getting inducted into the Hindu caste system. During the British regime, the movements were mainly against the British administration, although of course they too were invariably led by charismatic leaders and were rebellious in tenor and religious in colouration. The foreign missionary presence led to conversion movements which in turn brought about attempts at Sanskritization oriented to acquiring for tribals social status equal to that of the ritually clean-caste Hindus. Traditional tribal practices such as excessive drinking or sexual permissiveness came to be perceived as the main obstacle to development and the reason for low social status. Even these ostensibly religious reformist movements gradually came to acquire political colouration, got identified with the Indian National Congress with the spread of the national liberation movment, inevitably leading to confrontation with the great power—the British.

However, the pattern was not uniform for the country. In the north-east, British benevolence and Christian patronage in developmental activities, coupled with the awakening of tribal consciousness and identity, inspired movements. Among the encysted tribes, which are already semi-Hinduized, social mobility within the Hindu framework was the main concern. With independence, tribal movements irrespective of the religious persuasions of the participants—

Christianity, Hinduism or Animism—were directed against their exploiters, usually the 'outsiders' in tribal regions, and for a better deal from the government for socio-economic development. Conversion, Sanskritization and the policy of protective discrimination in turn led to the formation of endogamous divisions and the emergence of an elite sector among the tribes; and the deprived among them began increasingly responding to radical ideologies and movements as evidenced by the tribal involvement in agrarian rebellions such as in Naxalbari and Srikakulam.

Irrespective of the time at which these movements originated and the nature of the enemies involved, Mahapatra notes certain general tendencies. First, most tribal movements although initiated by charismatic leaders, gradually led to rationalization and institutionalization, resulting in a structural elaboration but not always effecting basic changes. This conclusion is in conformity with the current theorization regarding charismatic movements, namely, '...a charismatic movement cannot be an agent of any sustained change process, as its ideological appeal cannot be uppermost and its organizational base is necessarily weak' (Oommen 1972a : 182). Second, tribal movements, irrespective of their goal orientation, invariably appeared among the numerically strong, usually the settled agriculturists and the economically well-off tribes. Third, the primitive and small tribes of the north-east directly took to large-scale conversion and Westernization and the separatist tendencies are marked among them. Fourth, given the geographical distribution, ecological variation and different levels of development, a pan-Indian tribal movement is unlikely to emerge. Finally, democratic politics is fragmentary rather than solidary in character so far as primordial collectivities are recognized as the units of development, and this in turn blocks the emergence and institutionalization of civil collectivism. These tendencies clearly indicate that the types of movements which orignate and spread in a society are conditioned by the system characteristics and a theory of social movements necessarily implies a theory of social structure as noted in Chapter 1.

Surajit Sinha (1959:9-32, 1968:11-17, 1972:411-21) attempted an elaborate statement on the nature and types of tribal solidarity movements through several of his articles. He views the changing orientations of tribal movements in a time perspective. First came a series of sporadic tribal rebellions triggered off during the 18th and 19th centuries. Second, a series of reform movements oriented to emulating the cultural pattern of caste Hindus crystallized. Third, a variety of political movements emerged: *(a)* inter-tribal political movements and associations for separate tribal states, *(b)* secessionist movements among tribals located near international frontiers, *(c)* political movements connected with agrarian discontent usually initiated by communists, and *(d)* mobilization by Scheduled Tribes for better distributive justice from the state.

The political movements can be located in a series of social spaces as well. These are: *(a)* the isolated tribes who perceive their social, cultural and political independence as given and natural—therefore the need for asserting solidarity is not relevant to them, *(b)* those who are situated near the international frontier and consciously seek political secession from the Indian Union through the vociferous articulation of a self-conscious political elite among them, *(c)* tribal areas encysted by Hindus, which seek the formation of a separate state, *(d)* scattered groups asserting their rights as Scheduled Tribes, and *(e)* Hinduized and integrated groups seeking political dominance in their specific localities.

Sinha puts forward five major propositions regarding tribal movements:

1. The nature and degree of involvement of tribal groups in solidarity movements will depend on *(a)* the location *vis-à-vis* the core peasant matrix, *(b)* the size of tribal population *vis-à-vis* non-tribals in the region, *(c)* the degree of exposure and socio-economic and cultural interrelationship with the Hindu peasantry, *(d)* the level of economy of the tribe, *(e)* the level of education of the elite and the tribal masses, *(f)* the historical experience (friendly or hostile) in the encounter with the advanced peasantry and urban population, *(g)* the cultural orientation (Hindu, Muslim, Christian, European) of the elite, and *(h)* the pattern of articulation with non-tribal political associations.

2. The intensity of tribal solidarity/separatist movements will be positively correlated with an optimum convergence of the following factors: *(a)* ecological and socio-cultural isolation of the bulk of the tribal population *vis-à-vis* the core peasantry, *(b)* location near the international and inter-civilizational frontier, *(c)* a certain level of numerical and economic strength to provide the striking power, *(d)* a certain level of literacy and education to provide elite leadership,

(e) historical incidence and awareness of conflict with the peasantry, *(f)* the opportunity for political rank, combined with limited
scope for economic emolument, that is—a situation of status incongruity.

3. Conscious solidarity movements will be weak or absent under
the following circumstances:*(a)* small number and low economic
level which is inadequate for generating any striking power,
(b) absence of an educated elite to provide leadership, *(c)* high
socio-cultural integration with the Hindu peasantry to permit contra-
acculturative boundary-maintaining devices.

4. Those tribes which are too isolated and scattered with a
primitive economic base and the lack of literacy and a literate elite
would rarely be involved in solidarity movements. They seem to
prefer a policy of non-interference from others.

5. The major roots of tribal solidarity movements may be traced
to their ecological-cultural isolation, economic backwardness,
feeling of frustration about low status. While these movements are
guided by a minority of the emerging elite it could be an over-
simplification to consider them mere manipulations of a self-seek-
ing elite. On the contrary, these movements seem to indicate a
process of progressive enlargement of socio-political and cultural
experience beyond the primitive tribal units as well as a process of
drawing solidary boundaries around the expanded horizon
vis-à-vis the Indian core.

As a pioneering attempt Sinha's statements about tribal movements in India are elaborate and enlightening. However, substantial
empirical evidence is required to validate several of them. Further,
as they stand, there are several loose ends. We shall refer to a few
of them only as illustrative cases.

First, the time sequence of tribal movements in terms of their
nature does not seem to follow the order as posited by Sinha. For
instance, frequently one comes across the intertwining of the political and reform movements or, for that matter, the tribal rebellions
during the British period can be certainly characterized as political.
Similarly, one or more of the political movements, secessionist
movements and mobilizations for a better deal from the government for instance, may often coexist and in fact coalesce, rather
than operate in a mutually exclusive manner.

Second, the space series postulated by Sinha in terms of the
nature of political movements appears to be empirically incorrect,

at any rate, substantially overlapping. For instance, all tribes located at the international frontier do not articulate a secessionist tendency or the encysted tribes may simultaneously lead a separatist movement for a state and assert their rights as Scheduled Tribes.

Third, the 'propositions' are too clumsy, invariably overlapping, and do not fall into any graduated scale in terms of the attributes of tribes on the one hand, and the likelihood or otherwise of the emergence of movements among them on the other.

Fourth, these propositions do not attempt to link the nature of tribal collectivities with the types of movements which are likely to emerge among them, which is so critical for a meaningful understanding of movements as a social reality.

Finally, the major methodological flaws of the propositions put forward by Sinha about tribal movements are that *(a)* they are at once unilinear and circular, *(b)* exhaustive but not exclusive, both of which make empirical testing an impossibility, and that is the only route through which their validity could have been established.

Agrarian Movements

We began by noting that there had been a virtual explosion of movement studies by the third decade of independent India and even a quick perusal of these studies indicates that a large number of them are on agrarian movements.[11] While a few of these studies attempted to analyze Indian agrarian movements in general, most studies deal with particular movements with their anchorage in specific regions, or analyze one or the other aspect of these movements.[12] The general issues posed in the agrarian movement studies

[11] Although most writers use the term peasant movements to refer to these studies we prefer to employ the phrase agrarian movement. The term peasant refers to only one of the agrarian categories and movements are not confined to this sector; to label all movements of the different agrarian categories (for example the movements of the agrarian proletariat or the agrarian rich) as peasant movements is to mistake the part for the whole.

[12] Several studies of peasant movements have been attempted by political activists such as Swami Sahajanand Saraswathi, N.G. Ranga and P. Sundarayya, who were involved in one or another of these movements. Apart from these well-known accounts available in English, there are a large number of studies published by political activists in Indian languages. Valuable as these works are we consider them raw material for an analysis by social scientists. Therefore, these studies are not reviewed here. There are a few descriptive general accounts (e.g., L. Natarajan 1953; Choudhary 1971) of peasant movements which do not raise specific issues or do not follow or propose any analytical framework. Such studies have also been left out here.

relate to *(a)* the role of the peasantry in the Indian national liberation movement, *(b)* the revolutionary potential of peasants and the strategy to be followed in realizing the same, and *(c)* the tradition of peasant movements in India.

In considering the role of the peasantry in India's freedom movement, it is necessary to situate the peasantry *vis-à-vis* its enemies at that time : imperialism/colonialism and feudalism/capitalism. The basic question faced by the nationalist leadership in the pre-independent era was, against which of these enemies should it mobilize the peasantry first? It has been argued (see A.R. Desai 1979) that attempting the integration of the peasantry (ignoring its internal differentiation) with the rest of the nation in the context of the freedom movement was *(a)* to ignore its specific interests and *(b)* to thwart the crystallization of its specific consciousness. And yet, this is precisely what the national leadership did to mute the divisive forces of caste and communalism by promoting the idea that the peasantry is a single cohesive group. Further, the leadership posited the peasantry not only as the dominant element in the nation, but as its basic constituency, nay as the nation itself (Bipan Chandra 1979:328-67).

The failure to mobilize the peasantry as an anti-*zamindari*/landlord force but to utilize it as a resource against the imperialist forces led to the accusation that the national leadership 'exploited' the peasantry, and that their interests have been sacrificed at the altar of nationalism (Dhanagare 1975a:29-54). Others, while conceding that Gandhi played a vital role in mobilizing the peasantry for the cause of national freedom, accuse him of invoking non-violence to curb the peasants' tendency to fight against the landlord and the money-lender (Alavi 1965:241-77). However, there are others who suggest that the relationship between peasant movements and the national movement was one of reciprocity (Siddiqui 1978).

It has further been argued that the landlords were kept within the national movement by guaranteeing protection of their class interests, while the peasants, on the other hand, were mobilized through the ideology of nationalism. Even the left '...failed to establish a strong link between the anti-feudal and economic consciousness of the peasants and anti-imperialism.... The historical task was to *simultaneously* take up the peasants' class demands and to make them more militant anti-imperialists....Any effort to keep the peasant movement away from the anti-imperialist stream weakened the peasant movement itself' (Bipan Chandra 1979: 355-56). Further, until the 1920s the nationalist movement in India stood isolated from the potent forces of the peasantry and the communists scarcely began their work among the peasants by the mid-1930s, but even after they led agitations for broad peasant demands—for security of tenure, debt relief, cheap credit—they ignored the specific needs and interests of the poor peasantry (Alavi 1965: 241-77).

The above argument pinpoints the failure of the nationalist leaders as well as the leftist forces *(a)* to recognize the differentiation among the peasantry and the specific needs and interests of the different agrarian categories, *(b)* to organize them against landlords and *zamindars* through direct action, which in turn failed to foster the development of their consciousness. But the argument contains several contradictions and we shall only point out some of these.

First, this position denies autonomy of thinking and action to the peasantry and this is implicit in the accusation of nationalist and leftist forces that they either sacrificed the peasantry's interest or failed to mobilize it through an appropriate strategy of action, that is, the peasantry is at the receiving end, it does not possess the capacity to usher in the change process.

Second, if autonomy is denied to the peasantry it is logical to conceive the peasant movement as a tributary to the national liberation movement. Instead of admitting this logical position, it is argued that the relationship between the peasant movements and the national movement was one of give and take, of reciprocity. But reciprocity is possible only between those units which have a fair amount of independence and autonomy, which is denied to the peasantry.

Third, a candid admission of the logical position would imply that the relationship between the national movement and the peasant movements would be vertical, in that the latter derived its inspiration from the former. If so, the only viable course of action for the leadership (nationalist and leftist) was to identify and concentrate on the most *immediate* enemy and mobilize the peasantry also to liquidate that enemy first. Therefore, it would have been strategically unwise to have emphasized *simultaneously* the class demands of peasants and anti-imperialism, particularly because the strength of the immediate enemy, imperialism, was so stupendous.

Fourth, the analysis is naive in its understanding of the processual aspects of movements. Social movements, although informed by an ideology and buttressed by an organizational build-up, both of which indicate its long-term perspective, cannot pursue a strategy and tactics ignoring the immediate environmental challenges. A movement to be successful will have to cash heavily on the prevailing predominant sentiments, literally it has to live from moment to moment. Therefore, the movement leaders will have to give top priority to those issues which are most appealing to the largest possible constituency here and now, and adopt tactics which have the highest returns in mobilizational terms. This implies not only that the enemies are to be identified but they should be arranged in a hierarchical order as it were, and the top one, to begin with, should be concentrated upon. Further, the immediate target of attack will have to be demonized in order to mobilize and sustain the participants' commitment and enthusiasm. Any step which fritters away energy from this immediate goal will be catastrophic to the interests of the movement.

Viewed objectively, this is precisely what the leadership did during the freedom struggle. But its failure to mobilize the peasantry against *zamindars,* landlords and money-lenders soon after the attainment of independence is certainly colossal and indefensible. To confuse the role of leadership between the pre-independent and post-independent phase is to ignore the relevance of the *historicity of context.* As Gail Omvedt (1976) correctly argues, a national liberation movement must necessarily be carried out in two stages. First, it should be waged as a multi-class struggle against the forces of imperialism/colonialism, and second, against feudalism/capitalism. The first is a political movement for transfer of power from the imperialist power to the national elite and the second is a social-revolutionary one. And the latter in turn involves two processes, *(a)* anti-capitalist struggle of workers against the bourgeoisie, and *(b)* anti-feudal struggle against money-lenders and landlords. The struggle against the feudal money-lending category is bound to be a cultural revolt under Indian conditions, insofar as the categories involved are defined and perceived in traditional/cultural terms by the people.

Against the background of the on-going debate on the role of the peasantry in revolution in terms of Lenin, Mao, Fanon and others, Hamza Alavi (1965:241-77) suggests that the relevant issues to be investigated are: under what circumstances do peasants become revolutionary and what role do different sections of the peasantry play in revolutionary situations? In attempting to answer these questions with regard to India, it has been pointed out that India followed a parliamentary approach to peasant mobilization and the support came mainly from the rural upper class via the Congress, who were the main beneficiaries of land reforms. As for the communists, little work was done by them among the peasantry till 1936, the year in which the All India Kisan Sabha (AIKS) was formed. The two main consequences of land reforms were: *(a)* an upper stratum of tenants were able to acquire land and became employers of labour. Although this group participated in the anti-*zamindari* movements, they have now withdrawn (Kotovsky 1964); *(b)* mass eviction of tenants for self-cultivation, which created an explosive situation, but did not develop into a militant movement and this for two reasons. First, although the communists criticized the bureaucratic implementation and asked for peasant committees to be associated with it, they did not resort to direct action. Second, the political behaviour of peasants is based on factions of which there are two types : those which are vertically organized between masters and dependents and those constituted by independent holders.

Among the exploited section of the peasantry there is little or no class solidarity as they are vertically aligned with the masters through factional ties. The support to the leftists can come only from the poor and the independent holders and for this purpose the economic dominance of the rich peasants has to be broken. The poor peasants *initially* are the least militant, but as the anti-landlord and anti-rich peasant sentiment is built up by the middle peasant, the potential revolutionary energy of the poor peasant will be transformed into an actual revolutionary force. For this, the poor peasant is to be shown in practice that the power of his master can be broken. Once the poor peasant takes up the revolutionary role, the middle peasant will withdraw. Presumably then, the revolution will be successfully completed, now that even the doubting Thomases (middle peasants) are outside the orbit of revolutionary action.

In order to explicate his argument, Alavi analyzes two peasant movements in India: Tebhaga and Telengana. His analysis pinpoints *(a)* the initial vanguard role and the ultimate conservative role of the middle peasantry in the making of a revolution, (b) the initial dormancy but the ultimate capacity of the poor peasantry for playing a key role in the revolution, (c) the desirability of homogeneity in the social background of the peasantry and the sponsors of peasant movements (party workers), (d) the need to keep the orientation of the peasant movement within the orbit of nationalist sentiment, (e) the importance of accommodating the varying needs and interests of the different segments of the peasantry involved in the movement, (f) the significance of direct action to sustain the revolutionary elan of the peasantry, (g) the relevance of a clear understanding of the nature of the social structure which moulds the peasant political behavior in order that an appropriate strategy of mobilization is devised and operated. Alavi's argument is refreshing and insightful but its empirical explication is unconvincing. He seems to have found what he was looking for! His data is too meagre and his generalizations too sweeping. Subsequent analyses of these movements have pointed out several deficiencies in Alavi's position (see Dhanagare 1974: 109-34, 1976: 360-78).

Further, the internal consistency and the logical linkage between the points Alavi makes is problematic. For instance, if the economically independent middle peasantry withdraws after initiating the process of mobilization, how can we expect the dependent poor peasantry to carry on the struggle till its succesful completion, simply because it has been shown in practice that the power of its masters can be broken? If the answer is that the poor peasantry will have to be supported by an external agent, say party workers, to sustain the tempo of mobilization, what is the guarantee that the social background of these sections—poor peasantry and party cadre—will be similar so that one does not get alienated from the other? Is it possible to accommodate the differential interests of a highly stratified peasantry within the canvas of the same movement or association? Is it not necessary to think in terms of differing combinations and alliances of the different sections of the peasantry depending upon (a) the nature of the enemies involved, (b) the character of the state and (c) the phase of the struggle? These and several other questions cannot be answered within the framework of the analysis propounded by Alavi (cf. Gough 1969: 526-44).

Among the analysts there is no consensus as to whether India had a long tradition of agrarian movements. For instance, Barrington

Moore (1966:383) suggests that the tradition of peasant move-ments in India has been weak due to (*a*) the caste system, (*b*) the strength of the bourgeois leadership against the landlords and the British, and (*c*) the pacifying influence of Gandhi on the peasantry. K.C. Alexander (1975: 1551-60) notes that agrarian movements in India are based on a psychological perception of inequality in the system, an unanticipated consequence emanating out of the 'Green Revolution', thereby implying that these movements are of recent origin. As against this, Kathleen Gough (1974 : 1391-1412) argues that India has had a long tradition of peasant movements. While Alexander's conclusion is based on a patently ahistorical perspective, the divergence in the positions taken by Moore and Gough, both of whom take into account the historicity of peasant movements in India, can be traced to the varying emphases they place on the different dimensions of movements.

Moore seems to focus on the question, *who* are the participants, and taking peasants as an occupational/class category he excludes those movements in which the mobilization of participants is attempted, invoking their identities based on religion, caste, region, etc. Inevitably he finds that the number of peasant move-ments in India has been too few, considering its vast rural population. In contrast, Gough asks the question, *why* do people participate in movements? Having found that most mobilizations were against exactions of landlords, bureaucrats, money-lenders, the police and the military, she concludes that these are 'peasant' movements, although the collectivities involved were often primordial and the mobilizations were initiated by charismatic heroes and rebellious prophets invoking the participants' religious, caste and similar senti-ments, symbols and idioms. Admittedly, Gough finds ample evidence to conclude that India has had a long tradition of peasant rebellions. Thus, through a definitional twist, as it were, the two authors arrive at diametrically opposed conclusions.

Although we have illustrated this issue by referring to these authors, the problem besets most studies on movements. It is im-portant to recognize that three identities are basic to all partici-pants in movements: primordial/ascriptive, class/occupational and political/ideological. The frequent tendency on the part of analysts to ignore this multiple identity of participants (as Moore seems to do) and emphasize only one or another of these, has cluttered our under-standing of the real character of social movements. Furthermore, the goal orientations of movements are not always unilinear as Gough seems to imply; they are often multi-pronged. To emphasize just one of these goals to the neglect of all others is to do violence to the nature of social reality. This is evident from the classification of 'peasant' movements that Gough follows to which we will turn our attention presently.

Gough classifies Indian peasant movements (which were highly localized till the 1930s) into (a) restorative movements—backward looking, nativistic and promising a future utopia—to drive out the British and restore earlier rules and social relations, (b) religious movements—transformative and oriented to large-scale restructuring of society—for the liberation of a religious or ethnic collectivity, (c) social banditry, (d) terrorist vengeance, and (e) mass insurrections—all of which are initially reformative and aim at partial changes in society. But the third and the fifth have the potentiality of becoming transformative movements. It is clear that most of these movements cannot be designated 'peasant' movements if we view them as mobilizations of collectivities who perceive their identities as peasant, that is, who pursue their interests as class/occupational categories and whose consciousness is rooted in their peasant characteristics. But in her enthusiasm to discover a long tradition of peasant movements in India, Gough ignores all other aspects of human existence and social reality, for she writes: 'What is labelled interreligious or inter-communal strife is often, perhaps usually, initially a class struggle, but unity in the class struggle is all too often broken by the upper classes' appeal to and manipulation of cultural differences and under duress those most oppressed may turn on all the co-religionists of their oppressors' (1974:1433).

It is clear that an attempt is made here (a) to designate all conflicts in society as class conflicts, and (b) to label consciousness rooted in religion, caste, language, etc., as false, both of which are sociologically untenable. In fact, the confusion is further confounded as Gough refers to tribal secessionist and separatist movements, which are clearly sub-national or political movements focusing on transfer of political power, as peasant movements.

A large number of agrarian movement studies are analyses of particular agrarian revolts or rebellions at their intense mobilizational phases. We will discuss the more frequently studied among them to begin with—the Moplah uprising, the Tebhaga, Telengana and Naxalite movements. The series of peasant uprisings (33 in all) which took place in Malabar between 1836 and 1921 have been given detailed attention (Wood 1974: 5-33, 1976a: 97-106, 1976b: 543-58; Dale 1975: 85-97, 1976: 1-13; Choudhary 1977; Dhanagare 1977: 112-41; Hardgrave 1977: 57-99; Pannickar 1979: 601-30). It is significant to note that the recent proliferation of studies on the Moplah rebellion can at least partly be traced to the twin sources of the current interest in peasant movements and problems of communalism,[13] and the raging controversy about whether it was a peasant or communal uprising. A perusal of the above writings indicates that they belong to three categories in terms of their perspectives: those which consider the Moplah rebellion a predominantly peasant uprising, thereby underplaying if not completely ignoring the communal dimension; those which view these as a rebellion of Moplah peasants against the British-fortified power of the Hindu (Brahmin and Nair) landlords and therefore, at once an anti-British, anti-Hindu and anti-landlord struggle; those which look upon these outbreaks as essentially a religious revolt and argue that they cannot be understood as the result of Moplah peasant impoverishment because of the measures introduced by the British. The first and the third perspectives are the inevitable consequence of focusing attention selectively on one or another of the identities of the participants or dimensions of the mobilization, as we have pointed out earlier.

To grapple with this problem it is not enough to point to the multiple identities or dimensions as is attempted in the second perspective; it is necessary to allow for change over time and therefore pinpoint the predominant orientation and motivations involved in a given phase of the movement under which other aspects and identities are subsumed. Dale (1975:85-97), for instance, reports that the preparation for the rebellion often began several weeks before the event, prefaced by a period of intense devotional exercise; and of the 350 persons who directly participated in attacks, 322 died, which indicates that they were martyrs to the faith. While those who participated in the outbreaks between 1836-1919 belonged to a school which espoused a common body of religious doctrine devoid of formal organization and political ideology, the

[13] A couple of studies on the Moplah rebellion were published in the early 1920s. They are, C. Gopalan Nair (1921) and G.F.K. Tottenham (1922). But we do not discuss them here. All the studies discussed here were published between 1971 and 1979.

Khilafat movement endowed the participants of the 1921 rebellions with an organizational structure and a political faith. It is clear, then, that the Moplah rebellion cannot be described as a peasant revolt or an anti-British mobilization. Significant economic and political factors were inextricably intertwined with religious motives and commitments. That is, even as peasants fight for economic and political rights, insofar as religious symbols and values are invoked to mobilize them, the nature of the movement, its course, and even result, are bound to be influenced by this fact. To ignore this is to indulge in partisan analysis and to mutilate facts.

The two well-known peasant movements, Tebhaga (1946-47) and Telengana (1946-51) which began on the eve of Indian independence in Bengal and Andhra Pradesh, respectively, have been analyzed by several scholars: Tebhaga by Hamza Alavi (1965: 241-77), Sunil Sen (1972), D.N. Dhanagare (1976: 360-78), and Krishnakant Sarkar (1979: 469-85); and Telengana by Alavi (1965: 241-77), Barrington Moore (1966), Dhanagare (1974:100-134); C.M. Elliott (1974: 27- 47), Barry Pavier (1974: 1413-20), and K. Ranga Rao (1978:149-168). A large number of factors, the 1943 famine and the drive against *jotedars*, hoarders and black marketeers which followed it, the willingness of the emerging urban middle class to take up the leadership, the social solidarity of the tribals involved in the movement and, most importantly, the increased bargaining capacity of share croppers, facilitated the emergence of the Tebhaga movement. However, it has also been suggested that it was not the class position of *bargadhars* but the communal politics and the general political development which were decisive in the emergence of the movement. Although hailed as the first consciously attempted revolt by a politicized peasantry in India, it is accepted that the movement was limited in its impact and spread and was, therefore, ultimately a failure. Alavi lists the narrow base of the middle peasants in the movement and the social divergence among those who were involved in the movement—the peasantry (*jotedars* and sharecroppers) were mainly Muslims and the party workers, mainly Hindus—and the consequent wedge among them, as the main causes for the failure. According to Dhanagare, the lack of congruence between caste and class, the upper class manipulation of primordial loyalties within the peasantry and communal politics truncated the scope of the class struggle; and the limited goal which underplayed the oppressive character of the land control system and the cleavages between middle and poor peasants thwarted the possibility of the movement from developing into a massive peasant rebellion.

Although initially a success, the Telengana movement was ultimately a failure, according to Alavi, due to the communist support to the *razakars*—the conservative elements among Muslim population—against the Indian army, which ran counter to the nationalist sentiment and movement, and this led to the erosion of its legitimacy, and the incapacity of the movement to cater for the varying interests of the middle and poor peasants as well as the tribal population after the village Soviets were established. Having focused on the class character of the revolt, Dhanagare observes that the movement had a broad class base in that middle peasants, poor peasants and landless labourers forged an alliance and launched a combined attack on the handful of landlords; and yet he suggests that the movement was not a product of a sustained political organization of the peasants and that the involvement of the participants was spontaneous. While the movement did not make any lasting dent in the agrarian structure or lasting change in the conditions of the principal participants, viewed in terms of seizure of power and sustaining it for a considerable period of time, the movement was more successful than any other peasant movement in India.

Elliott attempts to explain the emergence of the movement in terms of endogenous political factors. The continuation of a Muslim monarch in a predominantly Hindu environment became untenable owing to increased pressure for a popular government. In such a situation, instead of being responsive to popular sentiments, the Nizam became more repressive and tried to sustain his power through the support of the *razakars* and acted as a puppet of the British regime. This infuriated the middle class—Hindus and Muslims—with whom the Nizam was reluctant to share power. The Telengana movement is thus an illustration of what befalls a political power which is incapable of responding to middle class aspirations.

It is clear from these accounts of the Tebhaga and Telengana movements that even those analysts who use the same framework differ in their assessment of the causes and consequences of these movements. Admittedly, those who differ in their perspectives emphasize different dimensions and hence their conclusions also differ. In such a situation, instead of treating one or another set of conclusions or evaluations as more valid than others, we must view them as illuminating different dimensions of the same phenomenon and hence as complementary.

Perhaps the most widely studied agrarian revolt in contemporary India is that which began in Naxalbari (West Bengal) in 1967 and spread to other parts of India subsequently. Several factors contributed towards this unusual attention to the revolt: (a) its anti-national slant as manifested in the Chinese support for it, its vocal denunciation of the Indian national leadership on the one hand and the unqualified acceptance of the Chinese leadership as the fountain of its inspiration on the other, (b) its declared intention to capture state power, (c) its tactics of liquidating the class enemies, which meant identifying and murdering specific individuals leading to substantial violence which spread despair among the people, (d) its emergence as a result of intense political factionalism among the leftists, (e) its being triggered off in West Bengal when the state was led by the United Left Front. Admittedly, these factors also influenced the perspectives which were brought to bear on its analyses. Thus, in terms of their dominant orientations the studies fall into one or another of the following categories : those which view it as an attempt to apply the Maoist strategy of peasant struggle to the Indian situation (Mohan Ram 1971; A.K. Roy 1975; Mohanty 1977), those which consider it from the differing perspectives of the communist parties and groups in India (Dasgupta 1974; A.K. Roy 1977: 31-41), and those which analyze the movement in terms of the relationship between social structure and social change (Mukherji 1978: 17-90). We shall confine our attention mainly to the last of these perspectives.

Most of the authors attempt a descriptive account of the origin, spread, strategy, ideology, organization, factions and splits within the movement. While some of them trace the eruption of Maoism in India to the late 1940s and consider the Naxalbari revolt as the culmination of this trend, there is unanimity of opinion that it was fundamentally an armed struggle against forced evictions from vested land and its redistribution. Later, however, it spread to urban centres, particularly to Calcutta where it took the form of a cultural revolt confined to educational institutions. Thus the locale of the revolt, the issues involved, and the tactics pursued attracted participants with irreconcilable socio-economic interests and politico-ideological orientations and motives: the socially cohesive tribals, the peasantry differentiated by caste norms and values, the urban-bred brilliant collegiates from elite families, the school dropouts drawn from urban social marginals, and the anti-social elements. This bewildering variety of participants, the sharp differences of opinion among the leadership *vis-à-vis* the terrorist tactics and the anti-national orientation which informed the ideology and activities of the movement resulted in its failure. Further, the violence it unleashed, the insecurity it created and its anti-national slant facilitated governmental repression which led to the erosion of the vitality of the movement discerned in terms of the mobilizational activities.

Although the declared intention of the movement was capturing state power, in reality '...the revolt was *not directed against the system* but against its excesses...the relations of production were not sought to be altered or transformed, it was the exchange of goods between the producer and the owner that was sought to be properly regulated' (Mukherji 1978: 73-74). The sudden revolutionary onslaught against the landed interest and the state through violent methods was a strategic error, it was the result of a natural cognitive lag between the requirements of a revolt and the demands of a revolution; hence the failure of the movement. In terms of its objective the Naxalite movement only attempted to bring about change *in* the system (it focused only on the excesses in the system) but it was the adoption of non-institutionalized means (use of excessive force and violence) which gave it a revolutionary colouration, argues Mukherji.

By implication what Mukherji suggests is that revolutionary means suit only movements which pursue systemic and not intra-systemic changes. This position implies that there is a logical fit between means and ends, which hinges on the assumption that collectivities behave rationally. But empirical realities do not always fit this expectation: the role of the irrational and a-rational is often substantial in collective behaviour. However, it is significant to note here that for the survival and eventual success of a movement the favourable response of the collectivity is critical. If the 'illegitimacy' of the non-institutionalized means employed by a movement exceeds the limit which can be tolerated by the collective conscience, the movement is doomed to fail, not only because this will lead to the alienation of the people at large and a section of the participants from the movement but also because such a situation legitimizes governmental repression. This seems to be what happened in the case of the Naxalbari movement (Oommen 1979: 305-9).

Apart from the peasant movements we have discussed so far, which secured the researcher's full attention, there are other cases of peasant movements which deserve notice but are inadequately analyzed. The studies relating to them focus attention on one or more of the following dimensions:

1. Associational aspect (Beteille 1970 : 126-37; Crawley 1971: 96-108; Alexander 1979). These studies usually discuss the role of agrarian associations, the easily observable and stable dimension of agrarian movements in specific geographical areas, to the neglect of mobilizational aspects. Even here, a systematic sociological study of the All India Kisan Sabha (AIKS) and similar agrarian organizations enveloping their micro- and macro-dimensions is awaited.

2. The relationship between politics and agrarian movements (Gough 1969: 526-44; Dhanagare 1975c: 66-77; Omvedt 1975: 40-54; Harcourt 1977 : 315-48; Hardiman 1976 : 365- 71). What is referred to as studies of agrarian movements is often the mobilizational programmes of organizations or parties for agrarian categories; during the pre-independence period those of the AIKS, and after independence the mobilizations initiated by the agrarian front organizations of political parties. Insofar as the main catalysts of agrarian mobilizaions are political parties, an analysis of the relationship between politics and agrarian mobilization is crucial for an adequate understanding of agrarian movements and yet this dimension is scarcely studied. The few available studies mainly discuss the role of either the Congress or communist parties in agrarian mobilization or the process of politicization the agrarian categories underwent over a period of time thanks to the activities of these parties.

3. The relationship between social structure and agrarian movement (Pandey 1971 : 201-38; R. Singh 1974 : 44-70, 1978 : 91- 148; Omvedt 1976). The revolutionary role of the peasantry and the participatory propensity of different categories of peasants (rich, middle, small) in movements have been discussed frequently. How ever, systematic attempts to relate the nature of the Indian social structure in its multi-dimensional context (caste, class, power) to agrarian movements are far too few. Most studies view peasant mobilizations in either/or terms—'caste', 'peasant' or 'political'—ignoring the interlocking of these identities leading not only to an

inadequate but erroneous understanding of the nature of the reality. We have made only a beginning in this context.

4. The relationship between the Green Revolution and agrarian movements (Oommen 1971a: 229-68; Alexander 1975: 1551-60; Mies 1976: 172-85; Yang 1976 : 9-13). The Green Revolution in India not only disturbed the traditional agrarian relations but it accentuated economic disparities and accelerated the social aspirations of the rural people. While a large number of studies discuss the agrarian unrest or conflict emanating out of this situation, only a few unfold the movement dimension. In fact, much of the agrarian mobilizations in India at present can be traced to the recent changes brought about through land reforms and the Green Revolution, which calls for immediate attention.

5. The relationship between agrarian legislation and movements (Oommen 1975a: 1571-84). While it is true that quite a few studies discuss the change brought about through legislation and movements as independent social forces, the dialectical intertwining of these is hardly studied. Movements not only cause legislation but they emanate as consequences of legislation. Similarly, unless there is an effective movement, the change attempted through legislation cannot be consolidated and institutionalized. Yet studies which analyze the dialectics between agrarian movements and legislation have scarcely been undertaken.

6. The relationship between mobilization and institutionalization in the context of agrarian movements (Oommen 1977b: 286-304). Conventional movement studies concentrate either on the mobilizational aspect (revolts, rebellions, agitations) or on the institutionalized segment (movement organizations). But no movement can continuously engage in an intense mobilizational process, neither can it ignore the organizational aspect. Therefore, the interlinkage between these two movement dimensions assumes great significance in understanding the processual aspects. Once again it is a scarcely researched area.

Most of the agrarian movements we have referred to so far are characterized by violent mobilizations. Even if violent confrontations did not take place in the course of several movements, it does not mean that they have consciously pursued a non-violent path. But there is a tradition of agrarian movements in India characterized by non-violence which can be traced to Gandhi. The two well-known agrarian mobilizations during the pre-independence era which were believed to have drawn their inspiration from Gandhi are the Champaran *satyagraha* (Mishra 1968 : 245-75; Pouchepadass 1974: 67-87) and the Bardoli *satyagraha* (Shah 1974 : 89-107). Though it is universally accepted that Gandhi was very successful in mobilizing the peasantry in the context of the national liberation movement (Dhanagare 1975b), no systematic effort to inquire into Gandhi's role in and his style of peasant mobilization, save the cases of the two *satyagrahas* mentioned above, has been made. This has led to the unquestioned acceptance of several popular beliefs. However, through an analysis of the Champaran *satyagraha* 'from below', Pouchepadass demonstrates that the people of Champaran hardly knew anything about the national movement, that the *satyagraha* was actually initiated by local leaders and that Gandhi was brought into the picture by them. Shah, in his study of the Bardoli *Satyagraha,* attempts to show the relationship between political mobilization and social structure in a traditional society and concludes that insofar as the traditional organizaitons, institutions, beliefs, values, etc., are used for mobilization, the social, economic and psychological commitment of people can be kept intact.

After the arrival of independence and the death of Gandhi, the Gandhian goal of reconstructing Indian society, keeping the welfare of the weakest links in society at the centre of attention, is being carried on through the Sarvodaya movement and its later development into the Bhoodan-Gramdan movement. The overall and ultimate objective of the movement is to evolve a participatory society from which exploitation is completely done away with. However, its immediate attention is on the agrarian front and involves collection of land from the rich and its distribution to the poor, and the evolving of self-governing villages wherein land is owned and cultivated collectively. Although the movement is unique in its approach to the agrarian problem and it is the most widespread post-independent movement in India, and although its record of collection and distribution of land is better than that of the state, it has hardly been studied save for one or two exceptions (Mukherji 1966: 33-41; Oommen 1966: 94-116 , 1970a: 44-45, 1972a).

Our review of studies of agrarian movements indicates that:

1. Notwithstanding the recent interest in the area, the prevalent tendency is to concentrate on the analysis of the more well-known

agrarian movements characterized by widespread violence and conflicts.

2. Analysts seem to concentrate on one or another dimension of the movements to the neglect of other equally important aspects, thereby leaving our understanding about the movements studied partial and incomplete.

3. Studies on several movements or several aspects of many movements are yet to be initiated, thereby leaving a wide gap in our understanding of this very vital social phenomenon.

Other Movements

The substantive areas we have discussed so far—religious, caste, tribal and peasant movements—are the more frequently studied ones in India although of course substantial gaps exist even in these areas, as has already been indicated. However, there are several other areas in which modest beginnings have been made and we club all these together for the present discussion not because these movements are insignificant as social phenomena (in fact quite the contrary) but because sociological studies in these areas are too few to merit an extended discussion.

Studies on the Indian national liberation movement can be grouped into four:

1. Those which discuss the movement in general either in terms of ideas (Brown 1961; Ghose 1969) or in terms of events (R.C. Majumdar 1963; Tara Chand 1983).

2. Those which deal with the struggle in specific regions (Halappa 1964; Venkatarangaiya 1965 ; Menon 1972).

3. Those which analyze specific events, such as the 1857 revolt, and their consequences (Metcalf 1965; Stokes 1970:100-18; Brodkin 1972 : 271-90) or those which deal with specific aspects or tendencies within the movement such as Swadeshi (S. Sarkar 1973).

4. Those which highlight the relationship between politics and national movement (Seal 1968; Johnson 1973; Suntharalingam 1974; Low 1977). It is widely acknowledged that the Indian independence struggle was a unique experiment and experience in human history and it is, therefore, expected that historians would analyze it; all the above-noted studies are by conventional historians. However, the challenging task of unfolding the human meaning and sociological contours of this unique event is yet to be

attempted, with one exception (A.R. Desai 1954). And even this study is largely historical in its orientation and too sweeping in character. Further, due to its ideological underpinnings the study fails to unfold the Indianness of this movement, namely, the predominantly non-violent character of the struggle, the peculiar Gandhian style of protest, dissent and mobilization, and the consequences of this for society in independent India.

A corollary of the development of nationalism in India was (a) the emergence of sub-nationalist movements which aimed at the formation of independent nation-states as manifested in the secessionist phase of the Dravidian movement (Hardgrave 1965); (b) movements which pursued the goal of forming separate states based on language within the framework of the Indian union as exemplified in the case of Andhra Pradesh (Leonard 1967 : 60-67; Narayana Rao 1973); and (c) movements which put forward the ideology of the sons of soil, as the emerging local middle class faced acute competition from 'outsiders' as in the case of the Shiv Sena movement in Bombay (Joshi 1970 : 967-78; Katzenstein 1976: 44-58; D. Gupta 1977 : 69-90). A large number of on-going movements in India belong to one or the other of the above types. The Naga and Mizo movements for independent nation-states (both of which we have discussed under tribal movements), the mobilizations for separate states within a linguistic-cultural region, such as the Telengana (Seshadri 1970 : 60-81), Vidarbha and similar movements, the proliferation of 'senas' espousing the ideology of the sons of soil, etc., are examples of these. Admittedly, given the difficulties involved in analyzing on-going movements and the prevalent methodological orientation (movements are invariably analyzed in terms of historical records) studies on most of these movements are yet to be attempted.

The nationalist movement had an overarching and unifying ideology in that there was consensus about the nature of the immediate enemy, namely, the forces of imperialism and colonialism. But beneath this unity lay substantial differences based on the differing perceptions of the role and character of the local enemy— the Indian bourgeoisie, capitalist and feudal elements—by the different ideological-political groups. This in turn led to the emergence of movements based on political-ideological orientations. However, the few studies in this context concentrate on 'leftist' movements (Brass and Franda 1973; Laushey 1975; Chowdhary 1977) and the absence of studies on 'rightist' ideological and political movements is striking. A few studies deal with the Sarvodaya movement (Ostergard and Currell 1971; Oommen 1972a) or with those which belong to the *sarvodaya* tradition, the Bihar movement, which was inspired and initiated by Jayaprakash Narain (Nargolkar 1975; Shah 1977b).

In sharp contrast to the current interest of social scientists in peasant movements, those among industrial workers are hardly studied in India. Although this is understandable against the predominantly agrarian background of India, given the fact that the absolute number of industrial workers in this country is more than the total population of several nation-states, this neglect is unfortunate. The few studies undertaken concentrate either on the trade unions, that is, the organizational aspect (Mathur and Mathur 1957; Pandey 1968: 243-68; Punekar 1970: 66-76; Revri 1972), ignoring the mobilizational dimension or else too sweeping in their coverage (J.S. Mathur 1964; Pandey 1966 : 14-39; Choudhary 1971; G.K. Sharma 1971; Saha 1978) so as to provide any significant theoretical illumination or empirical insights. Because there is a persistent tendency to use the notions of trade unions and labour movements interchangeably, it is necessary to note here that trade unions constitute the institutionalized core of labour movements. Similarly, some writers refer to the strike movement, although strikes constitute but one of the mobilizational strategies of movements.

The basic problem in referring to a trade union as a movement is its formalization of structure—membership enrolment, clear-cut boundary demarcation between ins and outs, an organizational hierarchy of leadership—all of which are typically absent in the case of movements. Yet, to deny the label movement to trade unions because of their organizational primacy is to ignore the nature of social reality. Industrial activity being highly organized, the nature of movements in that sector is bound to be influenced by it and hence it is realistic to designate the trade union movement as an organizational movement (Oommen 1972a) implying that the organizational aspect is critical, while not denying the importance of ideology, leadership, etc. Second, the very nature of trade unions implies that they pursue the welfare of workers, that is, the ideological orientation is in terms of instrumental collectivism.

The preoccupation of labour movement studies in India has been with three critical issues: (*a*) the role of the labour movement in the pre-independence era, (*b*) its relationship with political parties, and (*c*) the nature of its leadership. During the pre-independence era the immediate targets of attack by the labour movement were imperialism and colonialism, although the ultimate target was capitalism. Therefore, most of the organized and sustained labour mobilization was against foreign rule and it was undertaken in collaboration with the national movement. This meant that (*a*) the labour movement operated as a tributary to the national movement, and (*b*) the ultimate goal of the working class movement was relegated to the background.

The labour unions in India function as front-organizations of political parties and their relationship with political parties is vertical. Inevitably, the interests of political parties are accorded primacy in the activities of the labour movement, which in turn adversely affects the immediate welfare of workers. Further, the proliferation of and split in political parties based on ideological differences and factional interests invariably led to splits in the labour movement too, resulting in inter-union rivalries which eroded the strength and unity and consequently the effectiveness of the movement. Finally, given the fact that the labour movement operated first under the aegis of the national movement and later under political parties, the leadership of the movement came from the middle class—the nationalist freedom fighters or the sophisticated party workers. Since the vast majority of workers were illiterate, the possibility of a leadership emerging with the requisite skills but rooted in the labour class was further muted owing to the dominance of the 'outsider' leadership cadre. Inevitably the 'iron law of oligarchy' led to the reinforcement of the outside leadership, often eroding the growth of an authentic labour movement.

As in the case of movements among peasants and industrial workers, student movements also lacked autonomy for two reasons. In the pre-independence period it operated as a tributary to the national liberation movement (Reddy 1947; Weiner 1963 : 170-99; Altbach 1966 : 564-84; A.N. Roy 1967) and after independence as front-organizations of political parties. This situation often prompted several writers to stress the role of students in social change and nation-building, focusing attention on their role as citizens and thereby pointing to the students' role in wider social movements (Dasgupta 1974: Shah 1977b). On the other hand, student mobilizations relating to educational issues and campus problems are usually designated as 'indiscipline', 'unrest', 'agitations', etc. (Altbach 1968; Ross 1969; Vishwa Yuvak Kendra 1973), thereby indicating that the student movements lack an ideological base; that their mobilizations are spontaneous, erratic and ephemeral and that their power is coercive and destructive. Both these perspectives led to confusion about the very concept of a student movement.

Viewed sociologically, we can designate a movement as a student movement if it fulfils the following conditions: *(a)* it should emerge as the result of student needs and interests; *(b)* it should be initiated and led by them; *(c)* the major component of participants in the movement should be students, and *(d)* the ideology of the movement should be rooted in their consciousness as students. However, to insist either that students are a revolutionary vanguard, a militant minority, or an extra-parliamentary opposition (Altbach 1971; Cormack 1972: 21-25; J.R. Wood 1975 : 313-34), or to dismiss them as a deviant, indisciplined lot, is to ignore one or another aspect of reality.

The fact of the matter is that university students are simultaneously involved in two roles: that of students and of citizens, and their involvements are characterized by this duality. Further, student politics are bifocal, oriented to their needs and interests as well as concerned with the wider societal issues. Therefore, student power is at once both productive and coercive (Oommen 1975b : 10-38). While it cannot be denied that social scientists did show some interest in recent years in analyzing the mobilizational activities of students (largely because they attracted attention in the mass media and called for the intervention of law and order agencies) they have, by and large, ignored the study of student unions and associations which provide institutionalized support to student mobilizations, save for some modest beginnings (Oommen 1971b, 1974 : 777-94). Finally, we once again face the recurrent problem, that is, either the mobilizational activities or the institutionalized segment is studied, to the exclusion of the other, leaving the analysis incomplete as a study of movements.

The three social (occupational) categories whose role in revolution and change was considered to be crucial, at least until recently, were the industrial proletariat, the peasantry and the students. However, the role of women in ushering change and the change in the status of women as an index of social transformation are being discussed increasingly of late. The frequent verbal articulations and the occasional journalistic writings apart, only scarce beginnings have been made in women's movement studies in India. The few studies we have (Manmohan Kaur 1968; Asthana 1974; Chattopadhyaya 1975: 27-36; Basu 1976: 16-40; V. Majumdar 1976: 42-66; Forbes 1979: 149-65) mainly discuss the role of women in the freedom struggle and in the social reform movements.

As in other cases, the women's movement too has had a dependent status *vis-à-vis* the national liberation movement. This often thwarted the development of an independent ideology and an autonomous organization for the women's movement in India. With regard to the social reform movements, women were often the targets of change—abolition of *sati, purdah,* encouragement of widow remarriage, prohibition of child marriage—rather than the initiators. But the leadership role played by a few enlightened women and the mass participation are yet to be sociologically analyzed. At any rate, the study of the women's movement in independent India—both in its mobilizational and institutionalized aspects—has been totally neglected so far.

We must close this rather long review of substantive themes of social movement studies in India with a reference to what are frequently labelled as literary, theatre and art movements. These are certainly innovations in the realm of ideas or even ideologies but in order that a phenomenon be designated as a movement it should have an action—collective mobilization—component. While it is necessary, therefore, to recognize the literary and cultural background of particular movements as reflected in the literary and artistic creations of the time (George 1977: 357-67; Sanjeevi 1977: 345-53) these should not be confused with social movements *per se,* insofar as they lack the collective action component. However, it is likely that literary creativity may give rise to, accelerate the pace of, even endanger the very existence of a social movement. Finally, social movements and literary innovations may coexist and reinforce each other as in the case of the Dalit Panther movement. But to confuse the literary dimension of a movement (Bhoite and Bhoite 1977: 60-75) with the phenomenon of the movement itself is to mistake the core for the frills.

METHODOLOGICAL ISSUES

Notwithstanding the substantial increase in the number of publications on social movements in recent years, very little thinking has gone into the methodological issues involved in the study of movements. Although M.S.A. Rao (1978a: 13-14) raised what he preferred to call 'a methodological question', the issue is actually related to data collection techniques. It is suggested that social history is a legitimate area of social inquiry and therefore students of social movements should combine the skills of historians and sociologists, that it is possible to undertake social movement studies through participant observation and that it is not only desirable but absolutely necessary to resort to data collection through multiple techniques—participant observation, content analysis, informant interviewing, survey method—in social movement studies.

As noted in the first chapter, there are two methodological issues in the study of social movements: the problems relating to the scale of movements, and the issues relating to the units and levels of observation. The scale of a movement is influenced by the size and social composition of the participants and its time-span, all of which pose problems of operationalization. In order that a mobilization may be called a movement the minimum number of participants can be settled by defining it either in terms of absolute or in terms of proportionate number with reference to the universe under question. However, the issue of defining participants still remains a vexing one, as there are core, rank and file and peripheral participants in all movements. The social composition of participants in movements affects its scale: the greater the social homogeneity of participants, the smaller the scale; and the greater the heterogeneity, the larger is the potential scale of a movement. The issue is complicated because the participants simultaneously share three basic identities: primordial/ascriptive, class/occupational and political/ideological.

The widespread tendency on the part of researchers to ignore this complex and combined identity of participants and to invoke that specific identity which suits the researcher's perspective has often resulted in poor research pay-offs and led to misleading conclusions. An inadequate appreciation of the time dimension of movements also led to selective attention on the mobilizational aspect, usually on specific events, to the neglect of the institutionalized core, the organizational dimension, and vice versa. This in turn results in the dialectical intertwining between mobilization and institutionalization in the life-cycle of movements being ignored.

Finally, the prevalent tendency to view the movements from above concentrating on the macro-dimension—the ideology, the organizational patterns, the strategy and tactics—results in ignoring the view from below, the micro-dimension. That is, the level from which the movements are usually looked at are not conducive to yielding a comprehensive understanding. Apart from these, there are several other methodological issues which handicap the study of social movements. Some of these will be discussed later.

Although we have already referred to the issues relating to the units of analysis and levels of observation in studies of movements, a still wider, perhaps a more fundamental issue needs to be tackled. There are several authors who refer to intellectual protest, militant ideology or literary dissent (e.g., Brown 1961; Ghose 1969; Bhoite and Bhoite 1977: 60-75) as 'movements'. These tendencies can certainly be characterized as dissent in thought patterns and may usually facilitate the emergence of movements, but unless they are accompanied by protest behaviour they cannot be designated movements. On the other hand, as we have already noted, there are authors who mistake either the event structure or the institutionalized segment for a movement. It is important to keep in mind that a movement should have an ideology which often is an expression of dissent from the existing thought system, an organizational aspect which translates the ideology into concrete, here and now programmes to meet the interests and aspirations of the rank and file participants and mobilizational activities which impart a sense of involvement to them. To mistake any one of these dimensions for a movement as such is to commit the error of confusing the part for the whole.

Another widespread methodological confusion emanates from erroneous contextualization of the identity of participants. For instance, we have seen that several authors refer to the movements of peasants (Bipan Chandra 1979), workers (Revri 1972) and students (Reddy 1947) in pre-independence India. While the possibility of autonomous movements of these categories emerging and existing during the freedom struggle in India is not denied, insofar as the movements of these categories operated as tributaries to the national liberation movement and they fought against the forces of imperialism and colonialism, they were not fighting as students, workers or peasants, but as subjects against their colonial masters in order to gain freedom and become citizens, an aspiration which they shared with others of the then Indian society.

Similarly, the prevalent tendency to label a movement based on a specific identity of participants, even when the movement under consideration pursues goals which are not central to that category, creates confusion. Even if a specific category initiates a movement, plays the vanguard role and constitutes the principal participants in the movement, it is erroneous to label the movement after that category, insofar as the issue involved and interests pursued are not specific to it and the motivations and consciousness of the participants are not rooted in their categorial specificity. This is because the involvement of the category concerned in the movement may not be as students, workers or peasants, but as citizens of the country or as members of a caste or religious-linguistic group. To avoid this confusion it is necessary to define a movement in terms of what its goals and interests are rather than in terms of the participants, because the participants have a multiple not single identity. While it is plausible that in the case of a particular movement there may be isomorphism between the goals pursued and one or another element in the background of the participants involved in it, that these should coincide is by no means automatic.

Even a cursory perusal of the studies of movements that we have reviewed clearly demonstrates the preponderance of *ex post facto* analysis; typically, erstwhile rather than on-going movements are studied. Part of the reason for this lies in the fact that studies of movements have conventionally been the province of historians; most of the sociologists who have undertaken such studies tend to fall in line with historians and plead for the development of sociological history or historical sociology of movements. It is not only necessary but even desirable that sociologists respond to this appeal. But it is important to bear in mind that it is equally necessary and highly desirable to analyze on-going movements, although several peculiar methodological problems beset such a research endeavour. The leading among them are:

1. The phenomenon under investigations is in a flux, movements live from moment to moment and therefore it is very difficult to make any definitive statements about them.

2. The time-span of a given movement may be too long for any particular researcher to be involved in its continuous study.

3. Movements may trigger off suddenly and the researcher may not be mentally prepared to plunge into the study or may have to

face too many bureaucratic constraints to leave for the field immediately.

4. The study may involve too many physical risks if the movement operates from underground and/or it employs violent means to achieve its goals.

5. The researcher may have to be sympathetic to the means and goals of the movement if he or she has to gain accessibility as a participant observer—a task which may pose moral dilemmas to him/her.

In spite of these limitations, it is desirable to undertake the study of on-going movements because it is the only method through which the processual and micro-aspects of a movement can be understood. The *ex post facto* analyses which are based on records are bound to be one-sided as the records invariably reflect only the ideas and activities of the leadership, which give only the view from above, the macro-dimension.

The issues relating to the researcher's value position are much discussed and are still live ones in the social sciences. In the context of social movement analysis these issues are particularly important because the phenomenon of social movements anchors in contentions about the existing values and norms; it is essentially a confrontation between two or more competing value systems and normative patterns seeking to gain social validation. Therefore, it is almost inescapable that researchers should take one or another value position while analyzing social movements. In spite of this, it is necessary that this one-sidedness should not be allowed to blunt one's sociological sensitivity. Yet, this golden rule is not always followed. Let us illustrate, with an example. M.S.A. Rao (1978a: 11-12) writes:

> Normally, *status quo*-oriented attempts…spring up as a reaction to change-oriented movements. They are more in the nature of counter-efforts launched by the establishment.... The bases of collective mobilization among the privileged groups are self-defence, self-help, correction of self-image and consolidation of status. In contrast to the *status quo* maintaining attempts which emerge among the dispossessed groups, social movements which originate among the deprived sections are oriented towards bringing about changes in the structure of positional arrangements, values and norms.

It is clear from the above observations that collective mobilizations by the underprivileged can only be labelled as 'movements', a sociologically untenable proposition. In fact, Rao falls into a trap of his own creation as he assumes that (*a*) change-orientation is a basic feature of all social movements and he insists that(*b*) this change ought to be in a given direction. That is why he finds it inconsistent to use the term 'movement' to describe attempts to maintain the status quo.

However, it is well known that several social movements attempt to achieve system stability to arrest the onslaught of rapid social change; and even when the declared intention is system change, in actuality several movements have reinforced the existing values and norms rather than changed them. Further, it is widely accepted that a movement can be change-resisting or change-promoting in its orientation. Now, even if it is accepted that all movements are against the *status quo,* that is, their point of departure is the prevalent system, it does not follow that their *points of destination* fall in the same direction. This would be determined by the nature and intensity of the participants' deprivation. There are several possibilities here. First, some movements may bring about change viewed in a short-term perspective but they only reinforce the *status quo* if we take a long-term perspective. Second, there are. movements which aim at the purification of the system, those which are revivalistic in orientation. Third, there are movements which pursue change of the system—through the destruction and replacement of the old and induction of new structures. In all these cases the point of destination varies although the point of departure is constant. I would like to stress here that a particular researcher may or even should make his preference in favour of a given point of destination pursued by a movement, but he cannot pronounce the judgment that another movement pursuing another point of destination is no movement at all!

An important point which unfolds itself is the tendency to study those movements which pursued their goals through non-institutionalized means, unleashed substantial violence and were initiated by certain political parties or ideological groups, because they were more pronounced. Insofar as violence attracts the attention of the mass media, calls for the intervention of the formal agencies of social control, creates alienation among the wider collectivity and produces martyrs from among the movement participants, it is quite understandable that the social scientists should pay attention to it. But to consider the *amount of violence* unleashed by a movement as a *measure of its importance* indicates a distortion of perspective. It is quite likely that a violent movement may not make any significant impact on society and a non-violent movement may bring about substantial social change. Yet this conceptual plausibility and empirical possibility is ignored. For example, M.S.A. Rao (1978a: xii) suggests that two ideologies—*sarvodaya* and communist—have inspired peasant movements in India and adds that *significant* peasant movements such as the Tebhaga, Telengana, Naxalite and land-grab movements have emerged on the basis of the communist ideology. K. Ranga Rao (1978 : 149) refers to the Telengana peasant movement as the 'most important one' among the peasant uprisings before and after independence. There are several others (Dhanagare 1974 : 109-34, 1976 : 360-78; A.R.Desai 1979) who describe one or another peasant movement in a similar vein.

While every researcher should have the right to make judgments about the phenomenon analyzed, it is necessary to insist that the basis of such evaluations should be made explicit lest the judgment be dismissed as irrational, prejudicial and hence methodologically unsound. What makes a movement siginificant—its spatial spread, societal scope, declared intentions, actual achievements, social consequences? Unless this is made explicit, the judgments will remain personal opinions and cannot be considered scientific evaluations, which can be validated or rejected by fellow researchers. The instances we have cited clearly illustrate how social scientists tend to fall easy prey to political propaganda or simply, perhaps unwittingly, reinforce prevalent popular prejudices unless they are extremely cautious. We do not suggest for a moment that the social scientist should be value-neutral, the traditional and oft-repeated cliche, but would insist that the student of social movements should take a clear-cut value position rather than camouflage his values which can only create anomie in sociological analysis. If he considers a particular social movement more important as compared to other movements he should explicitly state why he considers it to be so.

The value orientations and ethnocentrism of researchers, it is widely recognized, shape their cognition of social reality and the conclusions they arrive at. This is particularly so in the study of social movements, as we have indicated above, since these are arenas in which value systems compete for legitimation by collectivities. This issue can be illustrated with a few examples of studies on religious movements. The earlier studies on Hindu religious movements have been attempted by those who were interested in proselytization and this often marred an objective study and assessment of these movements. For example, having attempted a comparative study of modern religious movements in India (1828-1913), J.N. Farquhar characterized the origin and spread of religious reform movements in India as a response to Western ideas and not as an indication of the crystallization of indigenous consciousness. Not only are these movements viewed as native attempts at condemning the materialistic West and eulogizing the spiritualistic East, but Farquhar concludes that these movements have been accompanied by the 'continuous and steadily increasing decay' of Hinduism and asserts that in spite of the multiplicity of factors at work in shaping these movements, 'Christianity has ruled the development throughout' (Farquhar 1924 : 431-2).

Another foreign author, of course not a missionary, writing exactly 40 years later, argues that social reform movements in India '...began with individual revolts against existing customs, took shape under the influence of Western methods of organization and propagation and recruited their supporters from men who were English educated or who had imbibed Western ideas indirectly' (Heimsath 1964 : 46), thereby indicating the primacy of Western ideas and organizational techniques in the origin and spread of social reform movements in India. In fact, the very definition of social reformers as those social innovators who attempted to adapt themselves to the new standards presented or sanctions enforced by British rule (ibid.: 4) and the statement that much social reform in India was started to counter the conversion threat (ibid. : 33) clearly indicates that in this paradigm the Hindu renaissance is described and explained in a simplistic need-fulfilment framework: influence of the West, impotence of the native tradition, and the nationalist response to a crisis situation. 'In this scenario, non-Christian religions were not, as a rule, viewed as internally evolving systems but merely as anxiety-resolving defence mechanisms used by the peoples concerned to meet the Western challenge (K.P. Gupta 1974 : 27). However, there is ample evidence to support the contention that there existed dissent, protest and reform in India

much before the Western advent (see Malik 1977), thereby implying that there has been an indigenous tradition of reform movements
in India. Further, even movements such as the Arya Samaj which
originated after north Indian exposure to Christianity can be viewed
as a parallel native effort to alter the traditional customs and practices which came to be perceived as evils by the local Hindu elite
(Suri 1977 : 214-26). Our purpose here is only to call attention to
the differing value stances which are embedded in the positions
taken by Western and Indian authors in the study of religious movements in India and the concomitant variations in the conclusions
they arrive at.

Ethnocentrism is yet another problem which figures prominently
in studies of movements. After analysing what he calls Messianic
movements in India, Stephen Fuchs concludes :

> The various racial, occupational, linguistic, social and religious
> population groups in India frequently rise up on the least pro-
> vocation in a narrow communal spirit to assert their particular
> rights, real and imaginary, often at the cost of other commun-
> ities... The widely propagated assertion that religious tolerence
> exists in India can safely be declared as a myth. India too had its
> wars of religion and this present history of messianic movements
> give abundant instances of religious intolerance (1965 : 284-85).

It can be argued with greater force that considering the deep historicity and wide variety of religious communities in India, it is
singularly laudable that inter-communal harmony existed and continues to exist in India and that the occasional communal conflicts
which erupt are negligible. To repeat, the point is that the conclusion
one arrives at is informed by the value bias one has. But it is of
acute methodological significance that this value bias should not
be allowed to result in patently prejudicial statements bereft of any
scientific validity.

I have already called attention (in Chapter I) to the selective
emphasis that researchers tend to give either to the mobilizational
aspect (event structure) or to the institutionalized segment (organizational dimension) of a movement, leading to the failure to capture
the movement dynamics in its totality. There is a related error,
perhaps a more fundamental one, which is frequent in studies of
movements emanating from the selective attention that researchers
give to one or another category in a socio-economic sector. This

can best be illustrated by studies on peasant movements. Peasants constitute just one category in the agrarian sector, the others being those who own land but do not work it and the agrarian proletariat. There are issues and interests which are peculiar to the land owners, peasants and agricultural labourers and consequently there are movements specific to each of them. Yet, the usual tendency is to talk of 'peasant movements' as a generic phenomenon, as if other categories are also encapsulated within the peasant category, which results in not only conceptual confusion but also in the neglect of mobilizational activities of other agrarian categories. This issue is a particularly vexed one because mobilizations of one category usually imply mobilizations of other categories too; mobilizations invoke counter-mobilizations. And it is the dialectical interactions of these which provide substance to any movement.

Again, insofar as there exist separate associations or unions (institutionalized segment of movements) for all the categories and it is the activities of these organizations which constitute the collective mobilizations, it is necessary to study all of them for a complete understanding of the phenomenon. Further, a given category, land-owners or agricultural workers, for instance, may have different organizations sponsored by different political parties or ideological groups. The mobilizational activities of all these organizations conjointly constitute the movement. To this extent, it is reasonable to view a movement as constituted by a stream of associations in action and confrontation. But there are hardly any studies of agrarian movements which pay attention to all the relevant categories, their mobilizational activities, interactions and confrontations. This is equally true of studies of movements of other social sectors—religion, caste, etc.

The inadequate appreciation of counter-mobilizational activities mars most studies on movements. For instance, although almost all studies on conversion movements from Hinduism to Islam and Christianity suggest that the introduction of *shuddhi* as a mechanism of reconversion to Hinduism by the Arya Samaj is a counter-mobilization piloted by sensitive Hindu elites, they do not analyze these two processes in conjunction. Parallel mobilizations by two or more contending collectivities lead to one or more of the following possibilities, depending upon the numerical strength, economic resources, political support and ideological commitment of those who are involved:

1. Blockage of the mobilizational efforts of the weaker collectivity by the dominant one, often leading to violent clashes;
2. Withdrawal from mobilizational activities by the weaker group;
3. Redefinition of the goal of mobilization (for example, giving up conversion as a goal and advocacy of a more puritanical and rigid religious framework as manifested in the Tabligh movement among Muslims);
4. A coalition between two or more collectivities which perceive a common enemy (as in the case of Sikhs and Hindus against Christian conversions).

A comprehensive understanding of the movement under study calls for an analysis of the interlinkages between these processes. And yet this remains neglected in studies of movements till today.

The discussion on the mobilizational dimension of movements brings to our attention the processual aspect, another neglected area in studies of movements. Although a large number of studies, particularly by historians, trace the course of events, rarely do we come across attempts at conceptualizing the processual trends and tendencies of movements. Available empirical evidence suggests that there are three specific patterns in the emergence of movements in India: (*a*) emergence and subsequent spread of a movement under the inspiration and initiative of a charismatic leader, (*b*) emergence of movements sponsored and coordinated by all-India structures such as political parties, religious organizations and caste associations, and (*c*) emergence of movements in specific areas or in situations independently, which may or may not subsequently get coordinated. In all these instances, the *movement process* would vary. For instance, in the case of movements initiated by a charismatic leader, the ideology, the organizational pattern and the strategy are transmitted *downwards* to the participants. In contrast, in the case of movements which originate independently and then get coordinated, the process of *upward transmission* is critical. In the case of movements sponsored by structures which coordinate them right from the beginning, there is a *division of labour* between the upper echelons and local leadership in regard to formulation of ideologies, devising the organizational patterns, evolving the strategies and tactics. It is necessary to recognize that the processual aspects of movements in each of these cases will vary substantially. However, the researchers are rarely conscious of these variations. Once again, this is the result of an inadequate appreciation of the importance of the linkage between the micro- and macro-dimensions of movements.

There is yet another neglected dimension of the processual aspect of movements, that which is related to the metamorphosis of its life-cycle. Once a movement emerges, there are several empirical possibilities: (*a*) getting institutionalized as an organization or party and ultimately reinforcing rather than changing the system, (*b*) continuing its mobilizational efforts vigorously along with sponsoring a party or organization to further its strength or gain entry into the formal framework of power, (*c*) persistent mobilization leading to revolution bringing about change of the system, (*d*) losing its vitality due to the irrelevance of its goal because of changed circumstances, (*e*) getting discredited by the collectivity or suppressed by the government due to the erosion of its legitimacy. It is of great methodological significance to understand these life-cycle processes of movements because only then can the researcher make an assessment of its impact on society. And yet, judgments about the significance or impact of movements are often made without taking cognizance of these processual aspects, thereby reducing these judgments to the level of ideological prejudices, or at best preferences.

3
Theoretical Framework and Empirical Research in the Analysis of Social Movements

In my academic career spanning a quarter of a century, one of the thrust areas of my research has been social movements centring around two major studies. The first of these, an analysis of the Bhoodan-Gramdan movement (*bhoodan* means land-gift and *gramdan* village-in-gift) with special reference to Rajasthan, began in 1962 as my Ph.D. research project and its findings were published in the early 1970s (Oommen 1972a). The second study, an analysis of the agrarian movement in 20th century Kerala, was initiated in the late 1960s and was published by the middle of the 1980s (Oommen 1985).

In this chapter I propose to pose and answer four questions: why did I study these movements? How did I arrive at the frameworks of these studies? What considerations went into the selection of the units of study? What bearing did my empirical research have on concept formation and theory construction?

BHOODAN-GRAMDAN MOVEMENT

The Bhoodan-Gramdan movement, the theme of my first study, began in 1951, a year before the Community Development Programme (CDP) was launched by the Government of India. These were then viewed by many as alternative approaches to socio-economic reconstruction of rural India. By the time I began my research in 1962, several social scientists had written extensively on CDP and most of these studies had been sponsored and financed by the different agencies of the government. But even a decade after its inception, hardly any researcher had made a serious attempt to evaluate the impact of the Bhoodan-Gramdan movement, although it was (and still is) the only agrarian movement in independent India with an all-India spread. However, this movement did generate some interest, as it was an attempt to reconstruct Indian rural society relying on voluntaristic action, and on faith in the goodness of human nature. It attracted the attention of a few foreign writers, none of whom was a social scientist, who characterized it in an idyllic fashion; the movement to them was a 'miracle' and a 'superhuman' achievement which could happen only in Gandhi's India (see Tennyson 1955; Del Vasto 1956; Hoffman 1961). Two social scientists, a foreigner (Yinger 1957) and an Indian (Sekher 1968), attempted an evaluation of the movement, based on secondary data, at the macro level. No investigation of the impact of the movement at the grass-roots, its real target, had been undertaken by any researcher, foreign or Indian. Therefore, I thought of studying the 'Sociology of *Gramdan* Villages'

When I started my research in 1962, the air was thick with the purported 'success' of the movement; the national press and All India Radio regularly reported its progress and the Planning Commission published statistics relating to the collection and distribution of land through the movement, in its evaluation of land reforms in India. Official patronage was readily extended to the movement and was very visible. Even the United Nations' documents on land reforms made references to the success of the movement.

At that time, two sets of questions figured in my mind. The first set included the following: why was it that no sociologist had ventured to make a thorough analysis of the movement, thereby either vindicating or contradicting the prevalent popular and official opinions and claims about the movement? Such a study had great potentialities for building a theory of rural social transformation not only for India, but perhaps for other developing countries as well. Further, such a study could have helped in examining the efficacy or inadequacy of several social policy measures initiated by the governments in developing countries to bring about rural social change. Why was it that such an opportunity was missed?

I do not intend to catalogue all possible reasons for this serious omission but let me list a few. First was the intellectual claustrophobia created by the professional conservatism of Indian sociologists. During the 1950s and the 1960s Indian sociologists studied religion, caste, family, village and urban communities. Any deviation from these 'sacred themes' was not only discouraged but even ridiculed. Second, as the movement drew its inspiration from the *sarvodaya* (literally, upliftment of all) ideology propounded by Mohandas Karamchand Gandhi and as it was initiated by Acharya Vinoba Bhave, his foremost disciple, most social scientists dismissed the movement as 'conservative' and hence not worth studying. Third, given the state patronage extended to and accepted by the movement, it came to be identified with the government and the party in power. Admittedly, the movement did not operate as a countervailing power to the state and therefore it did not attract much attention. Fourth, the movement was avowedly non-violent and hence non-controversial, had no nuisance value and hence did not attract the attention of the law and order agencies. Finally, hardly any material incentive in the form of financial assistance or a possible career advantage was available to those who could have undertaken the study.

The second set of questions which occurred to me were comparative in nature: If the movement was successful in certain regions or villages in tackling the basic agrarian problem of India, namely redistribution of land in favour of the tiller, what conditions favoured it? Were these conditions replicable elsewhere? And, if these conditions were recreated in areas where the movement was absent or unsuccessful, will it then spread to the entire countryside, thereby solving one of India's crucial problems: the concentration of land in the hands of a small proportion of absentee and non-cultivating landlords? I don't think that it is a *post factum* rationalization to state that while my enquiry was primarily motivated by intellectual curiosity it also had an indirect practical concern, namely the improvement of the lot of the rural poor, the landless agricultural labourers. This in turn moulded the content of my study.

Since I set out to study the impact of the Bhoodan-Gramdan movement at the grass-roots it was necessary to investigate whether its ideology had been adequately disseminated among *gramdan* villagers, the strength of their motivation to donate villages-in-gift, the economic and political changes in these villages following *gramdan*, the role of local leadership in effecting these changes (if changes did occur), and the value-orientations of the villagers.

As I proceeded with the investigation of *gramdan* villages I discovered that a meaningful analysis of the movement was possible only by conscious effort to view the village situation against the backdrop of the functioning of the movement at the macro level. Understandably, my initial theme, 'Sociology of *Gramdan* Villages' changed to 'Ideology and Social Change'. Broadly speaking, the movement had three layers: the micro (village and district), the macro (national) and the meso (state) levels. The macro level supplied the ideology, the broad organizational pattern and the top leadership; the meso level subjected the first two dimensions to a filtration process and moulded them to suit local conditions. For example, in states with a sizeable tribal population, *gramdan* rather than *bhoodan* was accorded greater importance considering the traditional tribal pattern of communal land-ownership. At the micro level the ideology was translated into actual programmes through organizations inducted into the system for the purpose. This realization led to a further shift in the emphasis of my study. While retaining the focus of investigation on *gramdan* villages, I started concentrating on the role of ideology in bringing about change which necessitated a macro-level analysis of the movement as well.

As I became familiar with the available writings on the emergence of the movement (Rambhai 1958, 1962), I found that its origin and spread could not be attributed solely to its ideology. During the pre-independence days Gandhi's *sarvodaya* ideology had been overshadowed by the nationalist preoccupation with the goal of *swaraj* (independence). Its tenets had scarcely been translated into concrete action, particularly in dealing with inequality in land distribution. Further, the movement needed a style of functioning, different from that of the anti-colonial struggle, and yet acceptable and appealing to the people. This was precisely what Vinoba attempted and his style of functioning was that of a charismatic leader. Taking my cue from this, I finally reformulated the theme of my study as 'Charismatic Movements and Social Change'. At that point I had simply assumed, following Max Weber, that charisma was a system-changing force in society. But by the time I concluded my study I had become convinced that charisma could as well be a system stabilizing force and hence the title of the book: *Charisma, Stability and Change*. In the book, I first attempted a general analysis of the movement in India based on its origin, ideology, organization and macro-leadership pattern before presenting details of its functioning at the grass-roots level in the *gramdan* villages of Rajasthan.

Based on this experience, I suggest that analyses of social movements should comprise two aspects, the macro and the micro. By the macro-dimension of movement I mean its ideology contained in the written and unwritten pronouncements by the leaders; organization, the machinery through which the ideology is sought to be propagated and communicated; strategy and tactics, the specific programmes, organizational devices and procedures adopted to put its ideology into practice. The micro-dimension refers to its actual operation and its consequences at the grass-roots level, wherein we observe the filtration or accretion process to which the ideology and organization are subjected, in order to meet specific local conditions and the mechanisms through which the movement ideology is put into practice. Thus, an analysis of the macro-dimension of a movement informs us of its ideology and organization, a study of the micro-dimension acquaints us with its actual functioning on the ground; the former offers us a perspective from above and the latter a view from below. In order to arrive at a meaningful understanding of a movement, then, we should view it from both these angles. And this is precisely what I attempted to do in the case of the Bhoodan-Gramdan movement, although my initial intention was to analyze the movement only from a micro viewpoint.

My analysis of the macro-dimension of the movement added new aspects to the study. In the case of the Bhoodan-Gramdan movement most of its basic tenets were contained in Gandhi's *sarvodaya* philosophy. In analyzing the ideology of the movement I drew upon the writings of its chief theoreticians—Gandhi, Vinoba Bhave, and Jayaprakash Narayan. Similarly, I found that its organizational core had pre-dated the emergence of the movement in its present form—the Akhil Bharat Sarva Seva Sangh (All India Social Service Society). When the movement started functioning as a concrete programme for the collection and distribution of land, the need for a specific new organization was keenly felt. In fact, soon after the first land donation in 1951 in Pochampalli village in Andhra Pradesh, Vinoba constituted a 'trust'—a tripartite committee consisting of the donor, local influentials and *sarvodaya* workers—to administer land distribution. As the number of donations multiplied, the need for coordinating organizational tasks arose. Thus, village, district, state and national level organizations developed gradually. Generally speaking, except at the village level, coordination of the movement activities had been taken over by the existing *sarvodaya* organizations. Therefore, it was necessary to analyze the organizational innovations of the movement at the village level in order to understand the problems of translating the movement ideology into practice.

Another 'feed-back' from the field provided the rationale for the shift in the focus of the study. My analysis of the communication pattern revealed that most of the villagers viewed Vinoba Bhave, the initiator of the movement, as a saint-on-march; they were gifting away their lands to a saint! Further, while analyzing the local leadership pattern of the movement, I observed a process of vertical transmission of charisma; local charismatic heroes donned the mantle of charisma and adopted a style of life akin to that of the national leaders and maintained their appeal through contact-charisma. This led me to conclude that the change propelling force in the movement was not so much its ideology as it was the charismatic appeal of the national and local leaders. I became convinced of the tremendous importance of the charismatic resource to mobilize people into collective actions. It was this realization which emboldened me to stick to the new focus of the study, 'Charismatic Movements and Social Change'. The point I want to emphasize is this: even as a researcher starts with a specific plan of study, the focus of his investigation is likely to change as he interacts with the field. What is important is his flexibility and ability to respond to the demands of the field situation.

An indirect pay-off due to successive shifts in the focus of study needs to be noted here. As indicated above, the analysis of the movement at the macro level showed the existence of an ideology and an organizational core prior to the emergence and spread of the movement in its present form. The critical factor facilitating the movement's spread was charismatic leadership. This led me to conclude that we could identify distinct aspects of any movement for purposes of analysis: ideology, organization and leadership. Any of these dimensions may emerge first and other aspects would crystallize subsequently. This led to the formulation of the life-cycle approach to the study of movements. Inevitably, a given aspect of a movement may have primacy over the other aspects at a specific point of time. If this is so, we can speak of three types of movements depending on which of these aspects emerges first in its life-cycle: ideological, organizational or charismatic, a typology I proposed in the study.

Reflecting back on the life-cycle approach proposed and the typology formulated based on that, I note two major omissions. First, I failed to account for the societal conditions which facilitated or thwarted the emergence of a particular type of movement. This lacuna emanated from the failure to systematically link the theory of social movements with a theory of social structure. A more fruitful analysis could be attempted by focusing on the system conditions more systematically. The crucial question then to be posed in a study of movements is: What type of movement emerges in what kind of society and why?

Second, I had overlooked the importance of analyzing the mobilizational activities of the movement. The main reason for this was the style of the movement itself. In the case of the Bhoodan-Gramdan movement, the most important mobilizational activity was *padayatra* (walking a long distance) by movement workers to propagate its ideology and to collect donations of land. Apart from this, the movement attempted very little mobilizational activity, partly because of the absence of any organized opposition to it. The cause the movement championed, land to the tiller, had been accepted by the government and most of the political parties. Further, the movement mobilized support by adopting non-violent means. Hence, there were no major confrontations between the supporters of the movement and their opponents and therefore mobilization was not a particularly exciting area of analysis. However, analysis of mobilization in a social movement is too important an area to be neglected.

As a young student initiated into the world of social research, my immediate problem was the focus of study. Although my field investigation was to be done in *gramdan* (village-in-gift) villages, my aim was not to analyze the social structure of these villages or even to understand the style of life of the villagers. My purpose was to evaluate the role of the Bhoodan movement to bring about social change and to observe the manifestations of this in *gramdan* villages. Therefore, the questions that arose in my mind were: How can one establish whether the changes, if any, taking place in *gramdan* villages are exclusively, or at least predominantly, due to the movement? Second, assuming that there are multiple causes of change, how can we isolate the specific contribution made by the movement in effecting changes in *gramdan* villages?

The fact that I began my investigation with a definite purpose called for the employment of an 'experimental' research design. It is widely recognized that a study of change is methodologically sound only if it is attempted either in a time perspective or in a space perspective. While in the former case the same working universe is subjected to analysis through time, the latter calls for a comparative study of at least two spatial units with the provision that the additional variable assumed to be causing the change is absent from one of the units. Since the Bhoodan-Gramdan movement was in existence barely for a decade when I started studying it in 1962 and, further, that the villages actually selected for the study were *gramdan* villages only for five or less number of years, it was felt to be unrewarding to attempt an analysis of *gramdan* villages, in a time perspective. Therefore, I decided to study two sets of villages, *gramdan* (experimental) and non-*gramdan* (control)[1], in order to understand the changes in the former set of villages, which may be attributed to the movement.

Since the movement operated all over India and over 5,000 villages were donated in *gramdan* by 1961, it was necessary to decide upon a specific locale from which the villages were to be selected. I cannot offer any specific rationale for selecting Rajasthan as the locale of my study, except that it was convenient as I was attached to one of the universities in that state at the time. However, discussion with movement leaders revealed that Rajasthan was one of the states wherein the movement was active and 'successful'. In 1961 there were 234 *gramdan* villages in Rajasthan and I had to select a few villages for intensive observation. Although a complete list of these villages was obtained from the coordinating agency of the movement in the state, the Rajasthan Sarva Seva Sangh, most of them could not be located or if located the requisite data to facilitate the selection of villages was not available. Therefore, I decided to select a few villages from among the 63 *gramdan* villages brought under the purview of legislation, the Rajasthan Gramdan Act, 1960,[2] since some preliminary information was available about

---

[1] The reader may note that the concept of property-space is implicit in our discussion of research design of the study at several points: *gramdan* (experimental) vs non-*gramdan* villages, revenue villages vs hamlets of villages, old villages vs new colonies. For a short discussion on the concept of property-space, see Barton (1955: 40-53).

[2] Two legislations passed by the State Assembly, the Rajasthan Bhoodan Yajna Act 1954 and the Rajasthan Gramdan Act 1960, were used as reinforcement mechanisms

these villages. Thus, the further delimitation of villages for selection to be included in the study was based on another social factor, namely, availability of data. The third social factor which influenced the selection of villages was limited resources—time and money. I was expected to finish this specific research assignment within a period of three years and funds available at my disposal were extremely limited, both of which restricted the scope of my study in terms of coverage.

These social factors apart, a few research issues conditioned the selection of specific villages. An examination of the details relating to the 65 *gramdan* villages brought under the Act revealed that these villages were, generally speaking, atypical, viewed in terms of their size of population and/or number of households, the area of land held by the villagers and social complexity viewed in terms of the number of social categories, castes and tribes, found in these villages, as compared with non-*gramdan* villages. There was yet another factor which contributed to the atypicality of *gramdan* villages. In the process of becoming *gramdan* villages they have undergone a process of bifurcation, usually in terms of the village 'core' and the hamlets.[3] Thus, if a 'revenue' village had three hamlets, apart from the village core, as a result of *gramdan* four 'villages' emerged out of it. The search for *gramdan* villages similar in size and social structural complexity as compared with non-*gramdan* villages, prompted me to select as far as possible unbifurcated villages. If I were to select typical *gramdan* villages they would have been atypical villages of Rajasthan. Thus, the *gramdan* villages selected were more or less typical of the villages of the region but were atypical *gramdan* villages.

---

for the successful operation of the movement. The legal requirements, for a village to be called *gramdan*, according to the Act, are (*a*) that not less than 51 per cent of the total extent of lands under private ownership in that village should be donated; (*b*) that the donors should constitute at least 80 per cent of the total number of persons owning land and residing in the village; (*c*) that not less than 75 per cent of adult persons residing in the village should have declared, in the prescribed form and manner, their desire to participate in *gramdan* community life.

[3] Generally speaking, a typical Rajasthan village has a number of parts attached to the village core or central village. The definition of the village for purposes of the Rajasthan Gramdan Act 1960, was the same as given in the Rajasthan Land Revenue Act 1956. According to this, parts of villages whether called *thok*, *patti*, *dhani*, *pura*, *fala*, *wada* or otherwise, are included in the village and are not considered as separate units. However, as many as 14.5 per cent of *gramdan* villages were former hamlets and this was the main reason for their atypicality.

The villages selected were atypical from another angle too. I wanted to examine the conditions which led to the successful operation of *gramdan* villages as communitarian enterprises, because the assumption was that the replication of these conditions in other villages would facilitate their being brought under *gramdan*. Therefore it was necessary to select 'successful cases' and this was precisely what I did. In consultation with the movement leaders at the local level I made a list of successful *gramdan* villages from the pool of 'typical' villages for closer analysis. Thus, the theoretical purpose and practical concerns of my study dictated the selection of *gramdan* villages.

A final consideration which conditioned the selection of *gramdan* villages was their spatial spread. On examination of the relevant data I found that out of the 65 *gramdan* villages brought under the purview of legislation, 62 were located in five of the 26 districts of Rajasthan and I decided to confine the selection of villages to these five *gramdan* 'clusters'. In turn, these five districts belonged to three major regions of the state—the Eastern Plain, the Dry (Arid) Zone and the Southern Highland. Two of the *gramdan* clusters each belonged to the Dry and Highland Areas and one to the Plain Area.

I decided to select one village each from three regions. In the case of the Plain area, since there was only one *gramdan* cluster, I faced no problem of selection. But there were two clusters each in the case of Dry and Highland regions and I settled on one or another of the clusters depending on certain practical considerations: relatively easy accessibility to the village, amenability of the movement leaders at the district level, etc.

However, the problem I had to tackle in the selection of villages was not yet over, as 12 per cent of *gramdan* villages brought under the Act were new colonies, villages established on land donated by local landlords or on government land. Since these colonies were established *de novo*, I anticipated their functioning to be on a different footing, as traditional animosities based on neighbourhood and factions may not be present in these villages. In order to give representation to this category I selected a fourth village (a new colony) from the Highland region in which the incidence of new colonies was the highest. Thus, I selected four 'successful' *gramdan* villages, which were also unbifurcated typical revenue villages, from four out of the five districts to which most of these villages belonged, the districts being drawn from the three major regions of the state. It may be noted here that the selection of villages from the three regions also facilitated the inclusion of villages with different sizes, quality of land and varying social composition (castes and tribes) in the study.

While four *gramdan* villages were selected only three *non-gramdan* villages need be selected because the category of new colonies was non-existent in the case of non-*gramdan* (control) villages. The three control villages were selected from the same districts, *talukas* and *panchayats* as that of the experimental cases, the distance between them ranging from five to ten miles in all cases. The selection of both the experimental and control cases from the same administrative units was intended to neutralize the impact of state-initiated programmes like Community Development and Panchayati Raj. The use of an experimental design thus affected the choice of control villages because of the need to select two sets of villages, the control set being comparable to the experimental set except in regard to the additional factor, namely, *gramdan*. Although sufficient care was taken to ensure similarity between experimental and control cases in regard to landholding pattern, size of population and social structural features, there were some differences between them. This is an inherent limitation in applying the experimental design to a natural setting. Thus, the control villages had more households, their complexity greater in terms of the number of social categories and the inequality of landholdings more telling as compared with their *gramdan* counterparts. However, these differences, I am sure, were not so crucial as to abandon the design itself. At any rate, instead of adopting a 'methodologically naked' design, I thought it was necessary to attempt a rigorous comparison since my purpose was to understand the rate and directionality of change.

I did not begin my fieldwork with an 'open mind'. The very fact that I had decided on the broad area of my investigation beforehand, made it incumbent on me to have an outline of what I was looking for in the field. The impression conveyed by some researchers which can be stated as: 'I went (to the field), I observed and I analyzed', is to my mind quite contrary to the 'natural' research process. On the other hand, the way in which one presents one's argument and data may impart the impression that the author started with a preconceived framework. For instance, readers of *Charisma, Stability and Change* may get the impression that I started with the argument stated in Chapter 1 and collected 'convenient data' to 'prove' my argument. This is quite contrary to my experience in evolving my strategy. I stated my argument at the very outset, in order to inform the presentation of data with some consistency and order. In fact, the argument, although stated in the begining of the book, was the end product of my research.

I started with the assumption, as noted earlier, that charisma is a change generating force in societies. Similarly, it was my hunch in the beginning that charismatic endowment existed only at the macro level, that it was a quality to be found only among the national-level leaders of the movement. Although I started with these assumptions and hypotheses it was possible to float counter-hypotheses, not always in a cut and dried fashion but as a sort of 'mental experiment'. Thus, in effect there was a constant inter-action between the assumption that I entertained, the concepts I employed and the empirical evidence I gathered. It was through this process that I arrived at my argument whose guiding principle was neither deduction nor induction but retroduction. Let me elaborate.

I gained my initial insight in characterizing the movement as 'charismatic' from the descriptions of the conditions under which the first land-gift was obtained and Vinoba's *response* to it (Rambhai 1958, 1962). However, as soon as I undertook my first field trip the empirical manifestation of charisma became clearer to me. The incidence of *gramdan* villages was high along the route of Vinoba's *padayatra*; the people were gifting away their land to a peripatetic saint. But gradually I noticed that the charismatic quality was also attributed to, or found in the regional- and village-level leaders as well and hence I started working with the notion of local or 'little charismatics'. The local leaders of the movement were often looked upon as charismatic heroes by the people, linking them with national ones. For instance, I came across Bagad Gandhi (Bagad being a folk region constituted by Dungarpur and Banswara districts of Rajasthan) and little Vinobas and Gandhis even at the village level. In the light of this evidence I postulated that there were two types of local charismatic leaders: (*a*) Those who came to don the mantle of charisma independently of the leaders of the wider system. This possibility obtained in systems in which leaders operated independently of the wider context, their independence being rooted in the cultural autonomy of their systems; (*b*) The mantle of charisma may be passed downward by the macro-level leader by grooming regional or local leaders or the latter may establish sufficient communication with the former thereby assuming the role of his spokesman at the local level. This vertical dispersion of charisma was designated contact-charisma.

The notion of local charismatics also led to a reformulation of the attributes of charisma. While the local leaders emulated the life-style of macro leaders in their dress, dietary practices and daily work schedule, they operated in a very limited locale. They were in constant interaction with the people and it was not possible to create a smoke-screen and mystify the relations between the leaders and the followers. Admittedly, we would search in vain for the charismatic qualities of a Gandhi or Vinoba in a local charismatic leader. Therefore, I argued that charisma was an amorphous attribute qualitatively different at different levels and contexts. I then reformulated the notion of charisma as follows: 'The attributes of charisma are not given for ever, they are contextual. That is to say, charisma is ultimately a product of social structure and it undergoes qualitative transformation concomitant to the changes in the nature of society' (Oommen 1972a: 6).

Another insight I gained from the application of the concept of charisma to a specific empirical context was the system-stabilizing function of charisma. Analysis of charismatic authority was crucial to Weber's explanations of social change. Within the framework of German historicism, Weber sought to explain the problem of change at the macro level through the concept of charisma. The charismatic leaders were innovators and creators who cause large-scale change, whom Weber distinguished from the maintainers of tradition. But I found that the means a leader employs would render him a charismatic hero even if he proved to be an agent of system stability. Further, I observed that the leaders of the Bhoodan-Gramdan movement were instrumental for system-conservation, at least in certain respects (Oommen 1967:88-89). Vinoba wanted to establish a society from which exploitation was rooted out, through peaceful means. Partly because of his approach to change, the movement could not effectively confront vested interests and unwittingly even reinforced them. Thus, in spite of its charismatic force, the movement often led to the perpetuation of the system.

Another instance of the bearing of empirical research on concept formation may be noted here. The prevalent tendency in
community power structure analysis was to emphasize a given
approach—positional, reputational or decisional—in locating
influentials which often led to the failure to net all the leaders in an
analytical framework (Oommen 1970b: 226-39). I employed all
the approaches to locate the leaders in the villages studied. In
gramdan villages there were two important formal bodies, the
executive committee of the *gram sabha* (village assembly), making
routine decisions and the Assembly itself constituted by all adults
in the village, those who were above 18 years, in which the ultimate authority for local affairs was vested. The usual practice in
the executive committee was to get the decisions endorsed by *all*
its members who appended their signatures or thumb impressions.
But the *gram sabha* meetings were too unwieldy to collect signatures of all present and, therefore, they were collected only from a
limited number of persons. The significant point to observe was,
who were the persons from whom signatures were collected and
what were *the bases* on which they were qualified to sign. In one of
the *gram sabha* meetings at which I was present, the secretary of
the executive committee was collecting signatures from a few
additional individuals *other than* the executive committee members.
On enquiry I was told that these were *khas admis* (men who matter)
in the context of village affairs. Such observations led me to a
fuller understanding of the nature of the power structure in villages
on the basis of which I made the following formulations:

1. All those who wield real power, *power reservoirs*, in a village
community may not be on the formal decision-making bodies.
2. The *power exercisers* who constitute the formal decision-
making structures have legal or formal power but they may not
wield actual power.
3. The *power pool* in a community is constituted by power
reservoirs and exercisers.
4. A power exerciser may be able to use his position to become
a power reservoir but one can be a member of the power reservoir without being a power exerciser. That is, membership in
formal bodies is a resource for acquiring actual power, but
actual power can be acquired independent of formal structures.
5. If the power reservoirs are not power exercisers or if the

power exercisers are not falling in line with the power reservoirs, political instability is likely.

6. Political stability is assured when power reservoirs are also power exercisers or power exercisers are controlled by power reservoirs.

Thus, an empirical observation in the field yielded fresh insights about the nature of the power structure and political instability.

The point here is that even as a researcher starts with a conceptual framework, it undergoes constant revision as he confronts empirical reality. The field situation offers him opportunities to reformulatè existing concepts and invest them with new meanings, if he has the required flexibility and openness. Additionally, the field situation also continously provides the researcher the context for enunciating new concepts.

AGRARIAN MOVEMENT IN KERALA

The three very well-known approaches in history to tackle agrarian problems are: violent uprising by deprived peasantry, legislative intervention by the state and voluntaristic non-violent action. A large number of studies on the impact of land reforms initiated by the government were completed in India by the 1960s, particularly by economists. Having analyzed the Bhoodan-Gramdan movement in India, the best-known non-violent effort in history to tackle agrarian problems, I came to the conclusion that in terms of its announced aim of establishing communitarian villages based on collective land-ownership, the movement was an abortive experiment. Ever since, I had been wanting to study an agrarian movement with a different orientation in rural India. An opportunity emerged in the late 1960s.

With the ushering in of the so-called 'Green Revolution' in India, the role of economic development in accentuating income disparities became a favourite theme of social science research. The widespread agrarian unrest in India's countryside, culminating in the emergence of the violent Naxalbari revolt in West Bengal in 1967, released shock waves throughout India. Unlike the non-violent Sarvodaya movement, the Naxalbari uprising was widely discussed, debated and analyzed. Everybody seemed to be attesting to the presumed linkage between the Green Revolution and rural unrest. Even the then

Home Minister articulated the popular stereotype when he declared in Parliament that the Green Revolution will turn into a red one if the strategy of rural change was not immediately reoriented.

Having followed this debate carefully for some time I made an initial effort to contest the widely heralded hypothesis, based on the data available in the Home Ministry report (Oommen 1971c: 99-103). I suggested that the presumed causal linkage between the Green Revolution and agrarian unrest was naive, simplistic and was not sustainable. But it was necessary to explicate my position with hard and detailed empirical data. My native district, Alleppey, in Kerala, provided an excellent empirical context to pursue the analysis. Although an Intensive Agricultural Development Project (IADP) district, Alleppey scarcely experienced the Green Revolution. On the other hand, Alleppey had a long tradition of agrarian unrest, very high agricultural wage-rate and low productivity. My detailed and intensive study of the district conclusively proved that the presumed causal sequential explanation; Development → Disparity → Discontent → Conflict, was facile and misleading. I found that mobilization of the peasantry and agrarian proletariat by a multiplicity of political parties competing for clients, substantially contributed to agrarian conflicts (Oommen 1971a: 229-68). This was my first study of Kerala.

Given my interest in rural social transformation and familiarity with rural India I favourably responded to a request from the Food and Agricultural Organization (FAO) of the United Nations in 1972 to undertake a study of agrarian organizations in one of the districts, as a part of a wider study covering 20 districts from all over India. Without hesitation I selected Alleppey district. The purpose of the FAO study was to collect and analyze data on agrarian organizations keeping in mind what factors facilitate or obstruct the building of organizations for the welfare of the rural poor.

I came across a large number and a wide variety of agrarian organizations in Alleppey. From the perspective of building organizations for the welfare of the rural poor, they could be classified into two: those sponsored by the government and those initiated by political parties. The archetype of the first being Harijan cooperatives and of the second being peasant and agricultural labour unions. In terms of their aims, while the cooperatives were dismal failures, the unions were a thumping success. One of the main reasons which accounted for this differential performance was the nature of leadership in these organizations. I therefore argued that if cooperatives were entrusted to the leaders who organized labour unions they may perform better (Oommen 1976: 177-96).

The FAO study clearly revealed the importance of agrarian unions in bringing about substantial change in rural Kerala. For a fuller understanding it was necessary to analyze their style of operation. This called for a new study. If the FAO study concentrated on the organizational dimension, the focus of the new investigation had to be mobilization. I then launched such a study with financial assistance from the Jawaharlal Nehru University in 1974.

As I have noted earlier in the Bhoodan movement study, the mobilizational dimension was neglected, partly because it was a non-violent movement. But in Kerala, what characterized the functioning of agricultural labour unions was their frequent confrontations with farmers' associations. Understandably, the focus in this study was on the varieties of mobilizations by a multiplicity of agrarian unions and associations.

Given the findings of my initial study of Alleppey district which dispelled the causal linkage between the Green Revolution and agrarian unrest, I was persuaded to enlarge the scope of my new study. The following questions became pertinent. Was there a tradition of peasant movement in Kerala? If yes, when did it emerge and crystallize? Were there basic differences in this tradition among the three regions—Tranvancore, Cochin and Malabar—which came to constitute Kerala? If so, what were the bases of the differences? What was the relationship between peasant mobilization and anti-colonial struggle? What changes, if any, did the agrarian movement undergo after independence? Which parties and organizations took the lead in mobilizing different agrarian classes? How did the collective actors define and perceive their identities and what were the consequences of this cognition? What was the impact of state policies in determining the course of agrarian movement?

I might not have satisfactorily answered all these questions in my book, *From Mobilisation to Institutionalisation*(1985). But I am sure that these questions shaped my investigation and they occurred to me precisely because of my previous studies and familiarity with the studies of fellow students of agrarian movements. And yet I believe that this 'prior knowledge' did not constrict and choke me intellectually.

Having stumbled on the idea of career of a movement (the life-cycle approach) while studying the Bhoodan movement, I was inclined to pursue the same strand of analysis in the case of the Kerala agrarian movement too. While the Bhoodan movement had a rather short career, that of the agrarian movement in Kerala was long and eventful. Further, while the former was initiated by a charismatic personality at the national level and had subsequently spread to distant parts of the country, the Kerala agrarian movement was autonomous to begin with but was subsequently linked to all-India movements (e.g.,the colonial movement) and structures (e.g., political parties). This facilitated the following conceptualization as adumbrated in Chapter 1

...in the origin and spread of movements in India we can discern two patterns: (*a*) independent local origin (at the micro level) either simultaneously or sequentially and then getting coordinated... (*b*) simultaneous emergence in different regions through the inspiration of charismatic heroes or sponsored by all-India structures such as political parties.

Given the fact that I was studying a movement which survived and continued for nearly a century, a question arose as to whether the nature of the movement remained the same throughout its existence. This prompted me to examine closely the goal transformations, value orientations, the nature of enemies and the styles of mobilization in the different phases of the movement. Based on this analysis, the movement was divided into four major historical phases: the pre-political, the anti-colonial, the anti-Congress and the pro-government phases. It is necessary to briefly explain the rationale behind this classification.

The pre-political peasant revolts and rebellions usually had independent local origins and were rarely coordinated at the regional level. Notwithstanding their economic goals these revolts were characterized by primordial collectivisms. Their ideology, organizational weapon and leadership were closely linked to and utilized the symbols of caste and religious collectivities. They were rarely exclusively agrarian in content and most of these movements were also cultural revolts. That is, an undifferentiated social structure gives birth to an amorphous 'agrarian' movement with multiple goals.

The anti-colonial phase was distinct in several specific ways:

1. Coordination of the movement on a wider, almost on an all-India basis.
2. Confrontation with a clearly identified and hierarchically ordered set of enemies, namely, the British, the 'feudal'/absentee landlord, the money-lender and the big landlord.
3. Emergence of political parties with distinct pro-landlord anti-peasant, and anti-landlord pro-peasant orientations.

In the first decade of independent India the peasant movement of Kerala was explicitly anti-government for the following reasons: First, the mobilization of peasantry and agrarian proletariat was undertaken mainly by the Communist Party of India, which was in the opposition. Second, the Congress Party, having acquired power, took or appeared to be taking a pro-landlord posture.

In the fourth phase, beginning with 1957, the Kerala agrarian movement took a different turn as the party or parties which were the chief mobilizers of the peasantry and agrarian proletariat either formed the government (intermittently) or remained as substantial opposition parties with sufficient political clout to challenge the parties in power. This rendered the possibility of the agrarian movement operating as an agent of the establishment and/or extension of the party in power.

Based on this empirical evidence I argued that any effort to generalize about the role of particular peasant classes irrespective of the contextual variations would be misleading. I have suggested that *(a)* the notion of the vanguard should be viewed in the spatio-temporal context and *(b)* the same agrarian class may play diametrically different roles in different historical phases. Much of the prevalent confusion relating to the analysis of the role of agrarian classes in revolution is the result of ignoring the *historicity of context*.

The conceptual distinction between party, voluntary association and movement is well-documented and widely accepted in sociology. This conceptualization is based on the empirical experiences of Western liberal democracies. But these distinctions are scarcely applicable to one-party systems and the Indian political situation. For example, what is labelled as a peasant or agrarian 'movement' in India is invariably the mobilizational activities of agrarian unions, that is, voluntary associations, which are front-organizations of political parties. Viewed thus, if one makes a comprehensive study of the activities of political parties that would encapsulate movement activities too.

In Kerala there are several agrarian front-organizations based on parties and classes. Thus, a particular political party may sponsor two or more such organizations (and in fact some of them do)—a peasant association and an agricultural labour union—while others may sponsor only one such association or union. The usual tendency among movement analysts is to concentrate on the activities of one set of these associations or unions—farmers' associations, peasant unions, agricultural labour unions—ignoring others, thereby mistaking the part for the whole. In reality, the agrarian movement is constituted by the cooperative and conflicting interactions between and among these unions and associations. Keeping these considerations in mind I defined a movement as a stream of associations in interaction. Such a definition helps to distinguish movements from parties and associations and to concentrate on the specific activity of movements as distinct from that of particular associations or parties.

Discussions on the role of the peasantry in the freedom movement in India are viewed from two perspectives: macro-holism and micro-individualism (Oommen 1985: 2-3). The first overemphasizes the political content and motivation and the second highlights only the economic grievances and interests of the peasantry. While emphasizing the specific attributes and motives of the peasantry, both these perspectives ignore the properties of the situation in which mobilizations take place. In reality, peasant collective action particularly under colonial conditions is largely prompted by political considerations, the aspirations they share with others to move from subjecthood to citizenship. But the concretization of this aspiration as far as the peasantry is concerned, is to be found in the redressal of its economic hardships. Even as the holistic perspective informs peasant collective action, the individualistic (class-categorical) interests and needs cannot be overlooked. That is, neither macro-holism nor micro-individualism can fully explain peasant involvement in anti-colonial struggles. Therefore I suggested *situational interactionism* as an adequate perspective which recognizes: *(a)* the *reciprocity* between local mobilization and national movement, and *(b)* the importance of the properties of the situation (Oommen 1985:3).

The tendency to juxtapose collective protest actions with state actions and hence movements and legislations is widespread in contemporary social science writings of the Western liberal democracies. But this conceptualization does not adequately portray the empirical realities of either the socialist countries or of the developing countries. The state in these countries not only initiates a series of legislative measures to bring about radical transformation but even sponsors collective actions either to legitimize its measures and/or to accelerate the process of social transformation. Further, legislation itself can be an initiator or indicator of change depending upon the role the state assumes. Keeping these considerations in mind, I tried to highlight the *complementarity* between legislation and movements. That is, legislation plays a pivotal role in order to institutionalize the changes initiated by social movements. Conversely, even when change is initiated through the instrument of law, collective actions become important to legitimize and complete the process of change. One cannot understand and appreciate these observations unless one conceptualizes the state's actions and collective actions as complementary, a pay-off obtained by recognizing the difference between our empirical situation and that of Western capitalist democracies.

It is widely recognized that the mould for the emergence of movements is provided by relative deprivation, its perception and articulation by the concerned collectivity. In contrast, very little theoretical work exists with regard to the termination of movements. However, it has been proposed that the specific processes which lead to the termination of a movement are: repression, discreditation, co-optation and institutionalization (Rush and Denisoff 1971: 367).

My analysis clearly showed that no effort was spared in the pre-independent phase and even in the first decade of free India by the then establishments to repress the agrarian movement in Kerala. In spite of this virulent repression the movement gained in strength, notwithstanding temporary setbacks. Therefore, the critical variable is not repression *per se*. but the collective conscience which bestows *legitimacy* on the agent of repression and attributes *illegitimacy* to movement participants. That is, insofar as the state is perceived by the collectivity as a 'legitimate authority' which should repress the 'illegitimate movement' which offends the collective conscience, repression will be an effective instrument for terminating a movement. On the other hand, if the state is perceived as an illegitimate intruder and/or supporting the vested interests in society, and movement participants are viewed as martyrs to a cause in the wider interests of the collectivity, then repression will not weaken but strengthen the movement. Thus, my analysis unfolds that, ignoring the properties of the situation leads to the formulation of erroneous theoretical propositions.

With the arrival of freedom and transfer of political power from the British to a national government, a critical proportion of people invested the Congress government with legitimacy. That is why the repression of agrarian movements by the Congress government was not viewed with the same disdain by the people at large. Conversely, the party in power tried its best to discredit the Communist Party of India (CPI) as it continued to pursue the path of violence. Recognizing the changed situation, the CPI opted for a policy of peaceful transition of socialism and entered into an alliance with the progressive bourgeoisie, that is, the party in power. This in turn led to partial co-optation of several movement leaders directly or indirectly into the establishment. But consequent upon the split of the CPI into CPI(R) and CPI(M) and thanks to the latter's refusal to 'cooperate' with the Congress, the possibility of co-opting movement leaders diminished. As CPI(M) front-organizations continued to be the most persisting factor in keeping the vitality of the agrarian movement high in Kerala, the strategy of co-optation did not produce the desired effect, namely the demise of the movement. That is, in order that discreditation and co-optation be effective means of terminating movements, a series of prerequisites should exist.

As noted earlier, I began the study of agrarian movement in Kerala within the framework of the natural history or life-cycle approach according to which institutionalization is an inevitable tendency leading to the termination of a movement. Baldly put, the argument runs as follows: the development of an organization, however rudimentary, is inevitable for the realization of movement goals. But the emergence of such organization inevitably sets in motion forces which defeat the very purpose which necessitated it. The instrument—the movement organization—becomes instrumental in frustrating the very purpose for which it emerged.

Contrary to this conventional theorization I found enough support in the empirical evidence available to me that there is no inherent tendency towards institutionalization. Further, even when it occurs, institutionalization does not necessarily stop or always decelerate the process of mobilization which is so fundamental and primary to the continuance of a movement. In fact, mobilization and institutionalization coexist and the latter may provide new possibilities for mobilization. Therefore I concluded: "...mobilization is not *displaced* by institutionalization but *both go hand in hand*....".

In the late 1960s when I began my study of agrarian unrest in Kerala, the most widely-studied territorial/spatial unit in Indian sociology and social anthropology was the village. But my effort to understand the Bhoodan movement through an investigation of *gramdan* villages revealed that if I were to link the micro-dimensions with those of the macro—ideology, organizational pattern, leadership—I need to go 'beyond the village' as my unit of study. This experience prompted me to consider the viability of a unit of analysis bigger than the village but manageable for doing fieldwork.

In arriving at the appropriate unit of analysis for a study several considerations are relevant. The most important of these are: the theme of the study, the spatial coverage of the phenomenon and its historicity. Generally speaking, a phenomenon such as social movement is rarely confined to a territorial entity such as a village and it may have existed for a long span of time. The Kerala agrarian movement, notwithstanding its independent and autonomous origins in the three regions which came to constitute Kerala—Malabar, Cochin, and Travancore—got coordinated during the freedom struggle and subsequently came to constitute and operate as a single stream with the emergence of Kerala state. Further, insofar as agrarian mobilizations in India are essentially activities of front-organizations of political parties, the macro-dimensions of agrarian movements are linked to a spatial unit bigger than the particular state in which they function. Thus, the agrarian mobilizations in Kerala initiated by parties such as the Communist Party of India (Marxist) (CPIM), Communist Party of India (CPI), and Congress (I), are tempered by the ideology and styles of functioning of these 'all-India' parties.

The above considerations make it clear that I could not have selected a 'fixed' unit of analysis while studying the Kerala agrarian movement. Rather, it was necessary to constantly shift the unit of analysis as a frame of reference depending upon the specific dimension under investigation. Thus, while analyzing the pre-independent phase of the movement the analysis of the event-structure had to be kept separate for the three regions of Kerala even as these mobili-zations were informed of the same spirit and ideology, namely anti-authoritarianism, be it against the British or the monarchy, and pro-peasantism.

Once Kerala emerged as a separate state it was possible to attempt the analysis on an all-Kerala basis. But whether or not this could actually be done would depend upon the nature of data available and to be generated. Insofar as one is drawing from various types of records and documents it is possible to construct a picture of mobilizational activities of a given region or state, say of Malabar or Kerala. But in those contexts and/or periods for which the documents are not available and the researcher generates data through field studies, he must confine himself to a very limited spatial unit. Thus, historical analysis usually undertaken on the basis of documents relates to a wider spatial unit as compared with field investigations done by the researcher. And this shift in the unit of analysis was inevitable. While analyzing the current phase of the movement about which I had to collect field data, my unit of analysis was one district, namely Alleppey. But wherein I deve-loped my analysis based on documents, the units are either a region (e.g., Malabar) or the state, that is, Kerala, as a whole.

Why have I selected Alleppey district as the unit of my field investigation? The fact that Alleppey is my native district and that I had already undertaken some fieldwork there were incidental but not decisive factors which influenced my decision in favour of Alleppey. The central focus of my field investigation was the nature and magnitude of mobilization of different agrarian classes and Alleppey was an excellent case befitting the purpose.

First, Alleppey had a long tradition of agrarian protest, the famous Punnapra-Vayalar revolt of 1946 occurred in two *talukas* of the district—Ambalapuzha and Shertalai. Second, while the agrarian mobilization in the Malabar region was largely confined to the peasantry, that of Travancore, enveloped both peasantry and agrarian proletariat. And, Alleppey was the epicentre of agrarian movement in Travancore. Third, with the implemen-tation of land ceiling legislations and abolition of intermediaries the erstwhile feudal landlords have disappeared as a class in Kerala. The emergence of the former tenants as owner-cultivators and the ushering in of the Green Revolution coincided and these two in conjunction led to the growth of a prosperous class of capitalist farmers. The latest phase of agrarian movement in Kerala is characterized by organized and continuous confrontations between farmers and agricultural labour. Twenty-three per cent of farmers in Alleppey district in 1971 were members of one or another farmers' association, sponsored by different political parties, probably the highest figure for the whole of India. Although only 12 per cent of the agricultural labour force of Alleppey district were union members in 1971, this was the highest figure for Kerala, followed by Trichur and Palghat districts with barely 5 per cent unionized agricultural labour force. All this convinced me that Alleppey was an ideal unit for my field investigation.

From what I have said above it is clear that in analyzing social movements one cannot confine oneself either to the micro- or to the macro-situation, one has to draw from both. This in turn means that one cannot rely entirely on field data or documentary analysis; it is imperative to combine both if one were to study an on-going movement with a long career. As the Kerala agrarian movement fits this description (that is, an on-going movement with a long career), I have resorted to collecting data from a multiplicity of sources employing a variety of techniques. However, even here the kind of perspective one adopts becomes crucial in determining the nature of data one collects. Let me illustrate.

Those who attempt to reconstruct the history of social movements usually rely on two major sources: archival records and the 'official texts' of the movement, both of which may provide a view from above. Archival records mainly relate to the correspondence between and among the administrative and movement elite. The official texts of a movement usually discuss its ideology, organizational pattern, strategy and tactics as conceived by the top movement leadership. Consequently, an effort to reconstruct movement history from these sources misses the view from below, the views and articulations of the ordinary participants. It was possible for me to capture a bottom-up view of the contemporary phase of the movement through the field data I have collected. To match this data I had to tap appropriate sources relating to the historical phase of the movement. The most authentic and useful data I could find was the writing by and on grass-root movement activists—biographies, memoirs, 'historical accounts', literary writings (novels, short stories, and dramas)—and informant interviewing, that is, 'oral history'.

An important source of information widely tapped by most researchers is reports by journalists. I have also used this source. But usually journalists report only when (*a*) the incidents are violent, and (*b*) political heavy-weights are present on specific occasions. Thus, the routine activities, particluarly at the grass-roots, go unreported. An invaluable source to get at these activities are police records, which are usually not accessible to researchers. Fortunately I was permitted to go through the police records and this helped me get a picture of the activities of different agrarian associations on a continuous basis. Once I knew that a particular incident did take place it was possible for me to pursue its investigation by collecting data through other sources. However, there is one disadvantage if one relies exclusively on police accounts of such incidents and activities. The usual tendency (and this seems to be based on official brief) is to concentrate on the activities of those associations and leaders affiliated to the oppostion political parties. But given the political situation prevalent in Kerala the associations affiliated to all parties get their 'attention' in turn as they circulate in and out of power. At any rate, the mobilizational activities are usually kept high by a party when it is in the opposition and therefore it is also natural for the police to concentrate on them.

I have defined the event-structure of the movement as the interactions between the different unions and associations. The record of activities kept by them was another important source of data for me. As is well known, the local (village) units of these organizations rarely keep comprehensive accounts of their activities. Even the decisions are taken in informal meetings. Therefore, the data about local units was invariably collected through informant interviewing, the informants being constituted by a pool of persons drawn from all the organizations.

Yet another source of data was the records of government departments of revenue, development, labour and newly-created organizations such as the Industrial Relations Committee (a tripartite committee to process disputes which arose among and between farmers and workers) or Land Tribunals (to settle the disputes between landowners and their tenants).

The foregoing account clearly unfolds that the major chunk of data for the study was drawn from records of various types and informant interviewing (with the help of interview guides devised for different categories of informants). In addition to this, I have had the opportunity to observe specific incidents of mobilizations and meetings of agrarian organizations for nearly a decade, although intermittantly, beginning in the early 1970s, during my several visits to Kerala, ranging from two to eight weeks.

CONCLUDING COMMENTS

My experiences in undertaking studies of two social movements reveals that a multiplicity of consiuerations go into the selection of research themes. The researcher may not be conscious of all these factors, particularly in the beginning. But it is rewarding to bring the unconscious elements into the realm of consciousness because that would at least partly reveal the value biases and preferences the researcher has. To be aware and conscious of one's value preferences is the first step in the journey towards objectivity.

There is an inevitable risk in choosing research themes which foment contemporary political and academic controversies. The possibility of getting grafted into one or another camp is fairly high. To take a position independent of the prevalent popular sentiments and opinions calls for tremendous courage and fortitude.. And yet, one has to do precisely that if one is to deserve the label of an impartial analyst.

Those who have a definite issue to investigate and questions to answer would invariably begin their empirical studies armed with a conceptual-theoretical framework. But this need not be an intellectual liability if one is sufficiently open, flexible and creative to reformulate one's framework in the light of one's exposure to empirical evidence. That is, while it is not possible to begin research with an 'open mind', one should constantly keep open one's partially-filled mind to provide scope for creative confrontations between concepts, theories and data. The captive mind is not simply a product of Western academic colonialism, but also of the inability to transcend trained incapacity and inappropriate indigenous work habits.

4

Movements and Institutions: Structural Opposition or Processual Linkage?

I deal here with two focal points: one relates to the inadequacy of Western thought to apprehend *even* Western reality, particularly in its processual dimension. Although the challenge posed by recent empirical developments (e.g., the Green Movement) prompted Western theorists to grapple with this problem, such efforts are but scarce beginnings. The other point is that at any rate the application of Western concepts to non-Western contexts would unfold their limitations. The argument is explicated with special reference to two concepts in wide currency—movements and institutions. As a prerequisite to the analysis it is imperative to state briefly the sense in which the two terms are used.

I

I have no intention of providing new definitions of institutions and movements; their definitions are aplenty. Therefore, what I propose to do is to describe the manner in which they are interrelated. Generally speaking, an institution may be viewed as a cluster of interrelated roles resulting from the institutionalization of socially desirable and legitimized values, norms, rules and procedures. But institutions are not eternally stable and institutional legitimacy is continually questioned. Thus, the response to institutionalization may manifest in different forms: conformity, differential inter-pretation, acceptance of values but rejection of the institutional role-incumbents, opposition, etc. This means institutionalization can occasion both bureaucratization and mobilization. That is, the process of institutionalization may and often does provide the moment for movements to emerge.

Movements are conscious collective actions informed of an ideology, aided by an organizational weapon and initiated by a core person/group to bring about change in any direction (past/future) using any means (violent/non-violent). That is, movements are deliberately initiated and guided collective mobilizations to bring about relatively rapid social transformation. But to consolidate and stabilize the gains of a movement one needs the instrumentality of the institution. Often the organizational core of the movement provides the nucleus of the institution. That is, a movement contains within it the embryo of an institution. In the process of institutionalization of a movement, the characteristic activity of the movement, namely, mobilization, is relegated to the background and becomes less salient. But the process of institutionalization carries with it the seeds of movement.

The point I wish to affirm is this: it is useful and necessary to make an analytical distinction between movement and institution. But it should not render us impervious to the empirical reality on the ground. What should matter is not the elegance of a tool but its efficiency in achieving the purpose for which it is designed.

II

Dichotomous constructions of human societies or their specific dimensions are very much a part of Western mainstream sociology. The tendency to conceptualize social phenomena in either/or terms is so ancient, common, virile, universal and internalized, that any effort to disabuse our minds of this mode of conceptualization is not simply a Herculean task but is often perceived as blasphemous in the kingdom of social scientists. Be that as it may, let me venture to suggest that this tendency has been and continues to be one of the major barriers to apprehending social reality.

To begin with, it is necessary to identify the leading sources which gave birth to this mode of conceptualization: Western epistemological dualism and the nature of the empirical base from which the construction of theory is attempted.

Epistemological dualism implies opposition between the subject and the object, matter and spirit, knowledge and belief, intellect and feeling, the whole and the individual. Understandably, the opposition and displacement syndromes came to be embedded in Western thinking. An important source of this seems to be monotheistic religions. With the persisting influence of religion, secularization notwithstanding, human thinking and conceptualization continue to be moulded by the religious ethos.

Social science developed and flourished in the liberal democracies of the West. It is but natural that social science theory is tempered by the empirical realities and the social contexts of its immediate origin. While this in itself is understandable, the obstinate tendency to generalize the Western experience for the whole world in spite of wide variations in empirical situations, needs to be questioned.

Analysts from and of liberal democracies counterpose the state with the party, the legislature with the judiciary, the judiciary with the executive, the party with the movement, movements with institutions, and obstinately insist that this should be so not only for these societies but for other societies as well. But this is simply not true. Let me recall a well-known example.

The primacy of the party in socialist systems attests to its importance as a structure/institution. And, the party is projected as the most important agent to initiate, guide and lead collective actions. That is, an institution is viewed as an instrument of collective mobilization. This is reflected in the formation and functioning of front-organizations for youth, peasantry, women, students or workers, of socialist parties even in non-socialist nation-states.

However, one needs to recognize at least three empirical variants of this situation. First, the party becoming the legitimizer of the state authority (e.g., USSR, China). To the extent that the party is perceived as an instrument of change by the people and the state is an instrument of the party, the rupture between people, party and state is conceptually non-existent.[1] But the possibility of a gradual rupture in the process of their interactions (wherein the issue of primacy would emerge) should not be ruled out, as is evident from recent events, in the USSR and China.

[1] However, when the party or institution is used as an instrument of collective mobilization, one comes across severe limitations and contradictions. Thus, in October 1917, when the elections for the Constituent Assembly of the U.S.S.R were conducted through secret ballot, the Bolsheviks lost. At the Second Congress of Soviets, elections were public and the Bolsheviks won. In all probability, the hesistant must have had their hand forced. 'Direct democracy' serves to mobilize the masses, facilitates quick decisions, but lends itself to the hegemony of an active minority. Understandably, Lenin dismissed 'representative democracy' as 'sham democracy' and held that direct democracy was a superior form of democracy.

Second, the party either does not attempt to legitimize state authority, or even when it does, it does not succeed in doing so. Thus, in spite of the overall supremacy of the party in East European countries during 1949-54, it could not legitimize state authority. And, when the party was confronted with the problem of legitimation by the mid-1950s, although it tried the separation of the state and the party, it did not succeed. Consequently, repression and army occupation were resorted to in the absence of a legitimized authority. Thus, the state-party rupture was not allowed to run its full course, thereby settling the issue of legitimacy.

Third, in countries once under colonial rule, the liberation movements invariably converted themselves into national parties. Given the nationalist expectancy, the party became the legitimate repository of formal authority. Conceptually, these are not one-party systems but are dominated by one party, although a number of smaller parties also exist. However, the general tendency is to identify the dominant party with the state, rendering the conceptual distinction between state and party redundant in the empirical context. The theoretical point to be noted here is that none of the above empirical situations warrants a neat juxtaposition of the state and the party, or, for that matter, institutions and movements as opposing elements.

It is instructive to recall here that the conventional party-movement dichotomy was obliterated in the West in recent times as exemplified in the relationship between the Green Movement and the Green Party. While the conceptual distinction between the two is maintained by the supporters, they seem to recognize the organic linkage between the Green Movement and the Green Party. This new understanding, I suggest, stems from the very nature of the movement itself.

Traditionally most of the movements in the West were segmental in their social bases, catering to the interests of one or another social category within the society. Consequently, mobilizations were sectoral in orientation. In contrast, the Green Movement is an umbrella movement encapsulating within it a wide variety of 'partial' movements ranging from ecological and feminist to peace movements. Further, it is holistic in approach, being a general response to the maladies of Western social formation. In Germany, where the Green Movement is particularly strong, it also represents a rupture with the Nazi past, which encapsulated the whole of of German society. Finally, the movement reflects the collectivistic orientation of the German people and society (see Galtung 1986:75-90). All this makes the Green Movement potentially capable of universal mobilization, thereby rendering the isomorphism between the movement and the party real.[2]

Epistemological dualism coupled with the narrow empirical base of theorization (Western democracies) has had two unanticipated consequences for comprehending and analyzing social reality. First, characterizing aspects of reality as polar opposites when they are not, and second, vociferous advocacy of the displacement syndrome while in reality there is only partial modification of the old (the denounced elements) and selective acceptance of the new (the adored aspects). Instead of acknowledging this simple fact of human life and attesting the sane strategy of selective retention and judicious rejection of specific elements (see Oommen 1983a: 253-63) to usher in social change, social scientists often indulge in theorization as if totalities are displaced: capitalism by socialism, dictatorship by democracy, hierarchy by equality, primordial ties by secularism, centralization by decentralization or *vice versa*. My present task is to demonstrate the artificiality of this exercise in regard to one aspect of reality, namely, institutions and movements, drawing upon empirical evidence from India.

III

In contemporary mainstream sociology, collective actions and movements are viewed as being disengaged from institutions and structures. This vein of thinking and mode of conceptualization cannot adequately account for several aspects of the emerging social phenomena. For example, the establishment of socialist and welfare states often necessitates that the state sponsor mobilizations, movements, and even 'revolutions' (see Oommen 1977c: 14-37).

In the 'new states' of Asia and Africa, movements are often piloted by organizations or associations of primordial collectivities. While these associations ordinarily operate as institutions, the

[2] The situation in socialist one-party systems is comparable in that by definition the party has a holistic orientation encapsulating the interests of the people in general. Similarly, national liberation movements by definition are totalistic in orientation, catering to the interests of everybody in the colony, thereby limiting the possibility of splintering participants based on specific interests.

mobilizational aspect is often encapsulated in them. Thus, one scarcely comes across the sharp disengagement believed to exist between movements and institutions.

There are several reasons for conceptualizing institutions and movements as if they were disengaged entities. First, the inadequate accounting of the time element in the analysis (for an exception, see Alberoni 1984). The transformation of movements into institutions, and *vice versa*, is generally gradual and seldom sudden. There is a *social state* between the two phases—movements and institutions—and social scientists have scarcely paid attention to this dimension of social reality. The initial, even if faltering, steps made to view society as a process [3] or an event would go a long way toward recognizing the interim social state between 'solid state' (institutions) and 'fluid state' (movements).

Second, the widespread tendency to confuse synergetic behaviour with collective actions. Synergism refers to the process wherein the isolated actions of an aggreate of individuals produce conditions of exigency which in turn result in social change. But the social actors are not consciously contributing towards change or motivated to bring about change (see Ogle et al. 1954). Quite a few of the social phenomena that are designated as 'collective' are only nominally so. For example, if individuals made independent decisions to improve their life chances through migration or planned parenthood (though these decisions could be collective as well), the impact of their independent action may have a group effect. But the impact is not the resultant of collective action only that of synergetic behaviour. The individual actors are not collectively aware but only individually conscious; there is no *interaction* between them. In contrast, there are instances which produce change precisely because participants interact and have or develop solidary relationships or collectively pursue the aim. The collective consciousness may be based either on an antecedent common identity anchored in an institution, or a newly emerging one, provided by a movement.

[3] Stark (1963) identifies the three fundamental forms of social thought in characterizing human societies as follows: Society as unity as upheld by philosophical realists, society as multiplicity as viewed by sociological nominalists, and society as process as conceived by the cultural school. The cultural school characterizes society as an event, a happening, an inter-human reality. Implicit in this characterization is the possibility of perceiving structures and processes, institutions and movements as entities which are intertwined and not estranged. However, this seminal insight remains an embryonic idea in social science even to this day.

In either event the identity is shared and acknowledged through the medium of either a movement or an institution which is interlocked and not disengaged.

Third, movements are usually defined and perceived as large-scale or mass efforts. Be that as it may, most movements, however large they might become eventually, would usually have small beginnings in the form of a small group, assocation or sect. That is, the formation of an institution or structure could be the starting point of a movement. Alternatively, a movement may emerge out of a sudden event or happening. But soon an organization becomes a necessary accompaniment for the survival of the movement. That is, there exists a processual linkage between institutions and movements (see Oommen 1977c: 14-37). Thus, one can conceive of empirical situations wherein the intertwining between movements and institutions is perennially present and continuing.

If institutions do not 'produce' movements, that is, if they do not respond to the challenges posed to them periodically, they will become structurally and culturally obsolete; they will perish. Therefore, institutions require movements for their very survival through periodic replenishment. Movements provide institutions with the possibility of re-legitimization, if and when the latter experience an erosion of their legitimacy. On the other hand, unless movements crystallize into institutions, unless the visions of movements are translated into reality through institutional mechanisms, they will embody mere aspirations. That is, institutions are the instruments movements employ to translate ideology into programme, theory into praxis, without which they remain shells without substance. In fact, every revolutionary ideology is in search of a structure—party, institution—capable of translating its vision into reality.

Movements emerge not only to correct the lags in praxis in the prevailing institutions, but to identify the gaps in theory as well. That is, movements not only produce collective actors but also provide them with new values. These values are to be rendered 'collective' to begin with, for which the involvement of people is a prerequisite. But if the resultant mobilization is left unchartered it will not lead to the pursued goal, the institutionalization of a new set of values. Mobilization and institutionalization are counterposed in contemporary social science theory, often forgetting that they fall into a continuum. The prevalent tendency is to view movements and mobilizations as *degenerating* into institutions and

institutionalization. In contrast, it should be noted that institutionalization of values pursued by movements is possible only through
building appropriate institutions.

It is true that movements surface when institutions fail and the
emerging collective conscience is articulated through movements.
Yet, if a movement does not create institutions embodying the
new values it upholds and articulates, it serves no purpose; it vanishes
without any impact. Sometimes movements tend to retain their
'glory' by dissolving themselves after achieving their goal.[4] But
what really happens is that even as a movement is disbanded formally,
it actually takes on a new incarnation either in the form of a political
party or as a new movement with a new goal. It should be emphasized
here that if a movement wants to translate its ideology into reality it
needs an institutional vehicle, for example, a party. This in turn leads
to institutionalization of power and authority which is an unavoidable
prerequisite. But the tendency in social science writings has been to
decry this development as pathological and undesirable.

Institutions and movements are reciprocally linked in three
significant ways. First, institutions and structures are *cleansed* by
movements. What are often labelled 'fundamentalist' or 'revivalist'
movements are essentially attempts to rescue institutions from their
current 'degeneration' and render them back to their original state of
pristine purity as defined by the visionaries of these movements.
Thus, a large number of religious movements are merely efforts to
cleanse the prevailing religious establishment of its undesirable
accretions which were not a part of the original vision. Even movements which challenge the bases of authority in the existing institutions
succeed only in cleansing the old structure. The student movement
attempted to question the basis of authority in the university
system but could only partially reform it (through institutionalized
student participation in decisional processes), as knowledge
remains the basis of authority. Conversely, institutions tend to
correct movements from their 'adventurism'. It is well known how
the rebels in institutions are contained or liquidated depending
upon the nature and intensity of threats posed by them to institutions.

Second, movements deliberately *create* institutions which are new
vehicles to fulfil the present visions and aspirations. Similarly, institutions

---

[4] A classic example of this is M.K. Gandhi's insistence on dissolving the Indian National
Congress which piloted the anti-colonial struggle against the British. In spite of the fact that
he was hailed as the Father of the Nation, his followers did not stand by his prescription.

may float movements to sustain their legitimacy. Third, movements tend to redefine old institutions; the effort being not simply to purify and inject institutions with new verve and vitality, nor to abandon them completely and create new ones, but to *recreate* them. The break from the past is evident but the link is not simply tenous. Thus, most feminists vehemently criticize family, but do not abandon it as an institution; they hope to *recreate* a non-violent and humane family. On the other hand, institutions tend to revitalize movements in such a way that the balance between stability and change is maintained.

It is important to remind ourselves here that the cleansed, created, and recreated institutions coexist: accretion rather than displacement takes place. Further, movements require institutions to concretize their visions; institutions need movements to sustain their legitimacy.

Having advanced a few theoretically plausible propositions, I should now like to provide some empirical evidence to support them with reference to religion and politics in India.

Hindu civilization is not the product of a movement and subsequent institution-building; it is the product of a gradual process which integrated many and varied streams. The date of its emergence cannot be easily ascertained; internally it is badly fractured through the ubiquitous and prodigious caste system. Further, it did not produce a Church which engulfed every believer. The solidarity of Hindu religion often depended on threats emanating from powerful protest movements dating as far back as the 6th century BC—Jainism and Buddhism—and fiercely persisting even in the 1980s—from Sikhism[5]. Intervening in between were not only the widespread *bhakti* movements for several centuries but also conquests and colonization by alien religious groups—Islam and Christianity. Each of these encounters created not only conflicts but also solidaritiec, leading to the crystallization of new collective conscience, the embodiment of which is found in new institutions.

Given the nature of Hinduism and the process of its formation, all religious protest movements of Indian origin were 'anti-Hindu', in the sense that they questioned the basic values and institutions of Hinduism. In this process, new religions—Jainism,

[5] It could be argued, and many do, that the current Sikh-Hindu conflict is hardly religious and patently political. Nevertheless, the social identities and boundaries are drawn on the basis of religion.

Buddhism, Sikhism—have emerged and they continue to coexist with the old and its numerous sects, *gurus* and cults. What happened and is still happening is elaboration and accretion and not displacement. Similarly, notwithstanding several centuries of Muslim and British conquest and rule, the dominant ethos in India is that of coexistence and reconciliation between the different religious collectivities.[6]

How can one explain this tendency? Part of the answer lies in the type of religious systems. In monotheistic societies, the exclusiveness of God was total; His sovereignty was absolute. The commandment was 'Thou shalt have no other gods before me'. In contrast, in polytheistic and pantheistic societies, a multiplicity of gods was an accepted maxim. As the Japanese Buddhist philosopher Ikeda put it:

> The difference between monotheism and pantheism is very telling in human civilization. Under conditions imposed by monotheistic faith, a great need to relate everything to an absolute being defines society and civilization and promotes the development of an all-pervasive uniformity. Because this makes the acceptance of alien elements difficult, when confronted with something foreign and new, a monotheistic society must undergo a win-or-loss, all-or-nothing transition. For this reason, changes in the historical current of the West have often been basic and far-reaching. In pantheistic societies, on the other hand, the value of alien ideas and things is recognized. The society is tolerant toward them; consequently, they can be introduced without the necessity of fundamental social alterations. No matter what new elements enter, the society remains basically unchanged (Toynbee and Ikeda 1976: 297-98)

[6] Two points may be noted here. First, even as powerful Christian protest movements emerged and challenged the existing church, all the denominations labelled themselves as Christians. This is equally true of Islam; both Shias and Sunnis claim themselves to be the more authentic Muslims. In contrast, the tendency to opt out of Hinduism is not unusual because it is possible for those who opt out to coexist with Hinduism. Second, if the religions of the conquered or colonized peoples were not 'developed' ones, the Semitic religions, particularly Islam and Christianity, displaced the native religions through conversion and proselytization as in Latin America and Africa. In contrast, the strategy was different in Asia as several highly developed religions already existed at the time of conquests and colonization. This, along with the ideology of tolerance embedded in polytheism and pantheism, seems to account for the emergence of the multi-religious societies of Asia.

The tendency to portray different dimensions of reality as if they are mutually exclusive is anchored in Western epistemological dualism which can at least be partly traced to monotheistic religions which predominate in them.

The Indian National Congress (INC) was the organizational weapon of the Indian national liberation movement. But this overarching movement encapsulated within it three types of solidarity, each of which created a series of movements. While civic and occupational collectivities such as peasantry, students or workers, and biological collectivities such as youth or women, did not pose any threat to the original vision of the INC, primordial collectivities did pose threats. Thus, communalism, that is, the claim of religious collectivities to establish exclusive sovereign states, crystallized as a countervailing solidarity to nationalism. The Indian nation-state could encompass within it the communal interests of all religious groups except that of the Muslims. And Muslim communalism was legitimized as nationalism when a new structure representing it, the state of Pakistan, emerged. But the process did not stop and with the crystallization of a new solidarity based on language, a new movement emerged, which in turn gave birth to a new structure—the state of Bangladesh. Similarly, in India a multiplicity of solidarities which lay frozen were animated, several of which created new structures representing their ideas and interests— political parties, trade unions, women's organizations. Thus, the interpenetration between movements and institutions is obvious.

After independence, Mohandas Karamchand Gandhi, the chief architect of the liberation struggle, advised the freedom fighters to dissolve the INC and constitute themselves into a body of voluntary workers for the social reconstruction of India. A minority of his followers did dissociate themselves from the INC and launched a new movement to pursue the second major Gandhian objective, namely, *sarvodaya* (upliftment of all), as the first, namely, *swaraj* (political freedom) had already been achieved. However, the majority of the freedom fighters either continued with the INC, converting it into a party, or established new parties. Almost all political parties in free India emerged out of the INC. Thus, the Congress Socialist Party, the precursor of the Communist Party of India (CPI) functioned as a 'group' within the Congress Party. In turn, the CPI was split into two giving birth to the Communist

Party of India (Marxist)—the CPI (M). Subsequently, the CPI (M) also split and the Communist Party of India (Marxist-Leninist) was born. The Indian National Congress too split several times, giving birth to several region-based caste-oriented and person-centred parties. But what is important to note here is that in each of these cases the new party and the old one were *linked* through a movement and/or mobilization. While the new parties claimed to be the genuine ones upholding the original vision, the old parties invariably tried to discredit them. Mobilizations and counter-mobilizations were inevitably involved in this process.

Thus, with the emergence of these parties, movements did not disappear. Many of them only redefined their goals and re-targeted their enemies. In fact, most of what are labelled as 'movements' in India are collective actions initiated and guided by these parties through their front-organizations. Alternatively, a large number of new 'movements' are the resultant of splits and factionalization of political parties. But this does not mean that once they move from the fluid state to the solid state they remain in that state forever. These parties often function as movements even as they develop elaborate party bureaucracies.

The attempts to differentiate in principle but combine in practise have created enormous problems for the smooth functioning of governments in India. Hence, the formal distinction in membership sought to be made between the Rashtriya Swayam Sevak Sangh (a militant Hindu voluntary organization) and the Jana Sangh (a political party sponsored by it) by some of the constituents of the Janata Party, which was a coalition of several political parties, led to the fall of the Janata government, till then the only non-Congress government in power in free India, although for a short period.

The situation in different regions and states of India is no different. The link between the Dravidian movement and Dravidian parties of Tamil Nadu; the Akali movement and the Akali Party in Punjab in north India; the Assam movement and the ruling party in east India, go to demonstrate the intricate and visible linkage between parties/institutions and movements in contemporary India. And yet the prevalent tendency is to counterpose them as if they belong to different social species, which imparts a sense of estrangement between conceptualization and empirical reality.

V

The prevalent tendency to view movements and institutions as mutually antagonistic is essentially in line with the natural history or life-cycle approach to the analysis of social movements, by now conventional in social science. The argument runs roughly as follows: The development of an organization, however rudimentary, is inevitable for the realization of movement goals. But the emergence of such an organization inevitably sets in motion influences which defeat the very purpose which occasioned it. A paradoxical situation arises: that which is needed as an instrument—organization—for the translation of movement ideology into specific programmes often tends to become instrumental in frustrating the very purpose for which it emerged. Thus, the emergence of movement organizations lead to routinization of charisma (Oommen 1972a), development of bureaucratic structures (Lipset et al. 1956), persistence beyond the purpose for which it emerged (Sills 1957), all of which invariably lead to the institutionalization of social movements. In this strand of thinking, institutions are viewed as degenerate entities emerging out of movements. In contrast, it is necessary to define and perceive institutions as indicators of goal fulfilment of movements. As and when institutions become rigid and non-responsive to the purpose for which they emerged, it becomes imperative to challenge and de-legitimize them. That is, the relationship between movements and institutions is dialectical and multi-polar. Second, there is no inherent tendency towards institutionalization of a movement and even when it occurs, it does not necessarily stop or even decelerate the process of mobilization which is so fundamental and primary to the very survival of a movement. In fact, mobilization and institutionalization coexist and, furthermore, the process of institutionalization provides new possibilities for mobilization.

The institutionalization of a movement is believed to occur as the goals it pursued are achieved, or an elaborate machinery for the implementation of movement goals emerges, or associational proliferation takes place leading to the substitution of the movement by these associations. I have demonstrated elsewhere (Oommen 1985) that the empirical reality is at variance with this strand of thinking.

The basic thrust of my argument has been that the process of mobilization and institutionalization are to be viewed essentially as two different dimensions of a movement rather than mutually inimical processes. However, the emphasis on different movement aspects would vary at different phases of a given movement (see Table 4.1

Table 4.1

Characteristics of the Different Aspects of a Movement at Two Phases

Aspects of Movement	Mobilizational Phase	Institutionalization Phase
Ideology	Very important emphasis on mass appeal, centres on issues of deprivation, stress on collective participation	Not so significant, emphasis on translating movement ideology into specific programmes, stress on implementation
Organization	Embryonic and rudimentary, leader-follower relationship emphatic. Stress on functioning as a propaganda vehicle, emphasis on martyrdom	Crystallized and complex, leader-follower relationship replaced by 'professional-client' relations, operate as interest groups, stress on administration of justice
Strategy and tactics	Stress on collective actions, (agitations, strikes, *gheraos*, *satyagrahas*, demonstrations etc.); emphasis on propaganda and communication of ideology to sensitize participants of their rights	Interest articulation (bargaining, submission of memoranda, petition, lobbying for legislation) emphasize the 'here and now' goal, namely, welfare of participants.
Leadership	Professional revolutionary (typical roles: prophet, charismatic hero, demagogue)	Institutional entrepreneur (typical roles: manager, bureaucrat, bargainer, legalist)
Membership	Inclusive, expansive, undefined	Exclusive and defined, clearer boundary demarcation

As a movement moves from the mobilizational phase to the institutionalization phase, several aspects undergo changes. Yet, it seems safe to conclude that: (*a*) at the initial stages of institutionalization of a movement, mobilizational activities are likely to continue unabated. In fact, the process of institutionalization may provide new occasions for the continuance of mobilizaional activities, insofar as the lag between the induction of a set of norms and their actual acceptance by the critical collectivity is universal; (*b*) the pace of mobilization may continue and persist, if the degree of institutionalization is kept within certain limits, that is, if the mechanisms of institutionalization do not attempt to formalize social relations beyond a point. In the final analysis, mobilization is not displaced by institutionalization but *both go hand in hand* to a large extent and often the latter process may *accentuate* the former. Admittedly, movements and institutions are to be viewed as processually linked. Institutions often trigger off movements; movements encapsulate within them seeds of institutions. Therefore, to characterize them in mutually exclusive terms is to create a wedge between concept and reality.

MACRO PERSPECTIVES: THE VIEW FROM ABOVE

5
Social Movements and Nation-State in India: Towards Relegitimization of Cultural Nationalisms

Available articulations on social movements in independent India unfold two broad value perspectives. One postulates these movements as pathological and indicative of the crisis in the system, and the other views them as inevitable accompaniments of the on-going process of social transformation. Among those who consider these movements as pathological there are three analytically distinct but often empirically overlapping sets of collectivities.

The political mainstream constituted by the leading Congress Party considers any challenge to the state authority at the centre as an onslaught on the very existence of the nation-state. The party seems to consider that it is the only agency in India which can save the plural society, that is India, from external threats and protect it from internal sabotage. The cultural mainstream, composed of Hindi-speaking, twice-born Hindus, considers that any mobilization against what it defines as Hinduism and/or Hindi is a threat to the nation-state. The economic mainstream constituted by the all-India bourgeoisie wants to maintain and nurture as wide a domestic market as possible under the prevalent state-protected capitalism and hence any challenge to the nation-state goes against its interest too. As opposed to this, the political parties which represent cultural nationalisms, marginalized primordial collectivities and political parties which articulate left-oriented ideologies, consider social movements as creative confrontations with their primary enemies—an obstructive state authority at the centre, an omnipresent cultural mainstream and an oppressive all-India bourgeoisie.

The two apperceptions towards the on-going social movements in independent India are rooted in value orientations buttressed by the existential positioning of those who hold them. Notwithstanding this polarization in perspectives one can characterize these movements as constituting a *hierarchy of threat* to the nation-state, a point often missed in the virulent controversies. As a prelude to the analysis, we must spell out our working terms and frame of reference.

I

By social movements I mean those purposive collective mobilizations, informed of an ideology to promote change in any direction, using any means—violent or non-violent—and functioning within at least an elementary organizational framework (Wilkinson 1971: 27). Inevitably social movements imply a series of confrontations between two or more contending collectivities, to gain or to deny critical societal resources—wealth, power, privilege. Social transformation refers to the reallocation of one or more of these resources in favour of the deprived and the oppressed so as to bring about a new system of relationships, a new social order.

Threats to a nation-state emanate from endogenous or exogenous sources. Here, we are mainly concerned with the former. These threats obtain when the constituent units, whatever may be the bases of their formation, act in a manner which weakens the overall national solidarity and/or questions the primacy of the nation-state as a political unit. By *cultural nationalism* I refer to the articulation of popular aspirations by the people to preserve and nurture their 'natural bonds' rooted in religion, caste, tribe, language or region. This is distinguished from all-India *political nationalism* based on common citizenship in the nation-state.

It is necessary to advert to the nature of the three mainstreams, albeit briefly. Except for brief interludes, India is characterized by one-party dominance. Thus, in the 1980 general elections to the Lok Sabha the Congress(I) secured 352 out of the 527 Lok Sabha seats and secured 43 percent of the votes polled. No other party could secure even 20 per cent of the votes polled. In the 1984 general elections the party improved its performance by capturing 401 out of the 508 Lok Sabha seats polled and 49.17 per cent of the total votes polled. According to the 1981 Census of India, 83 per cent of India's population is categorized as Hindu and 38 per cent are listed as Hindi-speaking. The biggest religious minority in India, the Muslims, account for only 11 per cent and no other religious minority constitutes even 3 per cent of the total population. As for linguistic groups, none other than Hindi account for even 10 per cent.

An analysis in the late 1960s of the 'nationality' background of the Indian bourgeoisie shows that 33 per cent of the total assets of India's 75 top monopoly houses, listed by the Monopoly Inquiry Commission, was accounted for by the Hindustani houses and 37 per cent by the Gujarati houses, although Gujarati-speakers constituted only 5 per cent of India's total population (A. Roy 1967: 22). Socio-cultural collectivities such as the Parsis, the Sindhis and the Sikhs also own a disproportionately large share of assets as compared to their population sizes.

A multiplicity of groups coexist and simultaneously mobilize themselves into collective actions to pursue their interests in a nation-state like India. In this endeavour, it is not unlikely that some of these collectivities would perceive a conflict between their goals and the 'national' interests. A classification of social movements for the present purpose should take into account at least two factors: (*a*) the bases of group formation, that is, the type of collectivities, and (*b*) the nature of goals these movements pursue.

Group formations based on a variety of factors obtain in all societies. However, for the present purpose I propose to categorize them into biological collectivities (e.g., sex, race, age groups), civil collectivities (e.g., workers, peasants, students, professionals) and primordial collectivities[1] (e.g., regional, linguistic, religious, caste groups). The rationale of the three-fold categorization of collectivities—biological, primordial and civil—should be noted here; they can be placed on a fixity-flexibility continuum. While the attributes of the biological collectivities are largely given, although often buttressed by socio-cultural stereotypes, the attributes of civil collectivities are invariably acquired, a product almost entirely of the socialization/enculturation process. In the case of primordial collectivities it is partly given and partly acquired. Given the relative fixity or flexibility of attributes, the possibility of crystallization of a collective conscience also varies among these collectivities. In the case of biological collectivities, it is almost natural, and in the case of civil collectivities it is gradual and prolonged. The case of primordial collectivities comes in between.

[1] Shils (1957: 130–45) talks of primordial, personal, sacred and civil ties. While there is a similarity between his classification and mine, they do differ substantially.

The nature of goals that social movements pursue may be categorized into two: instrumental and symbolic. Instrumental goals are those oriented towards the reallocation of wealth and power, and symbolic goals are those that are geared towards the redefinition of status and privilege. Movements may pursue any one of these goals or they may combine both instrumental and symbolic goals.

Social mobilization of a collectivity implies its active involvement and conscious participation in terms of the goals pursued. In turn, crystallization of collective consciousness is not only a precondition for mobilization, but takes place as the very process of mobilization proceeds. The understanding of this dialectical intertwining between the nature of attributes of a collectivity, the prospects of its mobilization and the shaping of its consciousness is of utmost importance for an adequate analysis of social movements.

If we tabulate the two dimensions, collectivity types and nature of goals, the following typology emerges (Table 5.1). These nine types of movements are not mutually exclusive. For example, even if the movement by the youth to increase the age at marriage may not achieve its goal, it may result in greater pre-marital freedom for them. Caste mobility movements begin with symbolic goals but may later tend to pursue instrumental goals as well. Similarly, a civil collectivity (e.g., agricultural labour) may have a predominently primordial base (that is, of Scheduled Caste origin) and hence may combine both instrumental (increase in wages) and symbolic (eradication of untouchability) goals. The point I want to make is that not only are there overlaps between the movements of a given collectivity but the goals they pursue may also undergo transformation over time.

The types of social movements as identified in Table 5.1 vary in terms of their consequences for the system. For example, movements which pursue exclusively symbolic goals (cases 1, 4 and 7) rarely question the basic values and principles involved in the prevalent distribution of goods and services, they only strive towards a change in the system. Similarly, movements which pursue exclusively instrumental goals (cases 2, 5 and 8) are capable of bringing about change within the system alone. But some of these movements may cause structural transformation, that is, change of the system, through an accretive process. For example, lowering the age of franchise can bring about a substantial change in the distribution

Table 5.1

Types of Social Movements Based on the Nature of the Collectivity and Goals

Type of Collectivity	Nature of Goals	Typical Examples
1. Biological	Symbolic	Movement for increasing/decreasing the age at marriage; right of admission to public places by women/blacks
2. Biological	Instrumental	Movement by women for equal wages; youth movement for lowering the age of franchise
3. Biological	Both Symbolic and Instrumental	Movement of a racial category for establishing a new nation-state
4. Primordial	Symbolic	Caste mobility movements; conversion or reform movements of religious collectivities; linguistic collectivities fighting for cultural autonomy
5. Primordial	Instrumental	Movement of religious/linguistic/caste/ tribal groups for political representation, economic opportunities, etc.
6. Primordial	Symbolic and Instrumental	Secessionist movements by religious, linguistic or tribal collectivities
7. Civil	Symbolic	Worker's movement to get May Day declared as a holiday; students' mobilization to abolish the compulsory attendance system
8. Civil	Instrumental	Students' movement for participation in university decisional processes; farmers' mobilization for agricultural subsidies; workers' demand for sharing of profits with owners
9. Civil	Symbolic and Instrumental	Most movements combine both symbolic and instrumental goals, the latter usually providing the thrust

of political power in favour of the youth, if they constitute a substantial proportion of the population, and political consciousness based on age crystallizes. Similarly, workers' movements for sharing of profits if successful can gradually undermine capitalism as a system.

The case of movements which combine both symbolic and instrumental goals is quite different. As for civil collectivities, such movements exist in large numbers but are rarely a threat to the nation-state, although of course the governing elite may be replaced through such movements. In the case of biological collectivities only race provides a basis for the emergence of movements which pose a threat to the nation-state. The possibility of the emergence of movements threatening the nation-state is the greatest when the collective actors are constituted by primordial collectivities such as religious, linguistic or tribal groups. Insofar as these collectivities pursue both symbolic and instrumental goals simultaneously, secessionism is almost the inescapable demand. As our present concern is to view social movements in terms of their potentiality to pose a threat to the nation-state, it is necessary to elaborate this point further. The kernel of a nation-state is its territorial integrity and political sovereignty. Any attempt to question the political sovereignty of a nation-state by the constituent units or any tendency towards extra-territorial loyalty by any section of its population is a sure indicator of national crisis.

Among the biological collectivities neither gender nor age groups can fundamentally challenge the existence of a nation-state, as they cannot form an alternate nation-state. One cannot conceive of a nation-state composed exclusively of the male or the female, as the process of biological reproduction would come to a halt in such a society. This is in spite of the fact that homosexual or lesbian settlements may exist as 'social isolates' or a handful of test-tube babies could be produced. Similarly, a particular age group—old, adult, youth—cannot constitute a self-perpetuating society and hence a nation-state. Among the biological collectivities, only race provides an adequate basis for the formation of a nation-state, as noted earlier. But in order that this goal may be actualized, the race concerned should have a territorial anchorage. On the other hand, even when race and territoriality coexist, these may not automatically lend themselves to state formation as in the case of Africa, wherein tribe or lineage may be an important element of social organization.

The civil collectivities do not demand the formation of a separate nation-state through a process of disengagement or secession. Some of these collectivities (e.g., industrial proletariat, peasantry, university students) may assume a vanguard role in bringing about fundamental social transformation, either through revolution (forceful capturing of political authority) or through reform (a gradual displacement of old structures and values through a process of accretion of new structures and values). But these cannot be construed as threats to the nation-state; they are attempts to redefine the existing values or to refashion the prevalent structures in favour of one or another civil collectivity *within* the nation-state. This means that the real threat to the nation-state emanates from primordial collectivities. I propose to explore this area at some length with special reference to India.

II

The bases of primordial collectivisms are several in the Indian context, the more prominent ones being caste (*jati*), tribe, religion, language and region. We will presently examine which of these factors poses a threat to the existence of India as a nation-state.

In a hierarchically ordered and socially repressive society like India, social status and prestige are of vital concern to several primordial collectivities, particularly to the Scheduled Castes, Scheduled Tribes and Backward Classes, to invoke the current socio-legal terms in vogue to describe the groups with traditionally low ritual status. The appalling poverty and ever-widening economic disparity and the persistent concentration of power in a relatively few hands and structures at all levels—union, state and local—have been constricting and debilitating the social development of various primordial collectivities. Viewed against this background, the content of social transformation under Indian conditions should be considered in terms of *distributive balance* in status and prestige, power and privilege, and wealth and income. To achieve authentic social change, the underprivileged primordial collectivities are bound to initiate and involve themselves in collective mobilizations, to correct the prevalent distributive imbalances. in all the above sectors.

Generally speaking, primordial collectivities pursuing symbolic goals cannot be viewed as weakening the national social fabric. This is so for two reasons: first, they attempt only changes within the system, and second, they do not question the legitimacy of the nation-state as an entity. However, it is likely that the changes initiated by these mobilizations are capable of releasing waves of repercussions which may not be viewed as conducive to social health by all. For example, if a lower caste tries to move up in the ritual hierarchy by imitating the life-style of the upper castes, and if the latter ruthlessly suppresses such attempts, it is likely to result in a series of violent clashes between the traditional status-holders and the new status-seekers. The situation may assume greater complexity if the status-seekers are capable of taking a recalcitrant attitude and adopt the life-style of the upper castes in a spirit of protest (Lynch 1969). But the very capacity of the lower castes to protest should be taken as an indicator of their emancipation from the clutches of the traditional debilitating values and norms, and hence, a welcome change. On the contrary, the tendency of the upper castes to preserve and protect their distinctiveness and to claim superiority on that basis should be seen as incompatible with the values of a democratic society.

Similarly, if vigorous proselytization is pursued by any religious group on a mass scale, which is likely to bring about a change in the demographic distribution of religious communities, the possibility of violent confrontation between the losing group and the gaining group cannot be ruled out. In contemporary India there have been several instances of the dominant Hindu community intervening to stop conversion from Hinduism, or attempting to re-convert those who have been converted to religions reckoned to be non-Indian in their origin (Oommen 1983b: 92-133). It may be argued that adopting a new life-style or voluntarily embracing a new religious faith is a matter of individual and collective choice and in a democratic society one should not intervene in such social processes. Yet, not only the majority or the dominant community but even the state in India intervenes to stem the process of conversion.[2] To conclude then, primordial collectivities pursuing symbolic goals may weaken the national social texture although they may not challenge the political legitimacy of the nation-state.

Mobilizations by primordial collectivities, insofar as they pursue exclusively instrumental interests, cannot by definition pose a serious threat to a democratic state, as bargaining and pressure-group politics are legitimate processes in such a polity. The constituent elements would demand economic justice and political rights

[2] For evidence of intervention by the state and the dominant religious collectivity in the process of religious conversion, see George Mathew (1982: 1027-34).

irrespective of the bases of their formation. But instrumental demands by primordial collectivities do erode the secular ethos of the
society, and of the state as well if it responds to such demands. The
expression of instrumental collectivism by competing primordial
collectivities would also invariably lead to conflicts between them,
which may often be perceived and described as 'communal'. To be
sure, the compulsions of electoral politics prompt political parties
to utilize every opportunity to champion the cause of the 'deprived',
irrespective of their compositions. Even the state apparatus is
geared to be responsive to these demands, rationalizing it as an inevitable compulsion of a democratic polity. Thus, mobilizations by
religious, caste, tribal, linguistic and regional groups for representation in legislatures and public sector employment, for admission
to educational institutions, for distribution of land or loans, are invariably conceded if the concerned collectivity has the requisite
political clout, often ignoring the fact that such demand-making
and demand-conceding may carry with it the seeds of threat to the
nation-state.

This brings us to the instances of mobilizations by primordial
collectivities that attempt to pursue both instrumental and symbolic
goals simultaneously. These movements pose the greatest threat to
the nation-state. Given the fact that these movements pursue both
instrumental and symbolic goals *simultaneously*, their approach is
totalistic and their tone is one of disengagement from the 'mainstream'. In the final analysis, then, we get a variety of movements
piloted by primordial collectivities, all of which pose a threat,
albeit in varying degrees, to the nation-state. The threat emanates
from two sources: the nature of responses from the deprived, *and*
that of the dominant collectivity. On one end of the continuum is
the eagerness on the part of the dominant collectivity to absorb all
other collectivities into its fold, leading to the crystallization of
assimilationist movements. If secessionism cannot be supported
from the 'nationalist' viewpoint, assimilationism cannot be defended
from the humanist perspective. In between these polar opposites
one may identify separatist, insulationist and welfarist movements.

The bases of *secessionist* movements in independent India are
basically three: language (e.g., the Dravidian movement at the
initial stage); tribe (e.g., Naga National Movement, Mizo National
Front); and religion (e.g., the movement for Azad Kashmir, the
movement for a separate Sikh state, Khalistan).

Whatever may be the bases of group formation, to the extent that the tendency towards extra-territorial loyalty persists or the 'aspiration' for disengagement from the nation-state continues, it is an indicator of inadequate welding of the constituents into the nation-state. While it is necessary to empathize with the aspirations of the people concerned and initiate steps to evolve satisfactory solutions to their problems, no nation-state can afford to ignore or tolerate movements of this kind. Social transformation in, or development of a constituent unit or units, cannot be achieved by endangering the very existence of the whole.

A few general points about the secessionist movements of Independent India may be noted here. First, the epicentres of these movements are regions situated on the international borders, or with natural boundaries. This provides these regions and the movements that originate in them with certain geo-political importance. Therefore, the state authority at the centre of the nation-state is often constrained to concede some of the demands of these movements, which it would not have ordinarily acceded to if put forward by units without this geo-political bargaining power. This invests the border regions with an undue sense of political importance and imparts a feeling of political insignificance to the encysted regions.

Second, the percentage of population involved in secessionist movements has been fairly small. The Tamils constitute about 8 per cent of India's population and only a negligible minority among them actively supported the formation of a separate Tamil nation-state even at the peak of Dravidian secessionism. As for the four frontier states of north-east India inhabited by tribes, they constitute less that 0.5 per cent of the total population of India. The population of Sikhs in India is less than 2 per cent and only a small proportion of them actively and consciously extend their support for Khalistan, a separate Sikh nation-state. The total population of Jammu and Kashmir is less than 1 per cent of India's population and secessionism is evident only among a small minority of Muslims inhabiting the Kashmir valley, one of the three distinct units which constitute the state, the other two being Ladakh inhabited predominantly by Buddhists and Jammu populated mainly by Hindus.

Third, of the three bases of secessionism—language, religion and tribe—in independent India language has come to be accepted as a legitimate basis of state formation within the framework of the nation-state[3]. Understandably, in independent India we do not have any more secessionist movements based exclusively on language. In the case of tribes, only among a section of the Nagas and Mizos of the north-east does the tendency towards secessionism persists. But these movements are also irredentist in that these tribes are distributed across other nation-states and into more than one state within India. The tribes of the north-east were late entrants into the British colonial system and were also insulated from the anticolonial struggle. Moreover, the inadequate development of transport and communication between this region and the rest of India also contributed to the relative isolation—physical and psychological—of these tribes (Guha 1982: PE 2-12).

Religion provides the most salient basis of secessionism in India. To begin with, it may be noted that all secessionist movements in independent India have had a religious content. Dravidian Tamil nationalism was not only against Hindi but also against Aryan Hinduism. The majority of Mizos and Nagas look upon themselves not only as tribes but also as Christians. But the two persistent secessionist movements—for Azad Kashmir (which is also irredentist) and Khalistan—are clearly based on religious ideologies, those of Islam and Sikhism. The epicentre of the first is the Muslim-dominated Kashmir valley and that of the second is the Sikh-dominated Punjabi Suba. In contrast to the isolated Christian tribes of the north-east (and even compared to the Tamils of the 'distant south'), both Muslims of Kashmir and Sikhs of Punjab were frontally involved in the anti-colonial struggle and constitute a part of 'Indian' tradition and heritage.

The secessionist movements of Kashmir and Punjab have their origin in the nationalist movement and the partition of colonial India based on religion. The Kashmiri Muslim leadership opted to stay with India, although they insisted on a special autonomous status, which was conceded vide Article 370 of the Indian Constitution. As for the Sikhs, although a minority wanted a separate status for Khalistan within Pakistan, the majority of Sikhs preferred to stay with India (Nayyar 1966). Efforts were made to solve the problem by conceding the Punjabi Suba in 1966, a state composed of 53 per cent Sikhs and dominated by them, although the ostensible

---

[3] However, the manner in which language is defined and is distinguished from dialect is problematic. For details, see Khubchandani (1983).

basis of conceding the Sikh demand was language, that is, Punjabi.
Both in the Kashmir valley and in Punjab, a minority deeply wedded
to their religious faiths—Islam and Sikhism—do seem to think
that their ultimate and full 'national' expression would be possible
only in nation-states founded on the principles laid down in their
respective religious scriptures. This 'aspiration' is ill at ease with
the basic spirit of the Indian Constitution which purports to separate
religion from politics and from the purview of the state.

The tendency towards proliferation of states within the nation-
state is a manifestation of *separatist* movements. Once language
has been accepted as the basis of state formation it is inevitable
that endemic demands for separate states based on language should
crystallize in a country like India with a multiplicity of languages.
Accepting language as the sole or even the dominant criterion of
state formation foments recurrent demands. Further, once language
is accepted as the basis of state formation, those cases where language and other factors coexist pose severe problems. The identification, although perhaps wrongly, of the Punjabi language with
Sikhism and Urdu with Islam are cases in point. The division of the
Punjab into two states, Punjab and Haryana, although said to be
based on language, came about as a response to Akali mobilization. Similarly, the wedge between Jammu and Kashmir runs
simultaneously on two lines—language and religion. The reverse
of this is equally significant. If the people speaking a language are
not concentrated in a definite territory, in all probability the development of their language and culture, for want of political patronage
and administrative nurture, would be adversely affected. The case
of Sindhi and to a certain extent that of Urdu are examples. This
would provide grounds for the emergence of separatist movements.

Once language is accepted as the dominant basis of state formation, other primordial bases would be used for mobilization:
region, dialect and tribe. The persisting demand for a separate
Jharkhand state bringing together the tribal groups belonging to the
border districts of Bihar, Orissa and West Bengal is simultaneously
a demand to recognize Jharkhand as a specific cultural region and
for tribal autonomy. The tendency in such contexts would often be
to rediscover traditional identities which lie frozen or even to
invent new myths of identity. Finally, the total neglect of administrative viability, ecological variations and developmental imbalances
and the sole reliance on language for state reorganization gave

birth to a series of regional movements such as the Telengana separatist movement between 1969-1971, and the resurrection of the erstwhile Vidharbha movement. The potentiality of such movements being triggered off is substantial, given the present disparity between the different regions which constitute a state. Consider the tension between the hill, eastern and western districts of Uttar Pradesh and the incipient mobilization for a separate state of Chattisgarh in Madhya Pradesh. The point I want to affirm is that in the absence of any set of rational criteria for the formation of political-administrative units the demand for further divisions can be endemic.

The logical extension of establishing states based on language is the emergence of animosity towards 'outsiders', that is, towards those linguistic groups outside the region, giving birth to *insulationist* movements. The widespread tendency to emphasize the rights of sons of the soil and the proliferation of *senas* are too well known. This type of movement usually emerges either in advanced urban-industrial towns or in backward rural belts. While the archetype of this variety of movement is the Shiv Sena of Bombay, the emergence of Bangla Sena, Lachit Sena, Kannada Chaluvaligars, etc., only indicate the widespread tendency in this direction. An extension of this tendency may also be discerned in the emergence of regional political parties such as the Bangla Congress, Kerala Congress and Dravidian parties. Similarly, the proverbial hatred and suspicion that the tribals have towards the outsiders or *dikus* is well known. Generally speaking, the contentions in this context anchor around employment, admission to educational institutions, licences for new economic ventures, etc. The mobilizations in Assam against Bengali Muslims, although originally from Pakistan or Bangladesh but long settled in the state, labelling them as 'foreigners', adds a new dimension to the already vexing problem (Oommen 1982: 41-64).

Two implications of this tendency should be listed here. First, in a country like India with single citizenship, the notion of state-based domiciliary prescription goes contrary to the national ethos. Second, the discriminatory treatment meted out to migrants will not only adversely affect the already low percentage of internal migration in the country (which is a prerequisite for economic development) but also accentuate the psychological deprivation and insecurity of mobile and enterprising groups who provide critical leadership at the initial stages of economic development. This is, however, not to ignore the domineering and exploitative tendencies of the outsiders and the inevitable resentment towards such tendencies by the local population. What needs to be emphasized here is that both blocking the aspirations of the local people and suppressing the initiative and drive of mobile groups are equally capable of weakening the process of social transformation.

The problems concerning the religious minorities of India are very complex, largely due to their long history and size in absolute terms. While Buddhism and Jainism took shape about 2,500 years ago within the country, Christianity came to India in the first century AD and Islam around 622 AD. Even Sikhism, one of the younger religions, is more than 400 years old. Further, although there are three dozen Muslim majority countries in the world, India has the second largest Muslim population in the world. Christians accounted for 16 million (or 2.4 per cent) and Sikhs 13 million (or 1.9 per cent) in 1981, bigger than the total population of several nation-states. Viewed against this background, to treat any of these religious groups as 'minorities' or 'outsiders' is extremely hazardous, yet this is what frequently happens in India (Oommen 1986: 53-74). This provides several occasions for mobilization of these primordial collectivities, be it for retaining or extending their rights and influences in the fields of education, politics or economy. The manipulation of religious collectivities in the context of electoral politics seems to be reinforcing communalism, although the exercise is presumably done in the name of secularism. Furthermore, this often prompts a communal response from the majority community. This kind of situation keeps alive communal forces and mobilizations of all varieties. Witness for example the recurring communal riots, particularly in north Indian Towns! The mobilization of Hindus through the Rashtriya Swayam Sewak Sangh or the Vishwa Hindu Parishad, of Muslims through the Muslim Majlis, of Sikhs through the Akali Dal, to meet communal ends does not serve the cause of strengthening the Indian nation-state.

While a culturally plural situation gives birth to the crystallization of identities and movements based on language, region and religion, a socially plural situation is likely to facilitate the emergence of identities based on social rank and prestige, giving birth to *welfarist* movements. These movements are geared to the welfare of their clientele in the broadest sense of the term. Given the fact that inequality was institutionalized in traditional Indian society through the caste system and the values and norms that were associated with it, it is not surprising that a large number of movements led by those who experienced deprivation under the rigidity of the caste system rebelled, particularly when the new democratic framework assured them equality, fraternity and freedom. The virulent anti-Brahmin movement in Tamil Nadu (Hardgrave 1965), the Mahar and Mali movements in Maharashtra (Omvedt 1976), the Ezhava movement in Kerala (Rao 1978), the Chamar movement in parts of Uttar Pradesh (Lynch 1969), are only some of the well-documented and more well-known movements of this variety. The mobilizations by religious groups (e.g., Muslims) or linguistic groups (e.g., Sindhis) without a territorial base also fall into this category of movements.

The caste groups which participate in welfarist movements belong to two categories: those who are above the pollution line, referred to as Backward Classes, and those below the pollution line, the Scheduled Castes. In the case of Scheduled Castes, the movements were invariably oriented towards status mobility at the initial stages. Thanks to their partial emancipation from the clutches of traditional ritual degradation due to social reforms and social legislations and the state patronage extended to them through the policy of protective discrimination, the Scheduled Castes have become increasingly aware of the need to continuously fight for their economic and political benefits, which triggers off several movements among them. However, the active groups in this context are only a few, such as the Mahars of Maharashtra, the Chamars of Uttar Pradesh and the Pulayas of Kerala. The emergence of an elite is in evidence among these groups and social tensions between the beneficiaries of the changes and those who are denied the fruits of development have already crystallized. Additionally, the dominant groups among Scheduled Castes practically monopolize the benefits of state patronage and this in turn creates discontent among those who are relegated to the background in the context of development.

In the case of Backward Classes, their position in the ritual and economic hierarchy was not very low. Yet, they too concentrated on status mobility in the beginning so as to obtain a firm position above the pollution line. Most of the castes included in this category are drawn from peasant or agricultural castes, constituted mainly by sharecroppers, marginal cultivators and small peasants. Typical examples of castes belonging to this category are the Ezhavas of Kerala, Nadars of Tamil Nadu, Ahirs and Kurmis of Uttar Pradesh and Bihar. Consequent to land reforms, many of these caste groups had become the owners of the land they tilled but did not earlier own. The gain in economic status coupled with their numerical superiority often facilitated their political ascendency. However, the near monopoly of the castes drawn from the twice-born varna categories (Brahmin, Kshatriya and Vaishya) in higher education, professions, top administrative and judicial services still continued. This status incongruity is frustrating to the Backward Classes and it is understandable that much of the mobilization among them is geared to a larger share in employment, seats in educational institutions and similar issues. Since the youth belonging to these castes are immediately affected by these deprivations their active involvement for mobilization in this context appears to be a natural response.

The status incongruence that I have referred to above seems to be applicable to several of the traditional land-owning castes, such as the Nairs of Kerala, Reddis of Andhra and Jats of north India, as well. Although economically well-off by local standards and politically often powerful, their position did not compare favourably with the twice-born groups in higher administration and professions. Therefore, these caste groups too demand a fairer representation in those sectors in which they are under-represented. Finally, we also notice a feeling of discrimination in the reverse on the part of twice-born groups, particularly the Brahmins, thanks to the special protection extended to Scheduled Castes, Scheduled Tribes and Backward Classes. The upper caste youth increasingly begin to feel that they are denied their rightful place in several secular contexts in society, precisely because of their superior ritual status. All these situations have enormous potential for instigating caste mobilizations pursuing instrumental goals.

Those who experience downward mobility in the secular context (e.g., twice-born caste Hindus) precisely because of their high ritual status, tend to share a pessimistic view of their life chances. They lose their confidence in social institutions—universities, the civic bodies, the bureaucracy, the courts—and values of equality and justice, and indeed it is difficult for them to fraternalize those whom they think are usurping their rightful place in society. That is, if aspiration levels remain high and expectation levels drop, widespread alienation from the system is sure to occur. On the other hand, those who experience upward mobility in secular contexts, simply because they have had a low ritual status, would come to look upon low ritual status as an asset. And yet, they are likely to experience a psychological degeneration because they occupy positions in a secular context, not because they are capable or have merit. This is psychologically debilitating and socially alienating. Indeed, the dilemmas India faces in its endeavour to build a nation-state which can provide an authentic sense of belonging are indeed vexing.

The *assimilationist* movement has been a part of the Indian ethos for centuries. Thus, through what N.K. Bose (1967) designated as the 'Hindu mode of absorption', the tribal people, particularly in south-central India, had been gradually assimilated into the Hindu fold. Similarly, through the process of Sanskritization (Srinivas 1962), the lower castes have been attempting to move up in the caste hierarchy. Among the religions of Indian origin, the Jains follow, by and large, a policy of socio-cultural assimilation with the dominant religious collectivity, the Hindus. As for the neo-Buddhists, the recent converts from Dalits, who constitute the bulk of Indian Buddhists today, the tendency is to assert their status in caste rather than in religious terms. Only the Sikhs aggressively assert their distinct socio-cultural and even political identity. Among the religions of alien origin the tendency to undergo a process of enculturation or Indianization of their life-style is clearly discernible.[4]

In the context of language too, the twin processes of assertion and assimilation are at work (Khubchandani 1983). The distinctiveness of most of the developed and major Indian languages is established and accepted. But in some cases, due to a variety of historical, cultural and political factors, one comes across a simultaneous tendency to assert distinctiveness and to pursue assimilation. Thus, the tendency among a section of Muslims is to assert the distinctiveness of Urdu but most Hindus and some Muslims prefer the amalgamation of Hindi and Urdu and the resultant Hindustani.

[4] For evidence with regard to Muslims, see Imtiaz Ahmad, (1981). The Christians have been consciously adopting a process of Indianization even in the context of rituals.

The situation with regard to Punjabi is different; the Sikhs highlight the distinctiveness of Punjabi written in Gurumukhi while the Hindus tend to prefer Punjabi written in Devnagri, thereby minimizing the distinction between Hindi and Punjabi and preferring an assimilative thrust.

The assertive and assimilative trends are persistent in the context of language-dialect relationship and these tendencies also change over time. For example, the percentage variation between 1951-61 for Bhojpuri and Magadhi in Bihar was +412,674 and +76,076, respectively. It is important to recall here that this assertive trend crystallized in the wake of the State Reorganization Commission in the mid-1950s. Each linguistic collectivity wanted to assert its specific identity so as to make a claim for a separate state, as language became the basis for state formation. But once it was known that these claims were not likely to be accepted, there was a decline in this assertive tendency. Thus, the percentage variation between 1961-71 for Bhojpuri (all-India) declined to +80 and for Magadhi to +135. As against this, an assimilative trend is exemplified by the decline in percentage variation in census claims by linguistic groups. For example, the decline between 1961-71 in the case of Maria Gondi in Madhya Pradesh was −104 per cent, Lamani in Maharashtra was −72.5 per cent and Parji in Orissa was −62.7 percent. It may be noted that all these are tribal dialects and the assimilative thrust is clearly discernible.

III

We began the present analysis by suggesting that the wide variety of social movements in independent India, if viewed as posing a threat to the nation-state, could be placed vertically. In the course of our analysis, five distinct types of movements have been identified. These movements have different consequences to the whole—the nation-state—and the parts—the constituent units within it, the micro structures.

It is clear from Table 5.2 that one cannot speak of consequences in neutral terms; these movements have negative or positive consequences depending on the perspective from which one looks at them. However, the prevalent tendency is to consider the boundaries and parameters of the nation-state as given, and view the mobilizations for identity and autonomy by local collectivities

Table 5.2

Types of Social Movements and their Consequences

Type of Movements	Consequences for Nation-State	Consequences for Micro Structures
1. Secessionist	Possible disintegration and re-drawing of boundaries	Independence, autonomy
2. Separatist	Erosion of state authority at the centre; emergence of a federal polity	Limited autonomy within the framework of nation-state
3. Insulationist	Weakening of the concept of unitary citizenship and hence of the overarching nature of nation-state	Confrontations between two or more local structures and hence hostility among constituent units within the nation-state
4. Welfarist	Possibility of traditional vested interests getting disenchanted and hence fomenting unrest	Social development of the traditionally under-privileged primordial collectivities and hence likely animosity from entrenched collectivities
5. Assimilationist	Consolidation of nation-state, but at very high social cost	Eclipse of local identities and culturocide.[5]

within it as illegitimate. I suggest that this strand of thought is unrealistic, particularly in the case of 'new nations', wherein the nation-states are characterized by loose textures and frayed edges. In less than 30 years erstwhile colonial India has been divided twice, leading to the formation of three nation-states. One may think of both fusion between and fission within the nation-states in such unsettled situations.

It is important to recall here that by the early 20th century we have *de-legitimized* not only colonial political dominance but also the institutions and values of the domestic society of the colonizer. An indictment of Western civilization (Gandhi 1938) served us well in mobilizing the Indian people against imperialism. But towards the close of the anti-imperialist struggle, the neat dichotomy between

[5] I use the term *culturocide* to mean a systematic annihilation of cultures, in preference to the terms cultural genocide or ethnocide (Oommen 1986: 53-74).

colonialism and nationalism became complicated with the entry of 'communalism' as an ideology into the Indian consciousness. Indeed, nationalism became the legitimate and communalism the illegitimate ideology; but this labelling unfolded not only the content but the social background of the collectivity using these labels as well. Thus, what the Hindus described as Muslim communalism was perceived as nationalism by the Muslims and vice versa. And this perception continued even after independence.

In independent India 'secularism' came to be juxtaposed with localism. While secularism and nationalism are defined as legitimate by the state and the dominant collectivities, all varieties of mobilizations which articulated the aspirations of the people at the micro/local levels, are invariably perceived as illegitimate. This does not augur well for authentic nation-building, because what is often labelled and dismissed as parochial, regional, sub-national, anti-national and secessionist in India, is invariably an expression of nationalist aspirations, in so far as nationalism is understood and defined in the European sense. Therefore, it is necessary to recognize the specificity of the Indian situation and accept *cultural nationalisms* as important ingredients of political nationalism. What we need is a *re-legitimization* of localism and decentralization, both of which are prerequisites to govern a nation-state of India's size and diversity.

6

Social Movements and State Response: The Indian Situation

I

Typically, social movement analyses concentrate either on the structural components of movements—ideology, organization, leadership, participants—or on their processual dimensions—strategy, tactics, mobilization, event-structure. Without minimizing the significance of such studies, I would like to suggest that unless we situate the movements in their environmental milieu, much of these analyses are unlikely to be sufficiently illuminating. The environmental milieu has two major dimensions: first, the state ideology and the means defined by it as legitimate, and second, the values of the society in which movements originate and operate. An assumption underlying this contention is that a movement essentially challenges and protests against the dominant authority structure and/or value system in a society. This in turn means that the nature of a movement is substantially conditioned by the character of the forces it challenges. Alternatively, the response to a movement is moulded by the type of authority structure and/or value system it confronts. Since our present preoccupation is with the state response to social movements, we will confine the discussion mainly to those movements which challenge the authority structure, that is, those which are predominantly political in orientation.

Viewed in a broad historical perspective, we may identify four major phases in the transformation of political authority structures and the concomitant variations in the nature of social movements. The first is the 'pre-political' or 'stateless' phase during which movements of the type we are familiar with since the 16th century did not exist. Most movements of this phase were akin to elementary collective behaviour or, if one prefers, spontaneous mobilizations. That is why the description of the activities of movements during this phase is often invoked through notions such as primitive rebellions, tribal outbreaks, slave riots, etc. The principal contenders of power in these contexts were primordial collectivities such as clans and tribes, often led by their hereditary chieftains operating in limited geographical locales.

As the scale of human communities increased, large aggregations and collectivities came to be organized under a limited number of central authority systems—the era of empires, nation-states, and colonies. Gradually, the notion of nation-state assumed wide currency and an increasing number of territorially bounded primordial collectivities—religious, linguistic, regional groups—came to claim the status of nation-states. The typical movements of this, that is the second, phase were anti-imperialist and anti-colonial mobilizations.

During the third phase, with the spread of science and technology following the industrial revolution and development of modern capitalism, the antagonism between classes grew and movements of particular class or occupational categories came into vogue—the working class movements and peasant revolutions. They either led to structural change, i.e., changed drastically the class character (not class composition) of those who wielded authority, or they facilitated the emergence of new wielders of authority who at least by definition identified themselves with the poor, the disadvantaged and the oppressed, exemplified by the political power holders of the socialist and the welfare states, respectively.

The final phase is marked by the consolidation of capitalism and socialism on the one hand, and the emergence of a limited number of 'post-industrial' societies on the other. They gave birth to the notion of a global division of nation-states based on the type of economy and the level of economic development—First, Second, Third, and now even Fourth, World. Concomitant with the emergence of superpowers, this phase has also witnessed a proliferation of international movements for human rights, dignity of women, disarmament, environmental protection, ecological balance, etc.

Admittedly, the above characterization of changes in authority structures and movements cannot be viewed as a sequence for the entire world, given the differing levels of development obtaining in different parts of the world and sometimes within the same nation-state. However, if our characterization is broadly correct, it may safely be asserted that the changing features of the authority structures alter substantially the nature of social movements.

Notwithstanding the fact that a segment of the human population still continues to be pre-political in terms of consciousness and that a minority of humanity has entered the post-industrial phase, almost the entire humanity is today organized into nation-states. In spite of the existence and proliferation of a large number of global organizations and movements and the increasing visibility of international public opinion, the effective authority structures exist only at the level of nation-states. Therefore, an examination of state response to social movement is crucial to an understanding of the environmental milieu in which they emerge and function.

A logical corollory of our position is that the nature of the state moulds the possibility or otherwise of the emergence of social movements, and this in turn influences its nature. Therefore, I find it difficult to accept the conventional wisdom in social sciences that all social movements are necessarily mobilizations *against* the state. Such a misunderstanding, I submit, emanates from two sources. First, it is an offspring of the limited empirical base—capitalist democracies of Western Europe and North America—in which the current theorization in this context is largely anchored. Second, the traditional view that the state is opposed to all social movements is based on an obsolete conceptualization of the state itself: that the state functions merely as a police state to protect the citizen from external aggression and to maintain internal peace through its national defence and law and order agencies as already noted in chapter 1.

In terms of the world situation today, we can visualize at least three possibilities of relationship between the state and social movements. First, the authoritarian states run by military juntas, religious fundamentalists, and racist groups invariably oppress, or attempt to oppress, all social movements which challenge state authority. Second, one-party systems oppress effective challengers of state authority but sponsor movements to their advantage so as to sustain and nourish state power. Third, a large number of social movements originate and proliferate in the multi-party systems but repression is resorted to against those movements which are explicit threats to the very existence of the state. That is, no state by its very nature permits the operation of movements which undermine its authority, notwithstanding the fact that the elasticity of permissiveness and the limit of tolerance admittedly vary according to the source of its authority. However, it should be recognized that a multi-party democracy provides the most fruitful empirical setting to understand the state response to movements, as it permits a variety of social movements to emerge and function.

An increasing number of states in the world today are accepting the welfarist ideology, inspiring and institutionalizing changes in a direction demanded by citizens. The ideology and the mode of functioning of states have undergone a sea change, which cannot be ignored when an effort at empirically rooted theory-building is attempted. Thus the most fertile empirical setting for understanding the state response to social movements is provided by a state which *combines* a socialist or welfarist ideology with a multi-party system. Such a setting exists in India and this is the justification for our pursuing the present analysis with special reference to India.

The following types of social movements may emerge in the kind of empirical setting referred to above: (*a*) social movements sponsored or supported by the government if a section of the 'national' population is perceived as a stumbling block in institutionalizing change in terms of state ideology; (*b*) social movements against the government by an overwhelming majority of the population either because it deviates from the professed state ideology or because the government perpetuates itself in power through state violence; (*c*) social movements against the government as well as against a section of the collectivity which supports it, to stem the aberrant tendencies which crept into the mode of functioning of the state. These possibilities obtain because the government in a multi-party system is supported by one of more specific political parties or organizations and the opposition parties and movements are permitted to exist and function.

It should be clear from our analysis so far that the state response to social movements does not fall into a unilinear pattern; it is dictated by the nature of mobilization attempted by a movement. Conversely, the character of the party in power is a critical variable in determining state response. Armed with this understanding, let us look at plausible patterns of state reponse. We can discern at least four empirical possibilities:

1. The ideology and the means of a movement correspond to those of the state. That is, both the state and the movement pursue the same goals, and the means employed by the movement are defined as legitimate by the state. In such a situation, state-sponsored

movements come to stay, and in all probability the state response is one of *facilitation*.

2. The ideology of a movement differs from that of the state but its means correspond to those perceived as legitimate by the state. The typical state response is that of *toleration*.

3. The ideology of a movement corresponds to that of the state but the means differs. That is, the movement and the state compete to attain the same goal but through different routes. The state attempts at *discreditation* of the movement.

4. Both the ideology and the means of a movement differ from those of the state. The state would spare no effort at *repression* of such movements. We present the differing state responses to the four types of empirical situations in Table 6.1.

Table 6.1
State Response to Social Movements

Type of Empirical Situation	Dimensions of Movements		State Response	Possible Outcome
	Ideology	Means		
I	Same as that of the state	Defined as legitimate by the state	Facilitation	State/movement distinction irrelevant; movement operates as an extension of state, reinforcing system stability.
II	Different from that of the state	Same as above	Toleration	Movement functions as an instrument exerting pressure to redefine state ideology; eventual reconciliation/ parting of ways.
III	Same as that of the state	Defined as non-legitimate by the state	Discreditation	Co-option of leadership, neutralization of movement through state welfare measures; eventual fading away of the movement.
IV	Different from that of the state	Same as above	Repression	Liquidation of the movement and its leadership; eventual termination of the movement. Alternatively, a new system may emerge: Revolution.

It is clear from Table 6.1 that the possible outcomes of state response to the different types of movements vary. But it is also significant that the mechanisms used by the state to cope with the challengers also vary. As I have indicated earlier, Situation 1 usually obtains in nation-states where one-party rule exists. But, as I will endeavour to show, in countries like India where different political parties come to occupy positions of authority at the centre (union) and the state levels, the state response to movements also consequently varies. The movements in such a situation are typically mobilizations undertaken by political parties in power through their respective front-organizations.

I would like to add one more caveat before we begin our analysis of the Indian situation. It should be recognized that the ideology and means of either the state or the movement are not constant. In a democratic polity the state is under constant pressure from the populace to respond to their needs and aspirations, and this may often call for reformulation of state ideology or change of its mode of functioning, that is, of the means. Similarly, the movements may have to redefine their ideology and means depending upon the state response, or, in response to the aspirations and demands of their clients.

II

As I have noted at the outset, traditional values and state ideology are the two components of the environmental milieu in which social movements originate and function. We shall deal with them briefly here.

The cardinal values of traditional Indian society were hierachy, pluralism and holism [1] (See Y. Singh 1973). Hierarchy implies the ordering of the constituent units of a system in relation to the whole in a superior-inferior gradation. While the ideology of hierarchy institutionalized inequality in every conceivable aspect of human life, it allocated a secure and definite place to each individual and caste. The valuation of the individual and groups and the distribution of social resources were based on status. Status was ascriptive, even though birth into a group was believed to be

[1] This section is an abbreviated version of an earlier paper (see Oommen 1983a: 253-63).

based on moral merit gathered during the previous birth, according to the theory of *karma* and reincarnation.

Pluralism implied tolerance of other styles of life while preserving one's own. Hinduism, the dominant religion of India, was largely tolerant. The faiths of Muslim conquerors, Christian colonial rulers, and Parsi merchants and traders not only survived but prospered and coexisted with relative harmony for centuries in India. The caste system provided an institutional basis for reinforcing the pluralistic tradition of Hinduism. Apart from this, given the linguistic diversities and cultural differences, castes operated mainly as regional entities. This resulted in a localistic orientation of castes which facilitated the coexistence of socially diverse groups.

Holism assumed a relationship between individual and group with the latter having primacy over the former. The individual was expected to perform his duties and claim his rights, always keeping in mind the wider interests of the community. The individual subservience to collectivity manifested in a multiplicity of contexts, be it familial communism, village democracy, or caste council meetings.

Notwithstanding the ideological prescriptions, practical aberrations were not uncommon. Thus, the hierarchy was sharp and clear only at the polar points of the caste system, the disputes over caste rank being almost endemic in the middle region, often facilitating mobility in spite of the rigid institutional framework. The indeterminancy over rank arose contextually, the king assuming superiority over the priest in secular matters and the priest claiming overarching importance of the sacred over the secular, thereby affirming his overall superior status. The problem of allocating status to certain groups either assimilated into the Hindu fold or obtaining outside of it—such as tribals, Muslims, and Christians—was also problematic as each person or group had to be placed in relation to others in the caste society. Similarly, while pluralism implied tolerance, it had frequently led to bigotry and domination, creating hostility between groups. And, while holism implied collectivistic orientation, it did not always impart the requisite altruism to sustain it. Individuals often felt the weight of the heavy yoke to which they were tied by group control, inhibiting their initiative, often leading to considerable tension in interpersonal and individual-group relations. All this is indicative of the dissensus between theory and practice, prescription and performance in traditional India.

The ideology pursued by the Indian state today is embodied in the Constitution. The ideological tenets are socialism, secularism and democracy. It is wrong to assume that everybody holds all aspects of this ideological package equally dear. Some think that socialism should be the most important goal to be pursued with immediacy, because the realization of other goals is contingent upon the establishment of socialism. Others bestow primacy on democracy and argue that the pursuit of other goals in a manner endangering democracy is worthless. That is, notwithstanding the overall consensus on the basic values, disagreements exist over their relative importance or over the mode and sequence of their realization. We ignore this dissensus while pursuing the present analysis.

The Indian Constitution envisions that 'the ownership and control of the material resources of the community are so distributed as best to subserve the common good'. Further, the Constitution requires that the 'operation of the economic system does not result in the concentration of wealth and means of production to the common detriment'. However, the word socialism found its entry into the Constitution only in 1976, quarter of a century after India became a republic.

Admittedly, Indian socialism is different in theory and practice as compared with socialism elsewhere. While recognizing the 'evils' of the concentration of economic resources, Indian socialism does not attempt collectivization of private property but only seeks to limit it. The legitimacy of private property as an institution is not yet fundamentally questioned; only its cautious restriction is aimed at.

Secularism in the Indian context meant, in practise, tolerance of other communities, particularly religious communities. Moreover, it meant not only non-interference in the affairs of other communities but also developing a positive appreciation of their distinct styles of life. The timidity in evolving a Uniform Civil Code for the different religious communities points to this feature of secularism. After independence, the need to recognize cultural autonomy in the regional-linguistic context became compelling. The official recognition of the cultural autonomy of regional-linguistic entities became explicit in the late 1950s when the Indian states were reorganized on the basis of language (which subsumed culture). This may be viewed as another aspect of Indian secularism, if tolerance of diversity is considered to be the basic thrust of the ideology of secularism. Notwithstanding the fact that secularism is fundamental to independent India, its institutionalization is far from being achieved; communal, linguistic and caste mobilizations are not infrequent.

While Indian democracy shares its form with other democratic societies and emphasizes equality of opportunity, its substance is different. Democracy assumes the existence of autonomous and independent individuals capable of participating in the decision-making process. In traditional India the individual as an autonomous entity making decisions for himself or herself was nonexistent. Consequently, the functioning of Indian democracy is substantially influenced by primordial collectivities such as religion, caste, and linguistic groups, and frequently mediated by traditional values and rigid institutional structures. Understandably, ideological polarization is often incomplete if not altogether absent in Indian politics.

Having discussed the fundamental ideological elements of traditional society as well as of the modern state in India, we now examine the possibilities of these being synthesized. For brevity and clarity the three fundamental value pairs are tabulated in Table 6.2. We examine only two aspects of the problem presently; first, the possibility of reconciling these value pairs and, second, unfolding their internal consistency or contradiction.

Table 6.2
Societal Values and State Ideology: Congruence and Conflict

Traditional Values	State Ideology	Prerequisites for Realization
I (a) Pluralism	I (b) Secularism	Tolerance and respect for others' style of life.
II (a) Hierarchy	II (b) Socialism	Status-based allocation of roles and resources for II (a) and need-based allocation for II (b)
III (a) Holism	III (b) Individualism	Renunciation of self-interest for III (a) and assertion of self-interest for III (b).

It should be clear from Table 6.2 that there is no basic contradiction between the traditional value of pluralism and the modern value of secularism since tolerance of others' style of life is basic to both. However, pluralism of the past was associated with distinct and deep traditions for each of the groups, which often provided legitimacy for special privileges and prerogatives. This in turn made those with a disproportionate share of privileges a dominating elite. But secularism as it is understood in India today calls upon the advantaged groups to orientate their behaviour consciously in such a way as to understand and appreciate the norms and values of the less privileged groups, the 'minorities.'

As pointed out earlier, hierarchy implied the principle of allocation of resources and distribution of rewards on the basis of birth. This is in direct contravention of the principle of need-based distribution implied in socialism pursued by the state. Perhaps one can try and seek a linkage here: in the traditional system status defined the need, and in modern times status is sought to be defined by the state on the basis of contributions made by individuals and groups for maintaining the system and for changing it in a direction defined by it. If those who occupied a higher status are also taken to be those who contributed most to the system, the contradiction between the two principles of allocation may be considered resolved. This, however, cannot be done. The basis of status in the traditional society was birth, while status is defined by the modern state on the basis of the individual's potential to contribute to the system. Hence the irreconciliability of the principles of hierarchy and socialism.

The traditional principle of holism required that the individuals renounce their self-interests at the altar of collective goals. Since hardly any autonomy was bestowed on the individual and he remained encompassed in the current of collective life, there was no basic problem. However, the introduction of democracy, predicated on the emergence of autonomous individuals, necessitated the assertion of self-interests, often ignoring collective orientation. This complicates matters because there are also extreme distributional imbalances of wealth, power and prestige, all a legacy of the antecedent social system. Thus, the principles of holism and individualism (consequently, democracy) are mutually inimical.

The values enshrined in the Indian Constitution are not fully translated into practice. Even as we recognize this lag in praxis, we should take into account the transmutations in the transitional stage during which a synthesis of the values of traditional society and the modern state is evolved. What we witness in India today is neither the continuation of all the traditional values nor the complete institutionalization of the newly introduced state ideology, but an intermediate situation containing elements of both. This complex empirical reality should not be dismissed as a transitional aberration but recognized as an evolving reality with distinct properties. It is important to remind ourselves that this perspective rejects the misplaced polarity often attributed to tradition and modernity.

Let us now examine the gap in theory in the two value packages, so as to see whether they are internally consistent. In traditional India, pluralism based on tolerance and holism based on collectivist orientation were not inconsistent, because tolerance implied a collectivity orientation. However, hierarchy, based on the principle of status, led to segmentation of the society into multiple groups, each imprisoned in its narrow grooves. Additionally, pluralism fostered local pride overlooking wider interests, thereby reinforcing hierarchy. In such a situation holism in effect meant the collectivist orientation of insulated communities. This situation naturally gave birth to a large number of social movements of primordial collectivities.

The basic inconsistency in the ideology package of the Indian state is between socialism, as we have defined it, and individualism. If the basic tenet of socialism is a pattern of need-based allocation of resources and distribution of roles keeping in mind common welfare, this calls for a high degree of collectivist orientation and altruism. In such a system one cannot insist on one's share based on one's status or on merit. One should be willing to contribute to the system as much as one can, that is, according to one's ability, but should be prepared to accept the principle of need-based allocation. The spirit of individualism implied in democracy rebels against this, as it ceaselessly emphaszies the importance of individual merit and bestows undue importance to the welfare of individuals. One may argue that maximization of welfare of all individuals will automatically lead to collective welfare and therefore common interests will not be endangered. But there are two problems here. First, such a system inevitably fosters acute competition between individuals for socially prescribed and legitimate goals. Second, no system can facilitate the maximization of welfare by all individuals who come to compose it, at any rate viewed from the subjective perceptions of its participants. And subjective evaluations are relevant to the heightening or lessening of psychological deprivations. These subjective perceptions, coupled with substantial disparity in the distribution of material resources, provide the context for the emergence of movements which pursue equality as their central objective.

III

With this understanding of the socio-cultural milieu of contemporary Indian society, let us look at the types of social movements which have emerged and operate in independent India. In terms of the schema presented in Table 6.1 we can conceive of four types of social movements. And, as indicated in Section I, movements whose ideologies and means are congruent with those of the state usually obtain in one-party systems. India has a multi- party system with one-party dominance, namely, that of the Congress, short interludes notwithstanding. However, there are instances of political parties whose ideological orientation is that of the one-party system, for example, communist parties assuming authority in a few states in India. We discuss here situation I as presented in Table 6.1, using as an illustration Kerala, the first state where the Communist Party of India (CPI) came to power.

The CPI was voted to power in Kerala in April 1957 and ruled till July 1959, when the CPI ministry was dismissed by the President of India, as a response to the 'liberation struggle' piloted by anti-communists. The communists came to power for the second time in Kerala in 1967 after a lapse of 10 years. But by this time there were two communist parties—CPI and CPI(M), the Communist Party of India-Marxist—due to the split of the CPI in 1964. Both the communist parties were in the United Front (UF) ministry which ruled from March 1967 to October 1969. Consequent to the tension that arose among the UF partners, a new ministry headed by the CPI came to power in November 1969 and continued till September 1970. In October 1970 a five-party alliance led by the CPI assumed power again and it completed a full term. The CPI(M) was not included in these ministries. However, the CPI(M) captured power again in 1980 as a leading partner of the United Left Front, which subsequently fell leading to the elections in 1982. Once again in 1987, after a lapse of five years, the CPI(M)-led Left Democratic Front captured power. But in order to understand the relationship between the state government and the movements sponsored by the communist party it is enough to examine the first phase.

Once the CPI came to power, a process of 'peaceful transition' to socialism, which was being advocated by the party since its electoral gains in 1952, was initiated. The relevant elements of the doctrine, for the present discussion, are:

1. Direct action through grass-root organizations should be accelerated.
2. Police should be neutralised.
3. Judicial organs should be directly used for transition.
4. The party directives should be implemented through local administration.
5. There should be laxity in crime administration (Fic 1970).

The Kerala pattern of peaceful transition to socialism was largely an improvisation based on local conditions. Perhaps success in electoral politics came to the CPI far too suddenly and theory formulations followed empirical experience. According to the Moscow Declaration of November 1957, after winning parliamentary majority the CPI in Kerala should have mounted a non-parliamentary mass struggle, supported by extensive use of the coercive state apparatus, in order to destroy the opposition forces. But this strategy could not have been applied in Kerala, as the overriding power rested with the Union Government in Delhi, which would have invited (and actually it did invite) intervention. The Moscow Declaration came eight months after the CPI rule began in Kerala, and was endorsed at the national level in the next party congress at Amritsar in 1958 through the adoption of a resolution on the peaceful road to socialism (see Fic 1969).

The acquisition of political authority by the communist parties led to substantial changes in the style of functioning of their front-organizations, namely, the industrial and agrarian labour unions as well as the peasant associations. It is well known that in India the so-called movements of workers and peasants are, by and large, mobilizations through the front-organizations of political parties. Since the communist parties were (and still are) the chief agents of mobilization of workers and peasants in Kerala, the state response to their movements has undergone a substantial change. The neutralization of police meant that the police should take a pro-labour stance in confrontations between workers and employers. The power accorded to the local party bosses meant that the bureaucrats had to follow their instructions. The top bureaucrats and judiciary too were expected by the CPI to support and rein-force the policy pursued by the party in power. To facilitate this process the CPI was said to have inducted a large number of its sympathizers into the state bureaucracy. Since the CPI had come to power once through election, the possibility of the party acquir-ing power subsequently could not be ruled out, and therefore, a section of the bureaucracy, police and judiciary became communist sympathizers, and the hostile attitude of others towards communists changed.

This social milieu facilitated the functioning of movements sponsored by the communist parties as extensions of the state apparatus, creating conditions favourable for the perpetuation of the party in power through mass mobilization. This situation supports the idea pointed out earlier of complementarity between the state and social movements in one-party systems. However, given the overarching presence of the central state authority, manned by a party with different ideological orientation and style of policy implementation, the response of the central government to communist-sponsored movements is bound to be different. We shall deal with this situation later.

The second type of state response to movements, namely, toler-ation, obtains when the means employed by a movement are perceived as legitimate by the state, although the movement's ideology may be radically different from that of the state. This situation is exemplified by the Sarvodaya movement in India. The basic differences in the ideological tenets of the Sarvodaya move-ment and the state are two. First, while the state has not yet ques-tioned the legitimacy of the institution of private property, Sarvodaya advocates collective ownership through trusteeship of property. For the Sarvodaya movement, the instrumentality of achieving this aim is neither coercive authority of the state nor violent revolu-tion, but reliance on voluntary gifts: *bhoodan* (land gift), *gramdan* (village gift), *sampatidan* (property gift) *budhidan* (knowledge gift) and *jeevandan* (life gift). As against the multi-party represen-tative democracy envisioned by the state, Sarvodaya insists on basic democracy through direct participation of people in the decision-making process. It rejects the power of the state and advocates *vichar shasan* (rule of ideas), or peaceful conversion of people to one's views through gentle and gradual persuasion, and *kartrittva vibhajan*(division of labour) or distribution of work among individuals without creating an administrative bureaucracy. As against the *rajniti* (power politics) of the state, the movement insists on *lokniti* (people's power) (see Oommen 1972a). To achieve its goals the movement pursues the path of non-violent militancy—*satyagraha* (passive resistance), *padyatra* (protest walk), voluntary donations—none of which is defined or perceived as non-legitimate by the state.

Notwithstanding the radical character of *sarvodaya* ideology, the state not only tolerated but explicitly supported the movement for several reasons. First, the movement's ideology was formulated initially by M.K.Gandhi, the Father of the Nation. Second, the movement was subsequently led by a band of outstanding Gandhian constructive workers who were widely acclaimed in the country for their integrity and for their cordial personal relationship with the political leaders in the country, particularly those who wielded formal authority. Third, the programmes of *bhoodan* and *gramdan* initiated by the movement were essentially in tune with the agrarian programme, namely, land to the tiller, which was accepted by the state. Further, the state was also eager to seize the opportunity by supporting the movement, as the state was not very successful in implementing its land reforms programme through the legislative apparatus [2]. Fourth, the collective actions pursued by the movement were such that they did not disturb the law and order situation in the country. Finally, and perhaps most importantly, by opting out of power politics, the movement did not pose any threat to the powers-that-be. Thus, the case of the Sarvodaya movement indicates that even as the ideology of a movement is fundamentally different from that of the state, if the movement is not an effective challenger of state power, the state response to a movement would be one of facilitation (not just toleration). Pursuantly, if indeed the movement changes its style of collective mobilization and if the state starts perceiving it as a threat, the state will attempt to repress the movement. This is precisely what happened in the case of Sarvodaya movement.

[2] For an account of the collaboration between the state and the Sarvodaya movement, see Government of India(1964).

It is necessary to recall here briefly the repertoire of events, not necessarily in a chronological order, which resulted in the change of state response to the Sarvodaya movement. It may also be noted that despite the state patronage extended to, and international a. a:m bestowed on, the novel method of rural reconstruction initiated by the Sarvodaya movement, disillusionment had set in by the early 1970s, two decades after its emergence. The events are as follows:

1. The praxiological deviations which crept into the movement *vis a vis* its proclaimed ideology, as well as the gaps in the movement's theory, unfolded by several scholarly studies (see, for example, Oommen 1972a);
2. The realization on the part of several top leaders of the movement (e.g., Dada Dharmadhikari) that there is a basic contradiction between *sarvodaya* (welfare of all) and *antyodaya* (welfare of the weakest), and therefore doubts about the feasibility of making a 'fetish of non-violence' and of being afraid of class war (Church 1978:11);
3. The introduction of the notion of *sulabh gramdan* (easily obtained village gift) by Vinoba Bhave, according to which the landowners in *gramdan* villages could retain hereditary rights over 95 per cent of their land, giving in gift only 5 per cent of the land for distribution, which meant a serious contradiction as the movement's ideology professed communal ownership in productive resources;
4. The declaration by Jayaprakash Narain (JP) in October 1971 that *sulabh gramdan* was a mistake;
5. The massive mobilization in Gujarat and subsequently in Bihar which drew inspiration and sought support from JP, leading to the fall of these state governments;
6. Vinoba's invocation of the notion of 'positive' *satyagraha*, which in effect meant explicit support to the state, and his taking recourse to voluntary silence (*maun*) during the emergency, thereby abdicating the responsibility of challenging a tyrannical state which concentrated and misused power and authority;
7. JP's appeal for the resignation of Mrs. Indira Gandhi as Prime Minister, following the Allahabad High Court judgement which accused her of corruption in election procedures;
8. JP's call for a total revolution, or comprehensive change, engulfing all aspects of contemporary Indian society (see Mukherji 1982).

These events led to the emergence of two factions in the Sarvodaya movement, those of Vinoba and JP. Vinoba and his supporters not only preferred inaction against state violence but took an explicit pro-government stand. In contrast, JP and his followers insisted on challenging effectively the violence perpetrated by the state. Further, the terror created and perpetuated by the declaration of emergency in 1975 was such that it provided a psychological climate for the disparate political parties and factions to make a united attempt to confront and challenge state power through massive mobilizations of people. JP was at the centre of this confrontation, the cementing force between the disparate elements. Although this confrontation was pursued through non-violent militant collective action, insofar as it challenged the state authority, the latter spared no effort to oppress the movement. And, this is evident in the appointment of the Kudal Commission to inquire into the alleged misuse of funds by the Gandhi Peace Foundation. the agency which supported the JP faction of the Sarvodaya movement.

In the third situation postulated, the ideology of both the state and the movement are similar but the movement resorted to non-legitimate means to achieve its goals. It is not suggested that the movements under this rubric would exclusively employ illegitimate means. In most cases such a movement may start with legitimate and constitutionally sanctioned means but it is typical of the state not to take cognizance of such mobilizations, unless of course it suits the designs and intentions of the state. The lack of response on the part of the state will eventually compel the movement leaders to employ such means as it may not only attract state attention but also retain the enthusiasm of the movement's participants. On the other hand, even when legitimate means are used by a movement as provided by the state in the Constitution, an attempt may be made by the state to label the means employed as illegitimate and thus discredit the movement insofar as it suits the purpose of the state.

A large number of social movements in independent India emerge out of the differing interpretations of and deviations from the practise of secularism, understood as the explicit recognition and fostering of socio-cultural pluralism, within the framework of the nation-state. The most telling empirical contexts, for the present purpose, are provided by movements for religious conversion and for formation of separate linguistic states. Given the nature of participants—primordial collectivities—and the nature of issues involved, most of these movements operate in regional-cultural contexts.

According to Article 25(1) of the Indian Constitution, '...all persons are equally entitled to freedom of conscience and the right freely to profess, practise and propagate religion.' Viewed against this background, conversion from one religion to another should not be a matter of state intervention. Yet there have been a few instances when the state intervened, not to deny the constitutional provision but to prevent 'illegitimate' means employed in converting people from one religion to another.

It is necessary to clarify two points here. First, the distinction between conversion and proselytization. Conversion is a manifestation of the psychological change an individual experiences—a spiritual rebirth—which may culminate in a shift from one set of religious beliefs to another. In contrast, proselytization may not imply an inner change in life, but a movement from one religion to another, usually accompanied by changes in one's style of life, manners and customs. Pursuantly, in conversion the individual is the unit of attention, in proselytization it is the collectivity. And this leads to the second point of clarification. Conversion from one religion to another in India has been invariably a collective phenomenon, a social movement. This is necessitated by the very features of Indian society—hierarchical organization, rigid stratification, group orientation, and social oppression. State intervention has been occasioned by the large-scale shift from Hinduism, the dominant religion of India, to the religions of the minorities, particularly the religions perceived as alien—Christianity and Islam. Most of the converts to these religions were drawn from among the lower castes—the Backward Classes, the Scheduled Castes—and tribes, the oppressed sections in Indian society.

The first case of state intervention in the process of proselytization in independent India was that of the government of Madhya Pradesh (MP) appointing a committee under the Chairmanship of M. Bhavani Shankar Niyogi, a retired Chief Justice of the MP High Court, in April 1954, to inquire into Christian missionary activities. The second case was that of the introduction of 'The Indian Converts (Regulation and Registration) Bill' in 1955 in the Lok Sabha, which was rejected. Third, in 1968-69, the governments in Orissa and MP passed the 'Freedom of Religion Acts' preventing proselytization. All this happened when the Congress Party was in power in the concerned states or at the centre. The Janata Party too, soon after it came to power at the centre, allowed Arunachal Pradesh to pass a Freedom of Religion Act in 1978. In December of the same year, a member of the ruling party in Parliament with an Arya Samaj background, O.P. Tyagi, introduced the 'Freedom of Religion Bill' in the Lok Sabha, which was subsequently withdrawn (for further details, see George Mathew 1982:1027-34).

The explicit aim of all the above Acts and Bills was to prevent conversion of low castes and tribes to Christianity and Islam by force, inducement, or fraudulent means. While on the ideological plane, given the commitment to secularism, the state finds it difficult to intervene in matters regarding the conversion, above interventions were justified on the basis of illegitimate means employed by those who attempted proselytization. They were essentially attempts to discredit the illegitimate means employed by conversion movements rather than question their ideology.

The other dimension of secularism we referred to earlier is acceptance of cultural pluralism, the most telling manifestation of which is found in the movements relating to the reorganization of Indian states based on language in 1956.[3] The broad principles enunciated by the Government of India for state reorganization were: (*a*) preservation of and strengthening the unity and security of India; (*b*) linguistic and cultural homogeneity; and (*c*) financial, economic and administrative considerations (Government of India 1955). These principles were difficult to apply because distribution of speech communities and size of language groups do not follow administrative need or financial viability.

Although the Census of India lists 1,652 languages as mother tongues in India, only 14 of them are listed in the VIII th Schedule of the Constitution as official languages. The numerical strength, development and distinctiveness of a language together seem to be the basis of according official status to it.[4] This situation created and perpetuates a distortion, whereby the underdeveloped and

[3] In order to develop the analysis on regional-linguistic movements here I have drawn substantially from a previous paper (Oommen 1982:41-64).

[4] However, this is not true. For an explication of this point, see Oommen 1986, especially pp.64-70.

numerically weak languages are neglected and even face the threat of extinction. Thus, a substantial number of Indians lose their linguistic-cultural identity, while the cultural identities of those whose mother tongue is one or another of the 14 official languages is defined and reinforced primarily in linguistic terms. This applies not only to numerous tribal languages spoken by smaller groups but also to several languages which are mother tongues of vast peasant groups. Thus, Bhojpuri, Braj Bhashi, Maithili, and Rajasthani, to mention only a few of such languages, are treated simply as dialects of Hindi, in the official efforts to project Hindi-speakers as the biggest community and to legitimize Hindi as the national language of the country. These languages are differentiated and spoken in regions which are culturally distinct, and the concerned speech communities recognize this fact, as manifested, for instance, in the Maithili movement.

The situation is complicated further because of a shift in the criterion of state reorganization. Although the division of Punjab into Punjabi suba and Haryana was ostensibly a continuation of the same policy, in substance it amounted to accepting religion as the basis of state reorganization. Gradually, a new criterion, namely, tribe, came to be recognized as the basis of state formation, leading to the creation of some of the smallest states on the north-eastern border, which are neither financially nor administratively viable. It is also noteworthy that while demands have been put forward for the formation of many new states, only those demands are conceded where the bargaining power of the agitators is substantial. The major source of bargaining power in these cases is their geo-political resource, that is, being border states which have the possibility of communication with nation-states on the other side of the Indian border.

At the time of state reorganization two broad views were articulated and persist to a certain extent even today. First, that the unity of India must not be imposed but fundamental, recognizing its 'social pluralism' and 'cultural diversity'; in other words, the strength of the Indian Union must be the strength it derives from its constituent units. Second, that in the past India was not an integrated political unit and efforts should be made to create a united India. The new concept of unity cannot be based on the re-affirmation or re-enunciation of old values such as those of religion and language, which are divisive rather than cohesive.

The unity of India should transcend community and language and recognize the nation-state as one integrated unit (Government of India 1955). As one looks at the situation in India today, one finds neither of these principles being adhered to and the deviations from them are far too many.

Given such a state policy it is not surprising that several movements emerged in independent India around the issues of linguism and regionalism. We can identify at least four types of movements in this context. First, when the linguistic identity of a state is threatened due to the immigration of a variety of people, resulting in cumulative domination over the locals by outsiders. The Assam movement is a case in point. The second type of movement crystallizes when the domination by outsiders occurs within a sub-region of a state. The tribal mobilization in Jharkhand for a separate state belongs to this type. The third type of movement emerges when mobilization against outsiders takes place in a metropolitan city. The typical cases are of the Shiv Sena in Bombay and Kannada Chaluvaligars in Bangalore. The fourth type of movement emerges for regional autonomy within a state even when it is populated by people speaking the same language. The well-known instances of this type are the Telengana regional movement in Andhra Pradesh and the Vidarbha movement in Maharashtra.

The ideologies of all these movements are essentially in tune with the state ideology of secularism as *practised* in India, which not only accepts but also encourages cultural pluralism. Yet, the state response has been one of discrediting these movements, labelling them as parochial, chauvinstic, and even anti-national. The discreditation is attempted by the state through several devices—labelling them as 'secessionist' and 'anti-national', initiating counter-mobilization of competing collectivities by the state from behind, or by accusing movement participants of indulging in violent activities.

The fourth situation visualized is the one in which incongruity exists with regard to ideology and means of both the state and the movements. Two types of movements fit into this category: leftist and secessionist. According to our schema, the state response to such movements should be one of repression. However, as we have indicated earlier, if these movements changed the strategy of pursuing their goals, the state response would vary concomitantly. A quick survey of a few cases from independent India seems to confirm this.

The fact that the ideology of the Indian communist movement and that of the state in India is at variance needs no explication. Although both pursue 'socialism', they pursue different brands of it, which in fact are different in substance as well. More importantly, while the Indian state with its overt commitment to political pluralism permits the existence and functioning of a multiplicity of political parties/movements, it enjoins upon them to pursue their goals through democratic means as provided in the constitution. On the other hand, the communist movement (I will be using the terms movement and party interchangeably as it is irrelevant to make the distinction in this context), following the classical line of thinking, attempted initially to achieve its goal of capturing political power through armed revolution. Thus, after independence, in 1948 the CPI made an abortive attempt to capture power through direct action. The party exhorted its members through a secret circular to subvert the government, annihilate capitalists, and seize arms and ammunition from the police and the military. Understandably the party was banned by the state. No effort was spared by the official apparatus to liquidate the party. But subsequently, the CPI abandoned the revolutionary struggle as a means to capture political power and accepted the electoral process to achieve its goals. Predictably, the ban on the CPI was lifted (in 1951). Subsequently, the party was sucessful in acquiring power through the ballot box in Kerala in 1957 and emerged as a significant opposition in several other states as well. However, despite the fact that the CPI attested to the policy of peaceful transition to socialism in 1958, it pursued the strategy of combining 'rule with struggle' in Kerala. This was one of the factors contributing to the surfacing of anti-communist forces through the so-called 'liberation struggle', which led to the intervention of the central government in dismissing the communist ministry.

In 1964 the CPI was split into two—CPI and CPI(M). While the former followed a policy of collaboration with the 'progressive' bourgeois forces, a euphemism for cooperation with the ruling Congress Party and support of state policy, the latter pursued an explicitly anti-Congress and hence anti-state policy. Admittedly, the attitude of the state to these parties varied: to the CPI it was friendly and to the CPI(M) hostile. However, even the CPI(M), as a participant in parliamentary democratic politics, was found to be functioning within the broad limits of legitimacy defined by the state. If indeed the party exceeded the limit in the perception of the state, the response has been one of discreditation and counter-mobilization. But a new party, the communist party of India (Marxist-Leninist) [CPI(ML)] emerged consequent to the split of the CPI(M) in 1967, which explicitly rejected the electoral route and consciously embraced armed struggle to capture power. This again brought forth the expected state response to the party, namely, repression. Subsequently, in the 1970s, a multiplicity of factions emerged within the CPI(ML) with varying strategies and tactics. The state response varied with regard to each of these factions, depending upon the strategy and tactics they followed; the more violent the means pursued the greater was the repression unleashed by the state (see Mohanty 1977).

The secessionist movements afford another instance of a complete disengagement between a movement's ideology and means on the one hand, and those of the state on the other. The kernel of the nation-state is its territorial integrity; the secessionist movements endanger precisely this. Any attempt to question the political sovereignty of the state by its constituent units or any tendency towards extra-territorial loyalty by any section of its populace is sure to meet with repression by the central state authority, as noted in Chapter 5.

The Dravidian movement, with its locus in Tamil Nadu and its anti-Hindi posture, was the first major secessionist movement in independent India. This was, however, a shortlived phase in the history of the movement. Subsequently, several political parties—Dravida Kazhagam, Dravida Munnetra Kazhagam, and the All India Anna Dravida Munnetra Kazhagam—emerged out of the womb of this movement (see Hardgrave 1965). All these parties have vigorously pursued Tamil 'nationalism' within the framework of the Indian Union. Since they acquired power through the electoral process they came to be accorded the requisite legitimacy characteristic of a democratic polity. Even during the secessionist phase, the Dravidian movement did not face much repression from the central authority for two reasons: first, it did not take to armed struggle, and second, the population involved was too large (nearly 30 million in 1951) to be contained through state violence.

The two persisting secessionist movements of independent India have been the Mizo National Front (MNF) and the Naga National

Movement (NNM).[5] Each of them has several factions encapsulated within it, with varying degrees of intensity in their violent activities and 'anti-national' orientations. Viewed as a whole, these movements have been taking differing postures and pursuing varying means to achieve their ends, that is, the establishment of independent sovereign nation-states. Consequently, the response of the state too has been redefined several times. As and when these movements overtly pursue their goal of secession and resort to armed rebellion to achieve their ends or to terrorize 'outsiders' in their territory, the state in turn matches it with a series of repressive measures (see Misra 1978:618-24; Rangasami 1978: 653-62). Conversely, as and when the MNF or NNM has showed an inclination to pursue its goals within the framework of the Indian Union and accepted constitutional remedies to redress their grievances, the state has been 'soft' to them, in that attempts have been made to arrive at decisions through negotiations. The signing of the Rajiv-Laldenga Accord and the return of peace to Mizoram exemplifies this.

IV

The preceding section attempted a brief review of state response to social movements in terms of the four logically plausible empirical situations postulated at the outset of this chapter. In the course of dealing with concrete cases, we have seen that our empirical anticipations have not always been correct. The state does not respond to movements in a logical or 'rational' manner. The state response has been pragmatic, at best. informed of expedient rationality. Its approach is one of tension-management, invariably taking a short-term view of the situation. We now examine the implications of this pattern of response.

There is enormous evidence to suggest that demands have been conceded to by the state only when the concerned movement has demonstrated its political clout (e.g., conceding the demand for separate states in the north-east or the formation of Punjabi Suba). In doing so, the state indirectly perpetuates conflicting situations and contributes to the proliferation of similar movements.

[5] Of the other two secessionist movements, one, the mobilization for a Sikh sovereign state, Khalistan, is of very recent origin. The other, the mobilization for a united Kashmir, became virulent recently.

Thus, paradoxically, the state response itself, insofar as it does not follow a pattern or principle, becomes a catalytic agent in the emergence of new movements challenging state authority.

To the extent that the state can manage tensions through co-option of the movement's leadership, it would invariably resort to this measure (e.g., the Telengana separatist movement, and the recent negotiations with the MNF). Such an attempt at pacification has its demonstration effect, giving birth to new movements often initiated by ambitious persons with spurious intentions—so much so that the mobilization of people becomes a project to fulfil personal ambition rather than collective need. Further, in such a situation, a multiplicity of leaders emerge, leading to the proliferation of factions within a movement, which is detrimental to its cause. On the other hand, in a democratic system, bargaining is an accepted mechanism but it may not always be done for the accredited purpose for which it is meant, namely, collective welfare. Here leaders' motives assume crucial importance. Unless the state makes the correct judgment it can cause irreparable damage to the very fabric of the state and society. It is likely that the state may attempt the 'neutralization' of the 'desirable' leaders and 'liquidation' of the 'undesirable' ones in such a situation.

Our initial postulate, that even if a movement's ideology is at complete variance with the state ideology, insofar as the movement pursues constitutional means the state may tolerate the movement, did not turn out to be correct. This is exemplified by both the Sarvodaya and the communist movements, though in different ways. In the first case, the state tried to use the movement to its advantage, to reinforce the official objective of rural reconstruction in general and of the agrarian programme of redistribution of land to the landless in particular. In fact, the vitality of the Sarvodaya movement has been substantially sapped because of its over-identification with the state. In the case of the communist movement, with the adoption of the policy of 'peaceful transition' and consequent cooperation with the progressive elements among the bourgeoisie by the CPI, we witness a phase of collaboration between the central authority and the movement.

It follows from the above that what moulds state response is not so much the ideology of a movement but the means it adopts. Even if a movement's goals are radical and in contravention of those accepted by the state, to the extent it pursues them

thi·'ugh peaceful and constitutional means the state response
will not ordinarily be hostile. Conversely, even when there is
ideological congruity between the state and a movement, if the
means employed by the latter are 'illegitimate', the state will not
stop at mere discreditation of the movement as we anticipated.
I may emphasize here that in a multi-party democracy the elasticity
of permissiveness is quite substantial. However, should the movement transcend the limit of legitimacy as defined by the state, it
will intervene to repress the movement, irrespective of the nature
of the movement's ideology.

It was my contention that if the movement's ideology is radically
different from that of the state and if the means employed by the
movement are 'illegitimate', the state response takes the form of
repression. We have no evidence to contradict this proposition.
But we have some evidence to suggest that even when a movement
pursues its objective through constitutional means the state may
repress it. This happens if the movement gains substantial political
clout so as to operate as a countervailing power to the state,
capable of threatening its very existence. Faced with such a situation, the state would employ two mechanisms to contain the
situation. First, it would attempt, through the party in power,
counter-mobilization against the movement, thereby attempting to
create a counter-collective conscience challenging the collective
conscience projected by the movement. Second, the state would
label the movement's mobilization as a law and order problem,
sometimes even creating 'appropriate' situations through agent
provocatuers, so as to legitimize the state violence unleashed
on the movement's participants. That is, in the reckoning of
the state the movements are arranged in a 'hierarchy of threat', as
it were, irrespective of their nature of ideology and the means
(see Chapter 5). The most telling instance of this is the Sarvodaya
movement. Although the JP faction of the movement attempted to
achieve its objective through militant non-violent collective action,
it posed a threat to the state, and hence the state intervened to
suppress the movement.

The state will not succeed in its effort if the degree of legitimacy
it enjoys is low and if the movement is successful in stirring the
collective conscience against the state. Faced with such a situation
the state may suspend its democratic mode of functioning and
resort to authoritarianism. The declaration of internal emergency

in India in 1975 was such a response by the state. On the other hand, if the state's attempt at repression is viewed by the majority of the population as the exercise of legitimate authority invested in it to maintain order and stability in society, the state will be successful in its effort. This seems to have happened in the case of the Naxalite movement.

The conclusion then is: a democratic state can effectively use the weapon of repression against a section of the population only when it is viewed as legitimate by the wider collectivity. Should the state authority experience an erosion of its legitimacy, it cannot sustain and continue its repressive measures against a movement. Thus, however paradoxical it may sound, the most critical variable in moulding state response in a democratic polity is the nature of response to state action by the collectivity.

7
Social Movements and Styles of Communication: An Overview

Social movements are among the least researched areas in Indian social science, although, of course, there has been a virtual proliferation of movement studies in recent years, particularly since the beginning of the 1970s (see Chapter 2). However, a large number of interconnections between movements and related aspects which determine their character and course still remain unexplored. Social movements and styles of communication is one such area. Therefore, the present attempt is bound to be exploratory in its tenor and orientation. I propose to deal with only three aspects: the interrelations between the nature of society, social movements and communication; the linkage between communication patterns, social movements and their environmental milieu; and communication within social movements. As a prelude, it is necessary to make a few introductory remarks.

I

The concept and hence the phenomenon of social movements as we understand them today are largely a creation of the 19th century; they are new. Not that there were no collective mobilizations before the 19th century; collective human actions are as old as human society itself. But the pre-19th century collective mobilizations were essentially *defensive actions* against aggressive designs of oppressors; there was no gradual building up of the tempo of the movement. Indeed they were more often than not sudden outbursts and hence they are described as rebellions, mutinies, uprisings, outbreaks, etc. Not that the causes of the movement did not exist or that they were suddenly invented by ingenious leadership, but the system did not permit the emergence and existence of social movements. What existed prior to the outbreak were the necessary conditions for the emergence of a movement; it was only a *latent movement*. To transform this latent movement into a manifest one it was necessary to communicate the shared deprivation and discontent. The societal ethos did not usually permit the sufficient condition—widespread communication of shared discontent—to operate.

The 19th century saw the rise of voluntaristic collective actions by groups of people commited to a shared identity, common goals and programme of action. To be sure wars and rebellions, the traditional forms of conflict, did continue. But conflicts are no more confined to two estabished authorities or between a delegitimized and an aspiring authority; they can also be between the social categories. Communication is crucial to these collective actions because mobilization of resources is essentially a collective enterprise; it cannot be done through a fiat from above. The rise of nationalism as a creed and an ideology in the ex-colonial countries rendered collective actions in these societies a massive and legitimate enterprise. Concomitantly, the thrust of communication shifted from micro to macro, from segmental to holistic concerns and considerations. This in turn meant ignoring temporarily the indigenous heterogeneity and evolving a communication strategy concentrating on the commonalities of actual and potential participants and emphasizing the differences between them and their enemy, the colonial intruder.

It is also important to note at the very outset that the styles of communication and the mode of articulating deprivations vary not only across time but also between the different contexts in a given society at a particular point in time. For example, the emergence of *guru* cults in Hinduism: while they were indicative of dissatisfaction with the established or mainline religion, the *gurus* did not necessarily confront or challenge the traditional religious establishment. Invariably they opted for a strategy of coexistence. In contrast, political parties, movements and associations attack the existing established structures—the inadequacy of the latter is the strength of the former; the strategy is one of displacement. The important point to be noted here is that the style of communication is markedly different in the two contexts and with regard to the two strategies. If the strategy of coexistence is reconciliatory in its orientation, the strategy of displacement is aggressive in its thrust. Admittedly, the style of communication opted for and required would be vastly different in the two contexts.

Third, it is necessary to dispel the widely-held naive notion that a social movement is a group, a collectivity. Indeed all movements have core and peripheral participants. But what is distinctive about a movement is that it is a *sustained interaction* between contending collectivities to bring about distributive balance in critical societal resources—wealth, power, privilege.[1] And sustained interaction implies, nay it is, communication. There are two types of communications here, *among* and *across* communications. Among communications take place between (*a*) the core participants, and (*b*) the core and peripheral participants. Communication among the core participants is concerned with policies and priorities of the movements; it is the process through which critical decisions are made. The communication to peripheral participants is geared to convince and carry them along. Across communication takes place between (*a*) the movement and its enemies, established authorities, counter-movements, and (*b*) the movement and its allies, potential and actual sympathizers from whom the movement seeks support. Admittedly, what is communicated and how it is communicated differ vastly depending upon to whom it is communicated. Communication to participants and allies is geared to strengthen and enlarge the support base of the movement. Communication about and to enemies is meant to expose them as unjust and oppressive elements in society.

II

Small-scale and closed situations and societies are characterized by face-to-face, personal, intimate interactions. In such a situation, any opposition to authority should necessarily be characterized by open estrangement. It is not a mere accident that the primitive rebel invariably physically attacked the established authority he was challenging, constituted by particular persons (cf. Hobsbawm 1959). The focus was on persons and not structures. Physical

[1] Sustained interaction and communication are prerequisites for societies, collectives and groups. But these interactions and communications are designed to sustain them. On the other hand, the sustained interaction and communication which takes place in the context of movements are steps to change the existing societies and groups.

violence was the only weapon he could wield against the structural violence of the establishment; expression of violence was communication. But in order to be able to do this the primitive rebel had to create a situation of social estrangement between him and the target of his attack. There are two possible routes to achieve this. First, consider and attack only those social categories which are traditionally defined as being socially distinct and distant as one's enemies. Second, create an estrangement between people and the object of their attack, if the latter was hitherto held in respect or perceived as socially close, that is, to create a mass (see Selznick 1951: 320-32). The process of depersonalizing human ties and creating social disengagement is as much a function of communication as building personal ties and social cohesion.

In contrast, confrontations in large-scale societies and impersonal situations need not be characterized by physical attack, to begin with at any rate. Physical violence in such social situations is an indicator of the breakdown of communication. That is, there is a gradual progression towards physical violence, it is the failure of the other modes of communication—petitioning, bargaining, demonstration—which are generally accepted as legitimate and non-violent, which eventuates in violent acts. It is instructive to compare the kind of *sudden violence* described in works of fiction like *Anand Math*[2] and the sudden actual violence which occurred in the uprising led by Birsa Munda[3] on the one hand, and the kind of *eventual violence* that gradually emerged in many contemporary and on-going movements. The capital role of the breakdown of communication in transforming non-violent movements into violent ones needs to be emphasized here.

In large-scale societies, the old form of face-to-face communication continues but sooner or later the mass media would become the more salient modes of communication for public interaction. It is not possible even for a band of dedicated persons to reach everybody in a large-scale society through direct contact. Mass media help reach the widest potential constitutency and render mobilization possible without physical contact. While modern technology makes it possible

[2] *Anand Math* was first published in 1882 in Bengali: several of its Hindi translations appeared subsequently. The first English translation appeared in 1904. The central characters in the novel are Hindus who constitute bandit gangs and plunder for altruistic purposes, the 'national' cause (see Chatterjee 1882).

[3] For a graphic description of the movement led by Birsa Munda see K.S. Singh (1966).

through transportation and communication to augment the scale of a social movement, whether or not this objective will be actually realized depends on its accessibility to movement leaders. The question of who controls the means of communication is crucial in this context.

In India the press is largely independent of direct government control. Yet it is not correct to say that the Indian press is supportive of social movements. Here it is necessary to distinguish between the press at two levels: the all-India English language press which operates at the macro level and is usually referred to as the 'national' press, and the micro level Indian language press which usually operates in the regional-linguistic contexts. The macro press is invariably owned and controlled by the big bourgeoisie in India and therefore it does not and cannot support any movements that lean towards the betterment of the poor. Not that it does not allow a handful of 'radicals' to let off steam. But I am talking about the main thrust. As far as movements based on primordial collectivisms—language, region, caste, religion—are concerned, the macro press perceives and dismisses them as parochial and anti-national. By and large the macro press in India supports only those mobilizations which would fall within the rubric of a capitalist-liberal-democratic framework. This renders the macro press in India largely redundant, in fact, invariably dysfunctional for most movements.

The response of the micro press varies depending upon a variety of factors. Regionally insulated and catering to readers in a specific linguistic-cultural area, the micro press is largely indifferent to the goings-on in regions which are physically distant and culturally distinct. However, the micro press becomes intensely involved in those movements which take place within their catchment area. This involvement is either for or against the movement, depending upon the clientele they cultivate. While the movement is *sacralized* by a particular section of the press, it is *demonized* by another section.[4]

The other instruments of mass communication—radio and television—are still owned and controlled by the government. There is hardly any possibility of these instruments being used by movement leaders to promote their cause as most movements are by their very nature challengers of authority. The government may

---

[4] The processes of sacralization and demonization are seminal to the very operation of social movements. For a discussion on this aspect, see Chapter 10.

provide its version of a movement through radio and television or even use these instruments to break a movement by allowing them to be used by those leading a counter-movement. To cite one instance, the prolonged, massive, and predominantly non-violent Assamese national (Assamiya) movement was invariably described both by All-India Radio (AIR) and Doordarshan (the TV network) as an agitation led by a handful of misguided and disgruntled youth whose outlook was parochial. Needless to say, the leaders and supporters of the movement described it in diametrically opposed terms.[5] Similarly, the current mobilizations in the Punjab are referred to both by the government-controlled media and by most of the macro press as the handiwork of a handful of terrorists. But those who participate in the violent activities believe that they are martyrs of faith. And, at least a section of the Sikhs, even as they do not participate in this violence, seem to sympathize with the activities and acknowledge that those who kill the 'enemies of the panth' are martyrs. The micro press is sharply divided in terms of its orientation to the Sikh violence and one finds both supporters and opponents among its ranks.

The point to be noted is that the control over instruments and channels of communication is of crucial significance in the context of presenting the 'facts' about movements. This is so because movements are centrally involved in contentions about values; they attempt to challenge and de-legitimize the existing established authority; they are group enterprises to create a new collective conscience and/or redefine the existing collective conscience. Admittedly, the same set of 'facts' will be differentially interpreted and presented by movement spokespersons and their enemies. The same event or act will be described as abhorrent and illegitimate as well as noble and laudable by two sets of interpreters; the same set of persons will be labelled as terrorists and criminals or martyrs and saints. The communication is about the same set of acts and persons, but *who* communicates and *how* it is communicated, the meaning assigned to the act/person, and *why* the communication perspectives vary are crucial issues in the spread or demise of a movement.

[5] However, once the movement succeeded in its objective and captured/political power by installing the political party it sponsored in power, both AIR and Doordarshan changed their attitude to the movement, the party and its leadership.

III

I have said that a movement has both enemies and allies and the nature of communication with them is radically different in orientation. But it is equally important to note that the enemies themselves are basically of two types: internal and external. If the enemy is external to the system as a whole, it is relatively easy to mobilize substantial support and de-legitimize and demonize the enemy; the reception of communication is easy. As is well-known and well-documented, the massive mobilization against the British in India in the context of the anti-colonial movement was successful largely because the enemy was perceived as external to Indian society—racially and culturally. Similarly, mobilizations against religions which are defined and perceived as alien to Indian soil are almost instantaneously successful (Oommen 1983b: 92-113).

However, in several contexts this juxtaposition of insiders and outsiders is not neat and tidy and hence the attempt to de-legitimize the enemy is not met with ready success. This is evident in the case of the Dravidian movement which projects Aryans as outsiders to India. But there are two complications here. First, the Aryans themselves do not accept this characterization. Second, even among those who are defined as Dravidians, the Aryan element (e.g., Brahmins) is not altogether absent. These factors make it difficult to mobilize one group against the other for a head-on collision.

There are yet other contexts in the Indian social milieu where the confronting primordial collectivities are undoubtedly perceived as 'insiders' to the Indian situation as a whole but perceived as 'outsiders' within the particular regional-linguistic-cultural context. South Indians in Bombay, Bengalis in Assam, plains people in tribal areas, Tamils in Bangalore, etc., afford examples of this. But given the conflict between state-ways (single citizenship) and folk-ways (ideology of sons of the soil), it is not easy for those who define themselves as 'insiders' to mobilize against 'outsiders'. Indeed, attack against and characterization of outsiders in derogatory terms often meet with disapproval from the state, a variety of outsiders and at least a section of the insiders. All this makes mobilization, and hence communication, extremely arduous and tricky.

The insider-outsider issue has yet another facet, the caste context.

Traditionally the caste system effectively operated only in the regional-linguistic context, and that too at the level of *jati*. In the modern democratic political context the effective unit is a caste federation, a product of the fusion of a set of *jatis*. The proliferation of caste *sabhas* and their political significance is too well-known to be recalled here. But it is necessary to note that although it is usually the proximate *jatis* which tend to confederate, each of these would consider others as different, at least in the socio-cultural context. Admittedly this has implications for communication and mobilization. To begin with, the effort should be to emphasize the bases of *unity* of a variety of *jatis* which should constitute the federation and then to focus on the *difference* between them and others.

As we shift our attention from the mobilization of primordial to other types of collectivities—biological and civil—the problems of communication also differ.[6] What I call biological collectivities are those which are differentiated on the basis of physiological factors: race, sex and age. Race, although a physiological feature, easily becomes a socio-cultural marker and this makes communication, mobilization and confrontation relatively easy. This explains why some of the most virulent conflicts and movements are inter-racial.

Sex is a clearly identifiable biological trait and through the process of socialization and enculturation, sex stereotypes are internalized in all societies. Notwithstanding this biological *and* social differentiation, it is extremely difficult to visualize male and female as two different social segments operating with autonomy. As of now one cannot visualize (test-tube babies and homosexual colonies notwithstanding) societies constituted exclusively by men or women. Therefore, communication, mobilization and confrontation exclusive to the sexes remain a remote possibility. It is clear then that movements of men and women will have to devise a communication strategy quite unique and peculiar

The youth constitute a transient bio-social category; nobody remains a youth for ever. The youth cannot define the non-youth—the adults and the aged—as permanent enemies as they themselves would eventually graduate into these stages. Once again, the object of communication is not to de-legitimize the 'opponent', but to sensitize one another of the needs and aspirations,

[6] For an elaboration of the three basic types of collectivities, their characteristics and potentials for collective action, see Chapter 5.

and to make each other aware of recognizing the need to share power and responsibility. Admittedly, the tenor of communication is bound to be different.

Civil collectivities are not bounded as in the case of primordial and biological collectivities; they cut across religion, language, caste, sex, race and age groups. Most of the movements of civil collectivities are mobilizations of occupational groups—rich capitalist farmers, peasantry, agrarian or industrial proletariat, black or white collar workers, professionals, students, etc. Precisely because the boundaries of occupational categories are shifting and their edges frayed—the poor workers may undergo a process of embourgeoisment, the black-coated worker may move up to become a white collar employee, the semi-professionals may succeed in acquiring the status of full-fledged professionals—it is all the more difficult for civil collectivities to develop consciousness exclusive to them. This is in contrast to the biological collectivities where categorial consciousness is almost natural, and the primordial collectivities where it can be easily nurtured right from childhood. Consciousness specific to the occupational categories is a function of occupational socialization which often crystallizes only when one enters adulthood. And, consciousness is a function of communication. As we have already noted, no movement can emerge and survive without communication. Pursuantly, the role of communication in mobilizing civil collectivities is most critical.

The styles of protest and modes of communication also differ between the various civil collectivities. The workers—industrial and agrarian—students and peasants have 'unions' which successfully attempt mass mobilizations through public meetings, protest marches, strikes, *gheraos* and *satyagrahas*. The black-coated workers and semi-professionals (e.g., nurses, school teachers) have 'associations' but they often take to the styles of protest and types of mobilization of workers. The traders, artisans, merchants, etc., have 'guilds' but they rarely attempt mass mobilizations and invariably resort to economic sanctions against their customers to express their protest. The white collar employees and professionals too have 'associations' but they rarely attempt mass mobilizations; their best bet is to impress upon the establishment above and 'clients' below their indispensability to run the system through appropriate tactics—go-slow, pen-down, providing misinformation, refusing cooperation etc. The point I want to emphasize is that the patterns of communication and the styles of protest vary with regard to each of the categories.

It is evident from the discussion so far that the milieu in which a movement operates substantially influences its mode of communication. Thus, in a predominantly agrarian or industrial society the mode of communication will have to be geared to its societal ethos. Similarly, communication styles would vary between the religious and secular contexts. There is yet another element in the societal milieu which critically influences the style of communication, the nature of the state. As I have detailed the relationship between social movements and the state in Chapter 6, I will only attempt here an analysis focusing on the styles of communication.

While most movements are anti-state enterprises, it is by no means untenable that a welfare or socialist state may facilitate or even sponsor some movements, to the extent that the goals of these movements accelerate the targets pursued by the state. On the other hand, the state response to movements even when negative would fall into a wide range. This would depend upon the nature of ideology and means pursued by the movement to achieve its goals and the assessment by the state of the threat posed by it. We may think of at least three distinct possibilities in this context: toleration, discreditation and repression.

If the state response is one of facilitation it would not only permit the movement to use state-controlled media but the state itself may propagate the movement. Admittedly, the identification of the state with the movement would sap the latter of its vitality but the movement would have a ready communication network. When the attitude of the state is one of toleration it will not pay much attention to the movement and will be indifferent to what the movement communicates.

The state effort to discredit a movement calls for considerable tact and careful handling of the communication system. First, the state has to prevent effective communication by the movement. Second, it has to present the movement to the public in such a vein that the followers of the movement are weaned away and the potential ones are scared away. Third, the state should carefully plan counter-communication so that the followers get alienated from the movement. If the state wants to repress a movement not only does it have to take all the measures with regard to discrediting a movement but it has to issue a warning that participation in the concerned movement is a 'crime', against 'national interest', 'social stability', etc. Liquidation of a movement is not simply a matter of using state violence against it, but also that of building up legitimacy in the employment of force. This is essentially a matter of communication.

I would like to conclude the discussion on the interlinkage between movement communication and social milieu by identifying three essential steps. First, abandoning those modes of communication which have proved inappropriate, ineffective or dangerous. The burden of our discussion was that communication cannot be viewed independently of the environmental milieu in which it takes place. Insofar as the latter changes, it is necessary to mould the modes of movement communication too. Second, adapting the existing or traditional means of communication to newer needs. While it is true that certain modes of communication are more appropriate to communicate specific types of content, the possibility of some of the old modes being adapted to communicate new contents is not ruled out. In fact, this is being done increasingly— *Harikatha* is used for both political propaganda and popularization of science.

Third, invention or adoption of new modes of communication to suit new goals and new contents. In the pre-independent era when most mobilizations/movements operated in small-scale situations, communication techniques were face-to-face and often involved physical confrontation. With the gradual 'massification' of the freedom struggle and Gandhiji's assumption of leadership, the modes of communication drastically changed. Being non-violent, the new modes such as *satyagraha, padayatra and swadeshi,* made it possible for people from all sectors of social life—including the middle classes, women, traders—who usually did not participate in violent activities, to become actively involved in the freedom struggle. The innovative techniques of communication evolved by Gandhi were of tremendous significance in enlarging the social base of the freedom struggle. This does not mean that violent activities suddenly and completely disappeared, but they were relegated to the background in terms of their comparative significance. In independent India new modes of protest are being evolved continuously, while some of the old ones are being retained and adapted. *Gherao*, *rasta-roko* and sit-in strikes coexist with hijackings, bombings and political murders.

IV

In terms of the agenda set out at the beginning of this chapter, we need to analyze the patterns of communication *within* movements. It has been established by now that perceived deprivation or shared discontent is the basis of all social movements. But for discontent to be shared, it needs to be articulated and communicated. In the beginning deprivation may be felt only by a small group, but unless the circle of discontent is constantly enlarged, collective mobilization is not possible. Who constitutes the initial recruits to the movement or how the circle of discontent is expanded depends on the mode of crystallization of a particular movement. Therefore, what is attempted here is to interrelate the processes of emergence of social movements and that of communication. There are several processually distinct possibilities, in terms of which dimension of a movement—leadership, ideology, organization, a precipitating event—surfaces first.[7] I propose to characterize each of these situations in turn.

A leader—ideologue, *guru*, prophet, charismatic hero—emerges and starts communicating to the people-at-large the reasons or underlying causes of the 'crisis' they face. This is a process of conscientization of the people by the leader. Since the leader has primacy, in the sense of sequential priority in emergence, the leader is of critical importance as a communicator. The communication in such cases would be direct and face-to-face, particularly at the incipient stage. The ideology of the movement will evolve gradually through the utterances of the leader, the organization will emerge when he wills it. Such a movement is built around personal loyalty based on direct contact with the leader. The leader, if he is to be socially validated, will have to conceptualize and present ideas in terms of the patterns of communication familiar and acceptable to the potential followers. But leader-centredness implies centralization of communication which in turn may lead to authoritarianism.

However, leader-centred communication cannot continue too long if the movement expands; one person cannot grapple with the

[7] I have argued in an earlier work (Oommen 1972a) that in the emergence of a social movement one of the three dimensions—leadership, ideology, organization—may surface first giving birth to three types of social movements. My subsequent observations and studies show that a movement may also emerge out of a precipitant event.

demands of a fast-spreading movement. There are two possibilities here: (*a*) That communication is mechanized or 'massified'. That is, if the communicaton is not a threat to the establishment, the movement can and may resort to mass media (press, radio, television). Alternatively, if these communication channels are not accessible or proscribed to a movement, it may resort to devices such as taping speeches or even making video tapes of the messages of the leader. That is, instead of the leader communicating face-to-face in flesh and blood he is brought into a face-to-face interaction through mechanical devices. To this extent, the movement will remain leader-centred not withstanding its massive spread; (*b*) A large number of lesser/local leaders emerge as mere disseminators of the ideas of the leader. These local leaders are usually recruited on the basis of their direct contact and proven loyalty to the leader. They are not men of ideas but channels of communication. This would invariably be the style of communication pursued if technological development does not permit resorting to mechanical devices or if the establishment it challenges is oppressive and too powerful.

Communication breakdowns may occur in the movement when (*a*) the initiator is physically and/or mentally incapacitated, (*b*) an accredited successor does not emerge after the death of the leader, (*c*) one or more among the multiplicity of local leaders deviate from their role as disseminators and take on the role of ideologues and interpreters of the leader's ideas. In such a situation, differential and even contradictory interpretations are likely, which implies the possibility of a split in the movement and its consequent weakening.

If a movement is to spread, it has to gradually change the leader-centred communication style. The ideology of the movement will have to be codified and either an oral or written text with specified meanings and interpretations should emerge. And, organizational vehicles will have to be established—*ashrams, gurukuls, sabhas,* parties, associations, training schools—which would disseminate the ideology of the movement. That is, for the survival of a movement, communication needs to be routinized. Stabilization of a movement and routinization of its communication should go hand in hand.

Let us look at another scenario for the emergence of movements. An existing ideology, say Marxism or capitalism, is perceived as the

most appropriate solution to grapple with the present evils, deprivation or discontent, because its vitality is already demonstrated in
concrete historical societies. Alternatively, a counter-ideology or a
new ideology is propounded when the existing ones prove ineffective
in solving the current problems. In either event, the primacy is of
ideology, the message, and not of the communicator. The content
of communication, that is ideology, does not just flow out of the
communicator as he speaks. But it is already there, well thought
out and even codified, whether it is the intellectual effort of one
person or a multiplicity of individuals. There is no one ultimate
spokesperson but a pool of persons, a think tank, which conjointly
interprets and articulates the movement ideology to the people to
win them over to the movement. A multiplicity of study circles,
propaganda groups and folk theatres may emerge as communication
channels. However, to avoid confusion through varying interpretations, every effort will be made to keep communication
structured. While a variety of forms—the written word, visuals,
theatre, songs—are employed, the message will be kept constant.

However, decentralization of communication carries with it the
seeds of confusion due to possible differential interpretations of
the message, in spite of adequate precautionary measures. Further,
the possibility of some of the communicators becoming more
effective and hence emerging as powerful and influential cannot be
ruled out. Further, a multiplicity of communicators would also
entail coordination if the communication is to be efficient. That is,
some amount of centralization of communication becomes inevitable
if the movement is to spread and effectively deal with premature
demise through splits.

Centralization of communication would necessitate the emergence
of coordinators of movement activities, which in turn would lead
to the crystallization of a central leadership. In turn, centralized
leadership implies centralization of communication. Rarely does a
movement escape this vicious circle. But in such cases, since the
leader has not emerged as an ideologue or as a charismatic hero,
he has to rely on an organizational weapon for effective communication and not on a band of loyal followers. This in turn calls for
bureaucratization of the communication flow; who can communicate
what, to whom, and when, needs to be specified. This rigidification
of communication flow will alter the style of movement functioning.
It may get solidified as an organization. But given the motivations

and value orientations of movement participants, discontent about the style of communication of movements would set in, leading to the emergence of a less rigid style of communication. If this does not happen, the authoritarianism of central leadership would come under attack eventuating in factionalization and splits.

The third possibility is that a group of discontented persons form an association/organization to fight an existing evil, which often becomes the nucleus of a movement. In the very nature of things, communication in an organizational set-up is structured. While leader-follower communication in a movement is typically open-ended, communication between organizational personnel and potential recruits to an organization is structured. But an organization working for the redressal of grievances or uplift of the deprived cannot afford to have a rigid pattern of communication, particularly at the initial stage. Therefore, such organizations tend to function more as movements than as organizations.

In contrast to other movements, an organizational movement operates with the organization as its nucleus. This is evident from vertical organizational elaboration and horizontal associational proliferation, both of which are expected to facilitate the process of communication between the organizational staff and their clients, actual or potential. Thus, depending upon the level at which an organization is established at the initial stage—national, regional, local—it tends to expand downwards or upwards. Similarly, once special-interest associations are established by or among a particular social category, the tendency is to establish similar associations among other categories as well. In either event—vertical expansion or horizontal spread—it is expected that the organization/association is brought closer to people facilitating face-to-face interaction between the leaders and potential recruits.

Associational proliferation and organizational elaboration call for codification and coordination of communication. This in turn would necessitate the creation of specialists who can handle communication efficiently. The professional manager, rather than the ideologue or charismatic hero, would be the typical role that would emerge in such a context. Clarity, specificity, target achievement, etc., rather than creativity or innovativeness would be the thrust of communication. In fact, social movement organizaitons keep movements going in most cases through communication (circulars, hand-outs, meetings, demonstrations), the resources for which are often raised independent of movement participants. A set of movement entrepreneurs emerge to efficiently manage the affairs of the movement.

A group of organizational professionals, institutional brokers, and participants collaborate to keep up the illusion that the movement is an on-going concern. However, gradually frustration and alienation might set in and challengers to the movement establishment would emerge. If the movement does not mend its style of functioning, a split is almost inevitable.

From the latter half of the 19th century onwards, we find the emergence of associations to redress grievances of particular collectivities in India. By the 1930s associational proliferation became so much a part of the Indian ethos that it is no exaggeration to suggest that almost every caste/community had its association. There are two empirically identifiable patterns here. First, small, dispersed sets of people begin making a demand or articulating a grievance which attracts more and more individuals and groups. Gradually, a set of activists and organizers emerge and try to co-ordinate the activities through the establishment of an association. Once mobilization spreads and the movement demonstrates its clout, power-holders start taking cognizance of the movement and respond variously—conceding some of the demands, co-optation of the leadership, repression. Second, an all-India structure, say a political party, sponsors mobilizations of specific categories (students, women, industrial workers, etc.) or in particular areas, through its cadre. Much of that which is labelled as 'movement' in India belongs to this mode of mobilization. What is important to be kept in mind for the present purpose is that while in both instances the communication flow is vertical, there is a basic difference in the direction of flow: upward and downward. This means that the content of communication, the manner in which it is formulated and communicated, drastically differ.

Finally, it is not uncommon for a movement to emerge out of a precipitant event. While the event itself may be unplanned and spontaneous, a latent movement ought to have been prevailing for long. The events that are referred to here, the womb out of which movements may emerge and eventually crystallize, should not be confused with mobilizations which are inevitable in all movements.

People may not be in a position to systematically articulate deprivation although they might have experienced it for quite some time because of the absence of *(a)* adequate leadership, *(b)* appropriate ideology, *(c)* viable organization. All the same, deprivation continues to accumulate and a precipitous act (e.g., physical assault, rape, sudden dismissal from employment) gives birth to a revolt, uprising or civil disobedience. When this happens there will not be any accredited leader, crystallized organization or formulated ideology. But the event itself might give birth to these in succession.

It is inevitable that a spokesperson should emerge on behalf of those who participate in collective actions; who becomes the chief communicator for the group and with the enemy. But if the instant leader is allowed to be the sole arbiter, in all probability he may turn authoritarian or opportunist, a risk the discontented can ill-afford. Therefore, the formation of an organizational structure, a committee, usually follows, which regulates activities of participants, puts forward strategies and steers the struggle. But the programme of action will have to be based on a philosophy, an ideology, a rationale, if it is to be sustained. The leadership will have to provide the rationale behind the proposed collective actions, which should be appealing enough to be accepted by the participants. Thus, the ideology of the movement gradually emerges. Admittedly, the process of communication involved in the emergence of such a movement is different as compared with the processes of communication described earlier.

V

It is my contention that even the bare beginning to systematically work out the relationship between social movements and communication is yet to be made. Having acknowledged the underdeveloped state of analysis in this context we could only attempt a few faltering steps.

It is suggested that the patterns of communication vary across societies situated at different phases of development—tribal, peasant, industrial. Therefore, the styles of communication adopted by movement leaders in different types of societies too would vary. The level of technological development and the nature of state authority are two of the most important factors which influence the patterns of communication, albeit in different ways. The type of collectivity—civil, primordial and biological—to which communication is addressed, would also influence the content and mode of communication because the internal milieu and the structure of consciouness of the constituent units of these collectivities also vary substantially.

Finally, the manner in which a movement emerges and what dimension of it would have primacy at the incipient stage also affect the styles of communication within the movement. However, it is our contention that neither extreme fluidity nor absolute rigidity in communication will be functional for the efficient operation of movements. Similarly, both over-centralized and uncoordinated communication styles are dysfunctional for movements.

MICRO ORIENTATIONS: THE VIEW FROM WITHIN

8
Agrarian Classes and Political Mobilization

The decade-old virulent debate among political economists, on mode of production in Indian agriculture, has produced more heat than light.[1] At least some of the participants acknowledge that the debate lacked an adequate data base to support one or another argument, that its concentration on the colonial period led to its failure to analyze adequately the qualitatively different processes at work in the post-colonial phase (see, for example, Omvedt 1981a A140–59. Couched in the broad evolutionary Marxian schema—feudalism, capitalism, imperialism—the debate demonstrated the preference of the one or another set of writers to fit the available scanty data into their preconceived or even newly-floated framework (e.g., colonial mode of production). The empirical reality on the ground is much more complex and often rebels against the framework.

While most political economists have assumed that there existed some variety of feudalism in India, whatever may be the specific term they used to label it—semi-feudal, pre-capitalist, non-capitalist—the historians still persisted in asking the question: 'Was there ₁eudalism in Indian history?' And, there is no consensus among historians on this issue. While the majority of Marxist historians seem to have concluded that there was at least an Indian variant of feudalism, it has been categorically asserted at least by a 'deviant' minority among them that there was no feudalism in Indian history (see Mukhia 1979). In the meantime, the majority of sociologists and social anthropologists were non-participant observers in these debates and still continued to highlight the importance of the caste system—both ideological and structural—to understand

[1] For a summary of the discussion see Thorner (1982: 1961–68, 1993–99, 2061–66).

Indian social reality but are rarely noticed by political economists and historians.[2] This acute division of labour,.splendid ignorance of and magnificent indifference to one another only defeated the primary aim of scholastic endeavour, namely, understanding social reality in its manifold ramifications.

I

Since our present concern is with political mobilization of agrarian classes, it is necessary for us to understand how far the mode of production debate is useful to identify agrarian classes in independent India. As the entire debate is about the nature and directionality of social transformation in India, let us begin by noting the problems it poses in relation to the different dimensions involved. In any discussion on social transformation three dimensions are to be recognized and dealt with: the point of departure, the process of displacement and the point of destination.

Much of the debate on mode of production in Indian agriculture centred around the point of departure and there is no agreement on the base from which change is taking place. The nature of mode of production in the pre-independent (particularly colonial) period is differentially perceived and described: feudal, semi-feudal, colonial, pre-capitalist, non-capitalist and finally the dual mode. This diversity in conceptualizing the point of departure predictably coloured the perception of participants in the debate in their conceptualization of agrarian classes in independent India, as and when it was attempted.

Further, the attributes of 'feudalism' or 'capitalism' varied enormously from one writer to another. For instance, while some would argue that tenancy is a feature of the feudal mode of production, it has been pointed out by others that (*a*) tenancy is not necessarily a characteristic of pre-capitalist relations usually referred to as semi-feudal (*b*) tenancy pre-dated and post-dated feudalism and coexisted with feudalism as well as capitalism (*c*) there is no sanction to associate tenancy with feudalism in the writings of

---

[2] Of course, one occasionally comes across some 'heretics' among Marxists who would concede the importance of Hindu social organization, caste system, Brahmanical ideology, etc. (see, for example, Rudra 1981: 2133-46). But even here only the importance of 'caste ideology' is recognized and there is no acknowledgement of the works by sociologists.

Marx or Lenin (see Chakraborty 1981: A5-14). To complicate matters, the prosperous capitalist farmers are reported to be leasing in land for cultivation in addition to the usually substantial land owned by them (see, for example, Jodha 1981: A118-28). Admittedly, the emergence of large farmers as tenants complicates not only the enactment and implementation of tenancy laws but also the mobilization of tenants against owners, insofar as the class composition of 'tenants' markedly differs. Similarly, while unfree labour is associated with feudalism, Nagesh (1981: A109-15) identifies 13 different types of unfree labour in India which may be arranged on a continuum of most-unfree to least-unfree labour. Admittedly, some types of unfree labour persist despite the development of agrarian capitalism, and it may not be correct to dismiss this phenomenon as a 'survival' which would disappear in course of time. This brings us to an important methodological issue which bedevils the entire social science research in India.

The underlying assumption in the debate on mode of production in Indian agriculture seems to be that, at best, semi-feudal or pre-capitalist elements are indicative of transitional aberrations and finally the 'new mode' will completely replace the old one. This assumption smacks of epistemological dualism and opposition, which does not seem to be true under Indian conditions. Even in Western societies the complete replacement of the traditional with the modern never occurred, as is usually believed. But the possibility existed given the crucial importance of epistemological dualism in Western thought which facilitated, if not accomplished, a win-or-lose, all-or-nothing transformation. In contrast, change in India has always been gradual, accretive, and reconciliatory in nature. Therefore, the displacement syndrome does not operate in Indian society as clearly and sharply. However, transformation implies a process of displacement and I am only calling attention to the style, strategy and process of displacement.

The process of transformation in Indian agriculture is discerned by the political economists mainly in terms of the development of agrarian capitalism in India. While there is enormous evidence that crystallization of capitalist relations of production in Indian agriculture is an important element in the on-going process of transformation, there are at least two other factors which critically mould this process: the state and political mobilization. It cannot be ignored that state-supported or sponsored capitalism is qualitatively different from free-market capitalism even if we concede that state intervention in India only reinforces and accelerates the process of capitalist development. At any rate, state intervention through the legislative weapon did play an important role in the transformative process taking place in India, although there could be honest differences of opinion with regard to the impact of these legislations.

Political mobilization of the agrarian classes on an all-India basis began during the freedom struggle, particularly by the early 20th century. And, this continues, even today although the spread and intensity of mobilization varies across regions, classes and time-periods. There is substantial evidence to suggest that the mobilization of rich farmers is accelerating the process of capitalist development in agriculture. On the other hand, the mobilization of the agrarian proletariat is moderating, if not halting, capitalist development in Indian agriculture.[3] Ignoring these aspects has substantially limited the scope of discussion and consequently the depth of understanding regarding the nature of agrarian classes.

Finally, the understanding of the participants in the mode of production debate regarding the point of destination was dictated by whether or not one is committed unequivocally or hesitatingly to the different phases of transformation. For those who believe that there is no escape from passing through the route of successive stages, the development of capitalism is an inevitable and of course logical one. Therefore, the immediate task is one of accelerating the process of capitalist development and agrarian classes are to be perceived and defined to suit this purpose. For those who reluctantly concede the possibility of 'skipping the stage', one need not wait for the maturing of capitalism and the inevitable contradictions ingrained within it, but collective actions could be planned and executed taking into account the specificities of the Indian situation, say, for instance, the caste system. For still others who define India as involved in the centre-periphery matrix as a peripheral capitalist country, the process of transformation is a global one.

[3] Let me just point out one example from my field study in Kerala. When the rich farmers in Aleppey district introduced tractors, the labour unions of agricultural workers successfully led their struggle against it so that the farmers had to agree that whether or not they used tractors, the land should be ploughed through bullocks/buffaloes at least for two rounds instead of the traditional three rounds in order that the labourers did not face further unemployment or suffer loss of wages. Predictably, tractorization has proceeded at a snail's pace in the district.

Logically, then, although it is not always explicitly stated or accepted, revolution is a project which should happen simultaneously on a global basis and there is no point in attempting a revolution even at the national level, let alone mobilization at local levels.

Notwithstanding the concern regarding the differential possibility of political mobilization, the role played by politics and political parties was hardly discussed. However, there is no gainsaying the fact that the role played by political parties impinges on social transformation not only in terms of the strategies of mobilization of agrarian classes, but also in terms of the performance and promises of political parties *vis-a-vis* the different agrarian classes.

Given such a state of affairs—the disagreement regarding the point of departure, ignoring the basic nature and factors involved in the process of displacement, confusion about the point of destination—one cannot draw much enlightenment from the discussion on the mode of production in Indian agriculture if one is interested in understanding the relationship between agrarian classes and political mobilization. And I may point out here that this is so in spite of the fact that most contributors to the debate are 'concerned scholars' and have a concern for working out praxiological implications of theoretical and conceptual formulations.

II

The revolutionary potentiality of the peasantry, an important dimension of our present concern, is a much discussed theme among historians, sociologists and social anthropologists. It has been argued with force by some that the middle peasantry is the most potent revolutionary force in peasant societies. Wolf, for instance, argues that subsequent to the penetration of capitalism the erstwhile rich peasants got differentiated into capitalist and tenant farmers. Those who experienced downward mobility refused to accept their subordinate role and provided the support for revolutionary peasant wars of the 20th century (see Wolf 1971, especially 278-82). Alavi (1973:56) arrives at the revolutionary potentiality of the middle peasantry through an analysis of agrarian social structure. He argues that peasant conflicts are organized on horizontal and vertical lines. Factional conflicts are intense among rich peasants and they mobilize their dependent tenants and agricultural labourers in support of them. In contrast to this, the 'independent' middle peasantry is not involved in vertical ties and middle peasants are bounded in intense kinship relations which acts as an insurance against the possible onslaught on them by rich peasants. The horizontal solidarity of the middle peasantry provides a conducive milieu for the development of class organizations and this explains their participation in revolutionary movements. It may be noted here that this is only an affirmation of Alavi's earlier position (1965:241-77) regarding the revolutionary potentiality of middle peasants. I have argued elsewhere that the 'middle peasant thesis' cannot be sustained either on logical or on empirical grounds (see Oommen 1985) and I will not repeat the argument here. However, it has recently been pointed out that the 'dominant peasantry' was the category which most actively participated in Indian 'peasant' movements and it is necessary to deal with this argument at some length.

After a careful analysis of the role of peasant classes in 20th century agrarian movements in India (1917-50), Pouchepadass (1980:136-55) notes that in most cases the movement developed on the basis of class collaboration. However, one can distinguish between three types of cases: first those movements, the majority, in which the initiative always came from the upper strata of the peasantry; second, a minority of cases in which the driving force came from the lower strata, and third, the two cases (Tebhaga and Telengana) in which the development of antagonism between the poor masses on the one hand and the rich peasantry and even part of the middle peasantry on the other, took place during the second phase. Pouchepadass (1980:141-2) asserts:

> In none of the three types of peasant mobilization did the middle peasantry play a separate role. In most of the movements, it acted in conjunction with the rich peasantry, but there were also cases in which at least some of its members followed the poor peasants when it was they who took the lead. In the other cases, the middle peasantry played no distinctive role. On no occasion did the middle category alone take the initiative in a movement.

The main thrust of the classical works in Marxian tradition by Engels, Lenin and Mao clearly unfolds that the middle peasantry is characterized by frayed edges, loose textures, ill-defined economic boundaries and political vascillations, in contrast to the proletariat on the one hand and rich peasants and landlords on the other. The middle peasantry is constituted by landowners or tenants or both; they cultivate their land with family or hired labour; they may be producers of surplus or indebted. 'The logical consequence of this heterogeneity is that the revolutionary potential of the middle peasantary is uncertain' (Pouchepadass 1980: 143). Having thus discarded the middle peasant thesis propounded by Alavi and Wolf and having considered the peculiarity and complexity of the Indian situation, Pouchepadass suggests that the category of middle peasant does not even correspond to living reality, let alone its revolutionary potentiality. In fact he warns that '.. the dogmatic use of this category in a social context to which it is ill-adapted tends to mask the true social composition of the movement under study' (ibid: 146)

Having demonstrated the impotence of the middle peasantry to act as a driving force, Pouchepadass suggests that the critical category in Indian peasant movements is the dominant peasantry, a notion initially used by Hardiman (1976: 365-71), although not elaborated by him. Pouchepadass identifies the dominant peasantry as:

> the oligarchy of rich and well-off peasants belonging to respectable castes who hold either as owners or as tenants the bulk of the land rights in each village.. a category which includes the whole group of peasants of respectable caste who hold enough land so that they can supply the needs of their families without having to go out for work for anyone else (1980: 147).

As a social force, the dominant peasantry, at the level of peasant movements is usually multi-caste but it may as well be a single caste. The mobilizing role of the dominant castes is facilitated by the fact that they are the power-wielding and exercising categories. Finally, the dominant peasantry is that group which the rural folk naturally consider as their chiefs.

Even if one accepts the description of the dominant peasantry as put forward by Pouchepadass as fairly accurate, there are serious difficulties in accepting his argument that this category is a driving force in peasant movements. But to begin, a comment on the concept itself. The very notion of dominant peasantry is scarcely different from that of dominant caste, except that the former category may occasionally be constituted by a multiplicity of castes in a given situation. If the crucial identity of the category is discerned in terms of caste it is confusing to refer to them as peasantry. For, caste, refers to an ascriptive/organic category whereas peasantry is an occupational/class category; it is an aggregation of individuals drawn from different castes; there is a qualitative difference in the character of consciousness of these categories. In a caste there can be landlords, rich peasants, poor peasants and agricultural labourers. The reference to a caste collectively encapsulates its entire membership; the peasantry, on the other hand, is drawn from *sections* of a multiplicity of castes. This is a crucial difference. Further, if the dominant peasantry is a category which 'hold enough land so that they can supply the needs of their families without having to go out for work for anyone else', it is simply an economically independent category. And this is precisely what the middle peasantry is: the only difference is that the dominant peasantry belongs to 'respectable' castes.

The dominant peasantry insofar as it is drawn from socially respectable castes, economically independent, and politically powerful, cannot be the driving force, as a collectivity, in a peasant movement. And this for several reasons. First, such a group has a vested interest in maintaining stability and *status quo* as they are not likely to gain anything by changing the system and in all probability they may lose some of their resources, power and status, if not wealth. Second, they are not likely to suffer from any serious deprivations as a social category and hence their involvement in movements is untenable. This is, however, not to deny that specific individuals from this group will not come forward to initiate movements if they are enlightened enough to challenge the *status quo*. Finally, insofar as the dominant peasantry is looked upon as the natural chiefs by the village folks, it cannot be the initiator of peasant movements. In fact, the dominant peasantry should be one of the targets of attack by the peasant movements as it is the repository of power and esteem in the rural context.

It is important to recall here that the evidence that Pouchepadass marshals to establish his argument—that (*a*) most of the peasant movements in India are characterized by class collaboration, and (*b*) the driving force in these peasant movements was the dominant peasantry—relates to the period 1917–50, the period during which the Indian national liberation movement was most vigorous.

His data and argument suffer from the fallacy of misplaced concreteness. The critical enemy during the colonial era was imperialism/colonialism, an external enemy. It is but logical that when the people in a society confront an external enemy they collaborate to fight against that enemy. Pouchepadass himself recognizes this fact when he notes that in the case of the two peasant movements inspired by Gandhi (Champaran and Bardoli) the enemy was exterior to the peasantry, the British. This was equally true in the case of peasant movements initiated by the *kisan sabhas*. Of course, it is true that the *kisan sabha* added another enemy to the list, the big *zamindar*. However, this does not mean that the external enemy ceases to exist or the fight against it is given up. That the peasant mobilization by the communists was an intense pro-national and an abject anti-colonial enterprise is borne out by the fact that Bhowani Sen, Secretary of the Bengal Committee of the CPI, appealed to the peasants who participated in the Tebhaga struggle not to launch direct action in 1947 so that the new government of independent India be given a chance to resolve the problems through legal instruments. In the case of Telengana, where the communists took a position which was against the prevailing national sentiment, they had to pay a heavy price. In the final analysis, then, the strategy of class collaboration was a natural corollary and a logical necessity of a peasant movement which operated as a tributary to the national liberation movement. The moment we recognize this it is easy to understand why the dominant peasantry could operate as a driving force in peasant movements during 1917–50. The critical variable here is not the attributes of the social category which initiated action, but the time at which it operated as a driving force, the nature of the enemy, and the purpose behind the mobilization.

Although Pouchepadass has not recognized the logical fallacy in his argument, the few empirical studies of peasant movements in independent India to which he refers clearly unfold this fallacy. The 'dominant peasantry' is no more involved in initiating peasant movements. In independent India peasant movements are organized on a clearer class basis and the poor peasants and agricultural labourers are the categories which are playing a leading role in these movements. The dominant peasantry, wherever it is involved, seems to be involved in counter mobilizational activities. This is so because the character of the enemy is different in the two phases: during the pre-independence phase the immediate and predominant enemy was external to the system, now the enemy is internal and within the system. Admittedly, the strategy of class collaboration, except within a narrow range and between proximate layers, has become redundant. The understanding and appreciation of this fact is of tremendous methodological significance in undertaking a programme of political mobilization of agrarian classes in India.

III

Having argued that neither the middle nor the dominant peasantry constitutes the most potent category to be mobilized into collective action, it is incumbent on us to identify the agrarian classes which are involved in political actions in independent India. As a prelude to this we need to identify (*a*) the agrarian classes, and (*b*) the strategy of mobilization pursued by political parties.

While the nature of agrarian classes of India is vigorously debated by several scholars, as we have already noted, and is likely to be an unending one, I follow a tentative categorization (see Oommen 1975c: 151-67). Regional variations apart, we can group agrarian classes under five major heads based on the ownership and control of land and management and work patterns on land. Admittedly these categories have distinct styles of life too, apart from their economic distinctiveness. The five agrarian classes can be described as follows:

1. **Landlords**: This category consists of those who live from rent and other exactions such as forced labour, who own but do not cultivate land. They may live either in the same village where they own land or may be absentee owners. Their style of life is 'feudal' in that they are a pleasure-seeking leisure class. Generally speaking, this is a shrinking category due to the introduction of agrarian legislations relating to abolition of absentee ownership, intermediaries, ceiling on landholdings and other reforms, and also due to the development of agrarian capitalism. They get the land cultivated through intermediaries such as sharecroppers. Most of them, if not all, are drawn from the traditionally privileged castes such as Brahmins and Rajputs.

2. **Rich farmers**: In one sense this category is a product of the Green Revolution in that it constitutes either rich peasants who are in the process of becoming 'farmers' or those who have taken to farming mainly to take advantage of the recently introduced state subsidies. However, they are not the real tillers of the land for they do not themselves work on the land, they only supervise agricultural operations and it is in this sense that they are cultivators. It is not uncommon that they lease in land for cultivation. I deliberately use the term 'farmers' in referring to them as they look upon agriculture as a business proposition and produce for market and for profit. They are capitalist farmers and are drawn from a variety of backgrounds, from retired military officers to the enterprising agricultural graduates. Their style of life approximates that of white collar employees, they are politically influential and economically well off. A majority of them are drawn from land-owning traditional castes such as Brahmins or Rajputs and the newly-educated of the peasant castes such as Jats, Ahirs, Reddis, Kammas and Nairs.

3. **Middle peasants**: The distinction between middle peasants and rich farmers is not based primarily on the difference in the size of their holdings, but on the fact that the former participate in the agricultural operations directly and hire labourers only for certain operations or at certain points in time. They are usually not educated and their style of life is rustic in the sense that it approximates the traditional rural pattern. Most of the middle peasants were erstwhile tenants and in one sense they are products of agrarian legislations which upheld the maxim, 'land for the tiller'. Although usually regarded as resisters of innovations, these peasants are shrewd men capable of making rational decisions provided they are convinced of the advantages of the new measures, and, of course, if they can afford them. Uneducated and unsophisticated, they usually lack the skills of dealing with the developmental bureaucracy. The caste background of the middle peasants is more or less the same as that of the rich farmers, except that the few land-owning backward and lower castes too fall into this category.

4. **Poor peasants**: These persons are mainly those who own uneconomic holdings and cultivate them by their own labour. Often their holdings are so small that they cannot make ends meet exclusively through the income derived from it and therefore also work as labourers for part of the time. They may also work as

sharecroppers or tenants of various types. These peasants find it difficult to secure the benefits available to them through the state because (*a*) these subsidies are monopolized by the first two categories, and (*b*) they lack the social skills and appropriate network to manipulate the bureaucracy. This category is drawn from almost all caste groups, although most of them may be from backward and Dalit castes.

5. **Landless agricultural labourers**: This category is constituted by those who do not own land; if they did, it is not more than *abadi* land on which their huts are situated. Their sole source of income is their labour and hence they are dependent on others—the first three categories—for their livelihood. The majority of these labourers belong to Dalit castes who occupy the lowest ritual status in the traditional caste hierarchy. The poor peasants and landless labourers qualify to be labelled as the agrarian proletariat.

What was referred to as peasant movements during the pre-independence phase was mainly the mobilization of agrarian categories against the British, though of course it was necessary to take up the issues relevant to peasants to get their involvement. At that point in time the primary enemy was the colonial master and the secondary enemy was its Indian agents, the feudal chieftains and landlords. After independence, what is labelled as peasant movements is largely the mobilizations of rural categories through the agrarian front-organizations sponsored by different political parties; although of course a few farmers' organizations have emerged latterly. Which specific agrarian category or categories a particular political party mobilizes into collective action is not simply a matter of its ideological orientation, but as much reflective of the political pay-offs it expects from such activities. We squarely recognize this vertical relationship between the national liberation movement and peasant mobilization during the pre-independence phase, and between political parties and peasant movements in independent India, which is of utmost importa' in understanding the true character of agrarian mobilization in India.

It has been frequently argued that the nationalist and left leadership ignored the internal differentiation among the peasantry and treated them as a homogenous class (see, for example, Bipan Chandra 1979). While most of them might have found it expedient to observe silence on the issue during pre-independence days, there were a few who did squarely recognize the heterogeneity of the peasantry and put forward cogent arguments of why it was necessary to avoid conflicts among them at any cost. For instance, Acharya Narendra Dev, the socialist theoretician wrote: 'The peasantry is not a homogeneous class. It has many class divisons among itself, whose interests are sometime conflicting. Our task *today* is to carry the whole peasantry with us' (1946:46). He recognized that there are basically three categories in the agrarian population: the landlords, peasants and the rural proletariat, and argued for the collaboration between the latter two against the land-lords. And the rationale behind this collaboration was informed of robust pragmatism and an astute strategy rather than ignorance of the internal differentiation of the peasantry. He made it clear that:

> If romantic conceptions were to shape our resolves and prompt our actions, we would aspire to organize first, the agricultural labourer and the semi-proletariat of the village, the most oppressed and exploited rural class which suffers the worst degree of eco-nomic and social bondage. Our conception of justice certainly prompts us to save first the interests of those who suffer most, but if we do so, we shall certainly be neglecting the huge exploited masses, consisting of small and middle peasants and the small land owners with small incomes who are no better than small peasants. The peasants in the mass would, in that case, remain aloof from the anti-imperialist struggle and we shall thus lose a much more valuable ally than the village poor (1946: 46).

But what is indefensible is the continuance of the same strategy even after independence; a strategy which ignored the specific problems of the different agrarian categories for sheer political expediency. And this is true not only of the 'liberal' congress Party but also of the 'revolutionary' Communist Party. I will only cite two instances here to illustrate the point. Pandit Jawaharlal Nehru who led the Congress Party and headed the Congress government for a long time said in one of his speeches at the Nagpur Congress Session in 1959, that 'though the imposition of ceilings would affect only an infinite small minority of landlords, and though its actual, practical gains would not be much, the *sentimental gains would be tremendous*' (emphasis added). The sentimental gains referred to here are the political advantages for the Congress Party in taking a pro-peasant posture. Thus, although the AICC Agrarian Relations Committee endorsed the maxim 'land to the tiller' as early as 1935, no concerted attempt to translate this principle into practice was made even after independence because its 'practical value' was considered to be negligible. At the same time, the need to put forward promises favouring the agrarian poor was recognized as politically expedient.

Broadly speaking, the communist parties of India were and still are in the forefront of mobilization of peasants. And yet, Indian communists rarely accorded sufficient weight to the poor peasants and landless in their organizational strategy and revolutionary mobilization. The CPI aims to establish proletarian dictatorship with the peasantry and rural poor wielding a major chunk of power under Indian conditions, if and when the party comes to power. Hence, peasant movements initiated by the party should be viewed as an instrument to achieve this goal. But even this argument does not hold as in 1958 the CPI adopted a programme of peaceful transition to socialism. Further, in 1961 the party propounded the concept of national democracy as the instrument of pursuing the non-capitalist path of development. While the capitalist class is the mainstay of 'bourgeoisie democracy' and the leadership of the working class decisive in the case of 'people's democracy', 'national democracy' is based on a class alliance; in it the proletariat shares power with the national bourgeoisie. If this is the goal, it is obvious that peasant movements have been used even by the communists as a mechanism of capturing political power, which would ultimately go in favour of the national bourgeoisie.

After the split of the CPI in 1964, the Communist Party of India (Marxist) was in the forefront of 'peasant' mobilizations. And yet it is not true that the agrarian proletariat was the main target of mobilization even for the CPI(M). This is evident in a statement made by A.K. Gopalan who was one of the top CPI(M) leaders spearheading the agrarian movement: 'We have to make them [the landless labourers] the hub of our activities. Reluctance to take up their specific demands, *fearing that this will drive the rich and middle peasants away from us, will have to be given up*' (Gopalan 1968: 5) (emphasis added). Needless to say political calculations weighed heavily even in the case of the CPI(M), a party which continuously declares its commitment to the agrarian poor in not mobilizing the real rural proletariat into collective actions. And this indeed was a continuation of the policy enunciated by the CPI, the parent party of the CPI(M).

IV

The question that has frequently been posed by analysts of Indian social reality is, what is the primary reality in India: caste or class? Consequently, one finds the answer one seeks depending upon one's value assumptions and methodological preferences. I suggest that the question is wrongly posed and at any rate to understand the nature of participants in agrarian mobilizations we must recognize that three identities are simultaneously salient: primordial ascriptive (caste, religion, linguistic, etc.), class/occupational, and polticial/ideological. The frequent tendency to ignore this multiple identity of participants and to emphasize any one or another of the identities has cluttered our understanding of the real character of social movements as I have argued in Chapter 1. Insofar as the participants in an agrarian movement are drawn from a multiplicity of castes and identified with different political groups even when they belong to the same class category, it will not be possible to mobilize all of them into class actions. The sources of their deprivations vary and consequently their perceptions of enemies and styles of protest.[4]

Agrarian movements in India are not simple and straightforward mobilizations of specific agrarian categories possessing certain class/occupational attributes. The class confrontations that take place in India are often conflicts between caste/religious collectivities which share certain class attributes; insofar as the congruity between caste and class is not uniform, class actions often break down in concrete situations. One of the problems that a social analyst of empirical realities often faces is the ordering of his data in a meaningful fashion; to see some pattern in the wide variety of facts he observes. And, he often resorts to typification of the phenomenon studied as a preliminary step. While a typology can provide

---

[4] I have argued in Chapter 9 that the Dalits of India were and still are deprived on three counts: cultural oppression, political repression and economical exploitation. There seems to be a hierarchy of deprivations in their cognitive map and it is no accident that the earliest mobilizations by Dalits were collective caste actions to fight untouchability followed by the demand for political rights, currently graduating on to class actions.

an all-embracing framework to fit the varieties of data collected or available, it should not ignore significant dimensions. Here the effort is to understand the phenomenon of political mobilization of agrarian classes and to that extent the crucial factors to be utilized for typology building are the class/occupational structures of rural India and the awareness based on deprivations stemming from this objective fact—consciousness. But for a population which is enveloped in age-old social and cultural repression (through the caste system), it is impossible to cognize their existential conditions exclusively in class/occupational terms. This is the reason why many of the agrarian movements in India are also caste/communal mobilizations.

Broadly speaking, agrarian classes in India have been analyzed from two perspectives: those who took a macro-perspective, looking at it from above, and those who pursued a micro-perspective, viewing it from below. The analysts employing the grand evolutionary schemas propounded in the Marxian tradition buttress it with aggregate data analysis and speak of the movement from the feudal to capitalistic to socialistic agrarian relations (in future). Here the equivalent identities are those of peasant/feudal lord, proletariat/capitalist farmer and free worker. The lack of fit between this schema and the empirical realities on the ground has often prompted those who undertook field studies to propose native categories of agrarian class structure. One of the earliest to propose such a conceptual scheme was Daniel Thorner who referred to *malik, kisan* and *mazdoor,* based on his observations in Uttar Pradesh. A large number of analysts have since invoked native categories to describe the agrarian class situation in different parts of India.

However, there are several difficulties in adopting these native categories. First, given the size and diversity of India there will be too many native categories and these would vary not only from state to state but even between adjacent districts. For an analysis even at a regional level, not to speak of an all-India level, therefore, these categories become dysfunctional. Second, the data is usually available based on administrative (state) and revenue (district, *taluka,* etc.) units and the native categories are essentially folk conceptions rooted in cultural regions. This lack of isomorphism between the conceptual categories and the accepted spatial units for administration and development creates difficulties in their application and limits their usefulness. Third, while these categories are useful in describing the agrarian world-view of the people, they do not illumine us as to why they hold it and how they come to formulate it. Finally, the native categories cannot cope with the substantial rural social transformation taking place in contemporary India. To illustrate, in Kerala, a state characterized by substantial change in agrarian relations, the erstwhile *jenmie* ('feudal' lord) has been replaced by capitalist farmers; the former tenants (*kanakkaran*) and sharecroppers (*vethakkaran*) have been replaced by owner-cultivators and the traditional attached labourers (*adiyans*), have been replaced by agricultural workers. The new 'native categories' in use are indicative of the changes in agrarian relations which do not seem to be specifically 'native', but share a much wider context. This increasing 'standardization' of agrarian relations therefore not only demystifies the native categories but makes macro-analysis more plausible. However, the problematic of the categories such as feudal, capitalistic, etc., is that they are essentially one-dimensional and ill-suited to comprehend the Indian agrarian social structure, particularly because the issues of identity and mobilization of participants are crucial while considering the relationship between agrarian classes and political mobilization.

As I have noted earlier in the context of Indian agrarian movements, three identities coexist and interpenetrate: status (caste), class (economic and occupational) and ideological (party/political). But there is no one-to-one correlation between these which renders the empirical reality extremely complex. Conceding the inevitable risk involved in attempting a 'neat' classification of such a complex phenomenon, I propose to chart out below the interpenetration between these three identities. This is necessary to answer the question *who participates in what kinds* of agrarian movements.

Notwithstanding the multitude of *jatis* and their regional variations in India, we can speak of three major caste groupings based on their traditional status: the twice-born varna categories (the high castes); the traditional peasant castes, the Shudras who occupied the ritual status above the pollution line (middle castes); and the ex-Untouchables, those who suffered from social stigma and degradation in the worst form (the low castes). Similarly, in spite of the overlap between the class-jural categories (e.g.. the landlord is also a tenant; the small owner- cultivator may also be a labourer), we can speak of three basic agrarian categories in India today;

landlords/capitalist farmers, peasants/owner-cultivators and agricultural labourers.[5] Finally, the multiplicity of political parties
apart, and in spite of the imprecision involved, we can speak of
three types of political parties based on their ideological orientations:
rightist,[6] centrist and leftist. While the central identity of participants in the context of agrarian movements is certainly their
class/occupational identity, the empirical situation in India
prompts us to consider the other two—status and party—identities
as well : the substantial congruence between caste and class and
the fact that most agrarian movements in India are nothing but
mobilizations sponsored by political parties through their agrarian
front-organizations lends empirical credibility to such an endeavour.

As there are three basic identities and there are three sub-
categories in each of these, we can logically work out 27 different
combinations. But our purpose is not to undertake a logically rigorous exercise in itself (which may be empirically meaningless) but
to identify empirically plausible categories informed of logical
rigour. These categories under conditions prevalent in contemporary India, particularly in those areas characterized by political
unionization of agrarian categories, are eight as shown in Table 8.1.

Those who tend to analyze agrarian classes invoking the notions
of dominant caste or dominant peasantry ignore the incongruity
between caste and class and merge the categories of 1, and 2; 3, 4
and 5; and 6, 7 and 8. They ignore not only the class element but
also the ideological identity of movement participants which renders
their categorization irrelevant for the analysis of collective mobilizations. In contrast, those who pursue 'class analysis' based on
aggregate data merge the categories of 1, 3 and 6; 2, 4 and 7; and 5
and 8. In this they assume class-caste congruity and possibility of
class-ideology incongruity. It is certainly important to recognize
the centrality of class identity of participants in agrarian mobilizations. But the fact that they are likely to be drawn from different
caste categories which would influence the chances of their universal

[5] It may be noted here that there is no basic variation between the five-fold agrarian classes we have postulated above and the present three-fold agrarian categories.
The first two agrarian classes (landlords and rich farmers) are owner non-cultivators,
the third category (middle peasants) are owner-cultivators and the fourth and fifth
categories (small peasants and agricultural workers) are non-owning cultivators.

[6] The rightist political parties include not only the existing ones but also some of
the erstwhile parties such as Swatantra, Congress(O), Bharatiya Lok Dal, etc.

Table 8.1

Identities of Agrarian Categories and the Types of Mobilizations

Category	Status Identity	Class Identity	Ideological Identity	Size of Actual or Potential Participants	Issues	Type of Mobilization
1.	Low caste	Proletariat	Leftist	Substantial	Land to the tiller, better working conditions	Radical
2.	Low caste	Middle peasants	Leftist/ Centrist	A few	Better subsidies, better prices	Reformist
3.	Middle caste	Proletariat	Leftist	Substantial	Land to the tiller, better working conditions	Radical
4.	Middle caste	Middle peasant	Leftist/ Centrist	Substantial	Better subsidies, better prices	Radical
5.	Middle caste	Landlord/ rich farmer	Rightist/ Centrist	A few, but likely to be supported by middle peasantry	Better subsidies, better prices, low wages for labour.	Reformist for self; conservative for workers
6.	High caste	Proletariat	Leftist	A handful	Land to the tiller, better working conditions	Radical
7.	High caste	Middle peasant	Leftist/ Centrist	Substantial	Better subsidies, better prices	Reformist
8.	High caste	Landlord/ rich farmer	Rightist	Substantial	Better subsidies, better prices, low wages for labour.	Reformist or self-conservative for workers

mobilization (as their cognitive maps and perceptions are shaped by their deprivations and life-styles) should be squarely recognized by an analyst who does not want to sacrifice and mutilate facts for the elegance of his theory. Those who opt for the elegance of theory tear up the total man into pieces, reducing him to a statistical entity, devoid of human qualities.

It is important to note that of the three identities the status identity is the most universal in rural India in that nobody can escape this; one is born into one or another of the castes or religions and the consciousness anchored on this ascriptive status crystallizes almost naturally. But those who are born into a caste or religion differ in terms of their material possessions, inherited or acquired. This fission within the caste coexists with the possibility of fusion with others drawn from other castes but sharing the same material base. But those who share these attributes remain a mere statistical entity (class-in-itself). In order that they should become a class (class-for-itself) they should be endowed with class consciousness. Again, all those who share the same material base do not necessarily develop this class consciousness, not even a trade-union or interest-group consciousness believed to be appropriate to their category. Therefore, only those who share the same material base and share consciousness appropriate to it become participants in mobilization. Thus, movement participants are necessarily much smaller in number and size as compared with those who share common attributes and hence could be potential participants or sympathizers of the movements.

Finally, as is evident from Table 8.1, the fact that the agrarian population is differentiated in terms of class and ideology points to the possibility of different types of mobilizations. Basically, these are movements of and by the agrarian proletariat, peasants and capitalist farmers, with specific interests and goals. Those who speak of 'peasant movements' invariably ignore the mobilizations by capitalist farmers and club together the mobilizations of peasants and proletariat, as if they belong to a blanket category. This does gross violence to the empirical reality. In contrast to this, not only should we recognize different types of agrarian movements, but the possiblity of the same agrarian category getting politically divided and organized under the auspices of different political parties or ideological groups.

V

In conclusion let me identify the major patterns of mobilization in the case of agrarian classes in independent India. To begin with, it may be noted that the issues have drastically changed over a period of time. The slogan 'land to the tiller' is scarcely heard now; it is widely believed that there exists hardly any possiblity of acquiring excess land from landlords to be distributed to the landless. The anti-tenancy mobilization has practically stopped, although tenancy exists—oral and hidden. More importantly, tenancy took a new pattern; it is no more the poor peasant alone who leased in land for eking out an existence but also the rich capitalist farmer. This diffuse class base of 'tenants' makes any mobilization against tenancy, a near impossibility. While 'intermediaries' in agriculture, that is, superior tenants who leased out land to peasants, have disappeared as a result of agrarian movements and land reforms, sharecropping continues based on oral lease. And the efforts of even left governments have not been hitherto successful in eradicating this exploitative practice.[7] In spite of this there is hardly any evidence of anti-sharecropping mobilizations being crystallized.

Perhaps the basic problem here can be traced to the conceptualization of 'peasantry' in India (including that of left parties), which was, and still is, anti-feudalist and pro-capitalist. A peasant was defined as a person who 'cultivated' land directly and in the Indian context this invariably meant supervising farm operations. The real tillers of land constituted mainly by Dalit castes were not tenants or sharecroppers. Consequently, the ex-tenants drawn mainly from middle castes who actually supervised farm operations secured land in the wake of land reforms and the actual tillers of the land continue to be mere labourers. In the meantime, the availability of state subsidies and the manner in which it was administered facilitated the emergence of a class of capitalist farmers.

Given the above situation we can identify three major agrarian classes participating in the mobilizational process. For brevity the details are presented in table 8.2 in summary form. I must add a few clarifications. First, the landlords as a category do not organize themselves into collective actions. This is so for two reasons: (*a*) no

---

[7] For the ineffectiveness of the programme, 'Operation Bargha' initiated by the West Bengal government, see the despatches of 'correspondents' published in *Economic and Political Weekly* during 1980-82.

Table 8.2

Agrarian Classes and Political Mobilization in India

Category	Identities	Mobilizers	Main issues	Chief enemies
I	Proletariat, drawn mainly from Dalits, Adivasis and Backward Castes	Political parties such as CPI, CPI(M) CPI(ML) and radical voluntary organizations.	Higher wages, better working conditions, political rights, cultural oppression	Landlords and rich farmers, drawn from rich and middle castes, and politically rightists; the bureaucracy and the police.
II	Middle peasantry, drawn mainly from middle and upper castes	Parties such as CPI, CPI(M), Congress (R), Lok Dal, etc.	Higher Prices for agricultural products, subsidized agricultural inputs	The rich farmers/ landlords (as they corner much of the subsidized inputs); petty revenue and developmental bureaucracy.
III	Rich farmers, drawn mainly from upper and middle castes	Parties such as Congress (R), Lok Dal; politically, 'independent' organizations such as Punjab Zamindari Union, Tamilnadu Agriculturists Association, Shetkari Sanghatana in Maharashtra, etc. However, left parties such as CPI and CPI(M) also extend limited support.	Higher prices, subsidized inputs; disciplining of wage labourers and if possible reduction of wages, etc.	The state, agrarian proletariat, industrial-urban India.

political party or voluntary organization seems to be willing to support them openly, and (*b*) given their small proportion in the population, any effort by them at mobilization is not likely to have much impact. However, this does not mean that the landlords do not indulge in oppression of the agrarian poc.. any more. This they do with the aid of locally hired toughs and dacoits to harass the poor peasantry and agrarian proletariat. Additionally, they also secure the 'cooperation and help' of the police, developmental and revenue bureaucracy.[8]

Second, while the agrarian proletariat and middle peasantry are mobilized into collective actions mainly by political parties, in the case of rich farmers a few independent organizations have emerged in those states where capitalist development in agriculture has been strong and visible, such as Punjab, Haryana, Maharashtra, Tamil Nadu and Karnataka. The main plank of these organizations is the disparity and unequal exchange between rural and urban India.[9]

Third, the schizophrenic attitude of left parties such as the CPI and CPI(M) is evident from the fact that they support the mobilization of not only the agrarian proletariat and middle peasantry but also the capitalist farmers. This in effect is a continuation of their old policy of class collaboration and indicative of pro-capitalist conceptualization of the peasantry, to which I have referred earlier.

Fourth, the agrarian category which suffers from multiple deprivations is the proletariat drawn mainly from Dalits, Adivasis and Backward Castes. While economic deprivation anchored in their class status is an important element in their mobilization, unless their political and cultural deprivations too are attended to simultaneously, it is unlikely that they will repose confidence in left political parties. That the erosion of confidence is taking place is already indicated by the emergence of several exclusive Dalit militant organizations. This poses a genuine dilemma with regard to what should be the axis around which mobilization should be attempted caste or class. But one thing seems to be clear: if the Dalits are to be involved in class actions, a cultural revolt is a prerequisite.

[8] The harassment of the agrarian poor by landlords is more prevalent in certain areas such as Bihar. For details, see the despatch from correspondents in *Economic and Political Weekly*, especially from 1976 to 1982.

[9] The archetype of this variety of farmers' association is the Shetkari Sanghatana led by Sharad Joshi in rural Maharashtra. For an understanding of its ideology and style of operation, see Omvedt (1981b: 1937-41).

9

Sources of Deprivation and Styles of Protest: The Case of the Dalits

I

While I have no intention of attempting an elaborate conceptual clarification, it is necessary to briefly specify the frame of reference of this chapter. In India, more than 50 per cent of the population lives below the poverty line, even by the official criteria of classification. On the other hand, nearly 22 per cent of the people are 'Scheduled' by the government (15 per cent Scheduled Castes and 7 per cent Scheduled Tribes), recognizing their traditional socio-cultural and economic disabilities. The continuation of economic exploitation and socio-cultural oppresssion have rendered them politically voiceless, although a handful of individuals from among them have recently experienced upward mobility. That is, notwith-standing the fact that the vast majority of India's population is underprivileged, viewed against the background of the contemporary world situation—levels of economic development, political partici-pation and socio-cultural involvement—there is a sub-stratum of the Indian population which is subjected to *cumulative domination* by the rest of the population in the country. When I refer to the Dalits in India, I have in mind this segment of the Indian popula-tion. But it is important to keep in mind that even they constitute a vast body of a hundred million people distributed into nearly 400 different *jatis* drawn from different parts of India.

Several terms—Exterior Castes, Outcastes, Depressed Classes, Scheduled Castes, Harijans, Ex-Untouchables—have been invoked by the clean castes, officials or social reformers to refer to this social category. However, the victims prefer to describe themselves as Dalits (the oppressed) which encapsulates all aspects of oppres-sion. Hence, I too refer to them as the Dalits.

Although the Scheduled Tribes in India are underprivileged both economically and politically, given their physical isolation they were not in constant social interaction with the dominant clean-caste Hindus. Further, being non-Hindus, they were not subjected to the ideological hegemony of the Hindu caste system and they were invariably outside the pale of purity-pollution, unless of course they got socially absorbed into the Hindu-fold. Therefore, the Scheduled Tribes were not subjected to cumulative domination as in the case of the Dalits. One also recognizes the existence of an extremely small sub-stratum of the economically well-off and politically privileged (but not entirely emancipated from socio-cultural oppression) among the Scheduled Castes. But when we refer to the Dalits, this section of the 'Harijan bourgeoisie' is left out. Similarly, we are aware that a substantial proportion of caste Hindus or non-Hindus, who are converts from clean castes, are also economically poor and politically powerless, but they do not suffer from socio-cultural oppression. However, these categories too are not subjected to cumulative domination and hence this analysis excludes them as well.

It is clear, then, that the sources of deprivation of the Dalits of India were (and still are) three: low ritual status, appalling poverty, and powerlessness. Understandably, the responses of the victims were organically linked to the sources of deprivation. But to understand this linkage, one should be clear about the identity of the population under reference. This is presented in Table 9.1.

Table 9.1

Types of Identity and Styles of Mobilization: The Dalits

Sources of Deprivation	Types of Identities	Nature of Oppression	Patterns of Mobilization
Degrading ritual status	Untouchable	Socio-cultural repression	Social reform movements for social equality
Powerlessness	Subject	Political disenfranchisement	Mobilization for political participation
Poverty	Slave	Economic exploitation	Bargaining for the betterment of economic condition

The problematic of analysis in this context arises mainly from the one-sided and ambiguous understanding of the identity of the collectivity involved. Broadly, two strands of thinking are

identifiable: (*a*) Those who concentrate on i   ... ... identity of
the Dalits and view them as erstwhile agres... slaves who became
proletarians due to the development of capitalism. Pursuantly, it is
argued that the current consciousness of the Dalits is proletarian
consciousness and their confrontations with the privileged sections
is a class struggle. (*b*) Those who focus on the caste identity of the
Dalits and suggest thät they strive essentially for social equality
and their present consciousness is basically caste consciousness,
which is buttressed by the policy of protective discrimination pursued
by the state. Concomitantly, it is suggested that the Dalit-upper
caste confrontations are essentially caste conflicts. But the advocates
of both these positions ignore that, first, all Dalits are not 'proletarians' and at least a small sub-stratum among the traditionally
underprivileged have undergone a process of embourgeoisement;
and, second, the Dalit consciousness is qualitatively different from
the proletarian or caste consciousness. If proletarian consciousness
is essentially rooted in material deprivations and caste consciousness is mainly anchored on status deprivations, Dalit consciousness
is a complex and compound consciousness which encapsulates
deprivations stemming from inhuman conditions of material existence, powerlessness and ideological hegemony. Notwithstanding
the compound character of Dalit consciousness there existed, and
continues to exist even today, a hierarchy of deprivations in the
consciousness of the Dalits. This is manifested in the nature of
responses articulated by them in the last couple of centuries.

It is logical to expect that a collectivity subjected to multiple
deprivations will protest first against those disabilities which it
perceives to be the most inhuman and unbearable. And, once
protest is perceived as a viable mechanism to deal with deprivation,
the importance of political freedom becomes self-evident. But
an important prerequisite to any sustained struggle is economic
resources of those who participate in protests. Therefore, it is no
accident that Dalit protests in India first crystallized against
socio-cultural oppression, particularly Untouchability. This was
followed by mobilization for political enfranchisement. Finally,
protests against economic exploitation gradually emerged. While it
is my contention that the sequential manifestation of these protests
is organically linked to the hierarchy of deprivations as perceived
by the Dalits, I must hasten to add two clarifications. First, it is not
suggested here that each of these protests has had an uninterrupted

life-cycle and replaced one another successively. The temporal sequence refers only to their initial emergence; more often than not they coexisted after initial appearance. Second, the possibility of a particular protest, encapsulating within it all aspects (ritual, political, economic) simultaneously, is not ruled out. In all probability, this is an empirical plausibility, particularly during the later phase.

A conceptual caveat may be in order before we proceed further. This relates to the notions of social change and social development. The notion of social change, whether it is positional or structural, assumes a point of departure, a point of destination and a process of replacement, occurring between these points. The concept of social change is neutral to the direction of destination; it is a value-free concept. In contrast, social development is a value-loaded concept.

...social development occurs when the process of replacement is taking place in a *specific* direction, when the point of destination is a *desired* and a *desirable* one... social development is that type of social change taking place through the active participation and conscious volition of the people, geared mainly to the welfare of the disadvantaged, dispossessed and disinherited, the chief target of development being the Wretched of the Earth (Oommen 1980: 7-8).

The above conceptual distinction is of signal importance to the discussion that follows. An examination of the available evidence suggests that the Dalits have made some advance in three contexts— partial emancipation from ritual degradation, acquisition of limited political clout and some improvement in economic condition. And yet no significant social transformation has been achieved in any of these contexts. It is our contention that this is because no authentic social development of the Dalits had taken place as their participation in bringing about change was extremely limited. The Dalits were relegated to the receiving end; their participatory potential has been scarcely tapped.

II

The initial protest movements of India, starting with the Buddhist revolt of the 6th century BC, were all geared to question the central

ideology of the concept of purity and pollution and Brahminic
supremacy. Our present concern is with the protests of more recent
times, which are essentially of three types: (*a*) *bhakti* movements
which attempted to purify Hinduism (in the 12th to 18th centuries)
of its evils and fought against the tyranny of the caste system but
subsequently crystallized as essentially Hindu sects; (*b*) movements
oriented to a reinterpretation of the doctrines of Hinduism so as to
cleanse it of its evil accretions and render it back to the original
pristine purity—notably the neo-vedantic movements; (*c*) movements which rejected Hinduism and led to the adoption of other
faiths, i.e., conversion movements.

The *bhakti* movements were charismatic in that their rise and
fall was roughly coterminous with the saints who initiated them—
Kabir, Ramanand and Raidas in the north, Chaitanya in the east,
Narsinh Mehta and Tukaram in the west and Ramanuja and Basava
in south India. As I have argued elsewhere, charismatic movements
may initiate a process of change but the internal contradictions
they develop render them incapable in sustaining this process and
not infrequently they become agents of system stability (See Oommen
1972a). Apart from this, all the *bhakti* movements shared the following characteristics. First, they were 'reformist' in that they only
attempted to correct some of the evils of Hinduism, particularly
the practice of Untouchability, without questioning the caste system.
Second, they were all initiated by caste Hindus and/or 'admitted'
clean-caste Hindus also into the movement fold. This eventually
led to the inevitable dominance of the priestly class, the Brahmins,
against whose orthodoxy the protests were initiated. Third, once
castes with differing ritual rank came to be associated with the
movements, the participants developed a dual identity: a religious-
ideological identity with fellow movement participants and a socio-
cultural identity with social collectivities (castes) to which they
traced their origin. The latter gained primacy in its day-to-day
interactions and transactions and finally the caste system got rep-
licated in the new sects and each caste group within the movement
was socially reabsorbed into the original groups. Fourth, none of
the *bhakti* movements had a programme of socio-economic uplift,
but confined its attention to the ideational realm. In the final
analysis, although *bhakti* movements became popular among the
Dalits, insofar as they did not change their socio-economic status,
the equality professed by them remained a mirage.

By the middle of the 19th century a new trend of protest was begun by Vivekananda and Dayananda Saraswati and later by Gandhi. Their movements may be designated as neo-vedantic movements (Shah 1980: 3-4). The kernel of this movement was the dissociation of the practice of Untouchability from Hinduism, the argument being that there was no scriptural sanction for this abominable practice. However, the neo-vedantists upheld the varna scheme as an occupational division of society and *varnashrama dharma* as an essential prerequisite for the preservation of harmony in society and purity of the soul. This doctrinaire unity of Hindu religion was sought to be extended to social life by the campaigning for temple entry of the Dalits and commensality or intermarriage with them. Secular sources of change, such as legislation, education, and improvement of material conditions were pressed into service for the welfare of the Dalits. However, both the *bhakti* and neo-vedantic movements were protests from *within* initiated by the caste Hindus. At best they brought about minor changes, helping the Dalits to make some adaptations and caste Hindus some concessions.

Against these adaptive movements came conversions to other religions which were essentially movements of disengagement from Hinduism. Essentially, conversion is a personal spiritual experience, but given the overarching hierarchical rigidity of the Hindu caste system and the absence of personal autonomy, it was collectivities—family and kin, *jatis,* an entire village population—which converted. This often meant a change in the life-style, customs and manners of the groups which embraced the new religion. This may be more appropriately called proselytization. Proselytization in India was started by Muslims during the medieval period, and later during the British period by Christians. Although a handful of twice-born aristocratic Hindus did convert to these religions, a vast majority of the converts were Dalits. Later the Dalits converted to Sikhism and Buddhism. Although the new religions embraced by the Dalits professed equality and brotherhood of men, the variations in the antecedents of converts persisted insofar as they were drawn from castes with different status: the converted Dalits came to be known as neo-Christians, neo-Buddhists, etc. (see Alexander 1972; Wilkinson and Thomas 1972). Thus the omnipresent caste system penetrated into new religions, whether they were indigenous off-shoots of Hinduism (e.g., Sikhism, Buddhism), or alien religions of conquerors or colonial rulers such as Islam and Christianity (see Oddie 1977b). However, conversion to Buddhism was qualitatively different in that it was more or less a conscious choice by the Dalits.

In spite of the fact that the *bhakti* and neo-vedantic movements were adaptive in their orientation to Hinduism, and proselytization was oriented to disengagement from Hinduism, they shared one thing in common: these movements were initiated by 'outsiders,' that is non-Dalits, caste Hindus in the first case and foreign and native missionaries in the latter instance, with the exception of conversion to Buddhism. The Dalits were not the initiators of change, they were at the receiving end. Even if some changes did occur due to the above protest movements, it could not have brought about social development of the collectivity concerned.

It is against this background that we should view the Dalit movements which emerged and spread by the turn of the 19th century. The critical difference between the erstwhile movements—*bhakti*, neo-vedantic and proselytization movements—and the new Dalit movements was that the latter were initiated by the Dalits themselves.

The oppressive as well as elastic character of the caste system and the failure of even proselytization movements to emancipate the lower castes, seem to have prompted many Dalit groups to improve their status through Sanskritization. Although the usual tendency is to view Sanskritization as a cultural process aimed at bringing about changes in the styles of life of Dalits, it had important structural ramifications in that protest orientation and counter-mobilization were necessary attributes of Sanskritizing movements (see Ahmad 1971: 164-91; Rao 1977: 60), as the Dalits often did so in a spirit of recalcitrance and the upper castes invariably opposed such attempts.

The central tendency in Hindu society was that the *jatis* in the twice-born varnas were the value-givers, norm-setters and institution-builders and others followed them. For once the Dalits provided the lead through the formation of their caste associations, which became the base for gaining self-respect and challenging upper caste authority. Two sub-types of these Dalit movements based on two factors can be identified: the resource base of the *jatis* (population size, the presence of at least a small section which was economically independent) and the consequences of the movement. First, those who had a favourable resource base and succeeded in crossing the pollution line ceased to be Untouchables. The Ezhavas of

Kerala and the Nadars of Tamil Nadu are classic cases of this type (Aiyappan 1965; Hardgrave 1969). Second, those who had a relatively weaker resource base (as compared with the first group) and did not succeed in crossing the pollution line in spite of a vigorous protest movement among them. This type is exemplified by the Mahars of Maharashtra and the Chamars of Uttar Pradesh (see Lynch 1969; Patwardhan 1973). Faced with such a predicament, the latter group preferred to opt out of the Hindu fold, as Ambedkar and his followers did by embracing Buddhism. But even then they may not be entirely successful in shaking off the shackles of Untouchability, to escape the label of 'Scheduled Castes' (see Fiske 1972: 127). Given such a situation they may attempt to build a parallel cultural system and refuse to get absorbed in the mainstream of Hinduism through upward mobility or build a counter culture to Hinduism through conversion. This is evidenced by the emergence of the Dalit Panther movement in Maharashtra which is gradually spreading to other parts of the country.

It is clear from our analysis that, unlike the earlier movements initiated by outsiders, the movements in which the Dalits participated consciously and voluntarily brought about a sea-change in their socio-cultural identity and self-definition. While some of them (like the Ezhavas of Kerala and the Nadars of Tamil Nadu) succeeded in emancipating themselves from the inhuman practice of Untouchability, others (like the Mahars of Maharashtra or Chamars of Uttar Pradesh), though not similarly successful, gained a new sense of self-respect and human dignity. However, the potential of these movements too was limited as they did not make a frontal attack on the actual framework of the caste system. In fact, the Dalits invariably invoked their caste status to wrest benefits from official agencies. This being so, all the Dalit movements—old and new—were at best reformative in their ideological orientations and they operated as interest groups to better their socio-economic conditions within the overall framework of the society. Therefore, these movements by themselves could not have brought about any substantial social change and development of the Dalits as a whole; their status as 'Untouchables' persists, although Untouchability is officially abolished and decried by social reform movements of all kinds. This hiatus between their official status as equal citizens before the law, and their being treated as Untouchables by the clean castes, can at least be partly located in Dalit powerlessness, the inadequate development of their political clout, the analysis of which we will now turn to.

III

The prevailing conditions of the Dalits could not have bestowed on them any political bargaining power, their substantial numbers notwithstanding. The mobilization of peasants and workers in the context of the anti-imperialist, anti-colonial national liberation movement also did not recognize the distinct identity and problems of the Dalits as a category. This is not to deny the Herculian efforts to eradicate Untouchability through constructive programmes enunciated by Gandhi. But as we have noted earlier, the impact of such efforts was limited. The thrust of the struggle for independence was against the British, an external enemy. But the Dalits did not perceive the British as their enemy; if anything the efforts made by the Christian missionaries (who were identified with the colonial regime) to bestow human dignity on them endeared them to the British. In the consciousness of the Dalits the enemy was essentially an internal one, particularly the upper castes who were also land-lords. Freedom, as such, had no meaning for them given the conditions of their existence. As the celebrated Malayalam poet of Ezhava origin, Kumaran Asan, observed in 1920: 'It was social oppression that people of this state (that is, the Dalits of Travancore) experienced more than political oppression' (see Balram 1973: 39). And the initial political participation of the Dalits in the national liberation movement was couched in terms of their socio-cultural emancipation, as manifested in their mobilization for temple entry and social reforms in the erstwhile princely states of Travancore, Cochin, Baroda and Kolhapur.

At the all-India level, the political articulation of Dalit interests and identity was first initiated by the great lawyer and constitutional expert, B.R. Ambedkar, a Maharashtrian Mahar. The first visible manifestation of this was found in his demand for separate electorates for the Scheduled Castes. Gandhi opposed it tooth and nail by undertaking a fast unto death as a protest against the vivisection of Hindu society. The controversy was settled through the Poona Pact wherein Ambedkar relented and accepted joint electorates. The Indian National Congress pledged to launch a vigorous and sustained effort to improve the condition of the Scheduled Castes.

In 1937, when popular ministries came to power all over India, an official programme for the upliftment of the Dalits was inaugurated. This programme intensified after 1947 with the attainment of independence.

The chief instrument employed by the state in India to bestow political power on the Dalits is the guarantee of 'reserved' representation to them in Parliament, state legislatures and local self-government bodies, roughly in proportion to their population. More important, it has come to be accepted as a convention by all political parties (irrespective of their ideological orientations) which succeed in capturing power, to give representation in the ministries formed by them, to Dalits. This co-option of the Dalits into the establishment was not without its political consequences, viewed in terms of their mobilization. To begin with, the competing political aspirants from among the Dalits get divided on party lines. They face the serious dilemma of competing loyalty between their ideological party affiliations on the one hand and the welfare of their constituency—the Dalits—on the other. Second, these Dalit leaders within the ruling party compete with one another to secure positions of power and pelf. This, in turn, leads to the emergence of factions and fissions among the Dalits within the same party. The net result of all this has been the political castration of the Dalits, rendering them a highly fractionated social collectivity incapable of serious bargaining with the powers-that-be. The unanticipated consequence of the policy of protective discrimination seems to be the vivisection of the Dalits!

The Dalit political mobilization on the national scene can be traced to the late 1920s when the British government initiated a series of Round Table Conferences to provide political representation to the Scheduled Castes. In the Second Conference in 1931, Ambedkar was invited as the representative of the depressed classes, but he soon realized that precious little could be achieved through the official channels. Ambedkar firmly believed that unless the caste system was destroyed the social evil of Untouchability could not be removed and he realized that to achieve this objective the Dalits should have political power. Keeping this end in view he established in 1942 the All-India Scheduled Caste Federation (AISCF) at an All-India Depressed Class Conference in Nagpur. In 1957 the AISCF was dissolved and the Republican Party of India (RPI) was formed. Although an exclusive political party of the Dalits, the RPI endorsed the fundamental tenets of the Indian Constitution and it pursued these objectives through the medium of parliamentary democracy. The specific aims of the party were fighting for the equality of all Indian citizens with a provision to give the Dalits some special consideration to bring about a balanced Indian society, and for the removal of exploitation of man by man and class by class (see Oommen 1977a: 179).

After the death of Ambedkar, the RPI gradually weakened and a large number of its followers joined the Congress Party. In 1970 with the formal split of the RPI, two factions emerged, one openly favouring the Congress policy and getting co-opted into it, while the other maintained its distinct identity, although without much political clout. The visible indicators of the party's existence at the national level are the periodic charter of demands it submits to the government, and the very infrequent and often ineffective collective actions it launches, focusing on the problems of the Dalits. However, through its persistent demand the RPI was successful in getting the government to pass the Protection of Civil Rights Act 1976, which prescribed more stringent punishment for those who practise Untouchability, replacing the Untouchability Offences Act 1955. The RPI failed to make an impact at the national level for the following reasons:

1. The party was too weak and localized and even in those pockets where it existed, its ranks were not united.
2. The party in power commanded the resources to extend patronage to the aspiring Dalit leadership through the policy of protective discrimination. These leaders emerged as seriou challengers of the RPI leaders.
3. The party did not have an ideology or an action programme radically different from that of other parties.
4. The RPI leaders were often co-opted into the ruling parties at the state and central levels, thereby eroding the potentiality of the party for any serious and sustained mobilization of the Dalits.

Faced with such a predicament the Dalit youth gradually got restive. The visible expression of their mental unrest was first manifested in finding a 'voice ' for themselves; the Dalit literary movement gradually emerged (Bhoite and Bhoite 1977: 60- 75). By 1972 the Dalit Panthers came into being as a distinct cultural-political group with their anchorage in urban Maharashtra, particularly in Bombay and Poona.

The Dalit Panthers are disillusioned with conversion to other religions (most of them are neo-Buddhists) and participation in parliamentary politics. Notwithstanding their continued allegiance to Ambedkar, at least part of their ideological kit is drawn from Marxism; they consciously opt for confrontation or total revolution. At the same time they do not attest to the Marxian understanding of the Indian reality in its entirety as they think it overemphasizes the economic factor and practically ignores other dimensions of social reality. According to the Dalit Panthers the problems facing the Dalits are multiple: bare economic needs, social discrimination, political oppression and physical torture. These problems cannot be tackled through the mechanisms of appeasement, 'tokenism,' in the form of economic concessions or political reservations. The way out is to capture political power. The Dalits declare: 'We want to rule over the entire country. Our target.... is not individuals, but a whole system rotten to the core' (Oommen 1977a: 184).

It is significant to note here that the Dalit Panthers count not only Scheduled Castes and Tribes and neo-Buddhists as Dalits, but all the toiling masses—industrial workers, farm labourers, land-less tenants, poor peasants—not all of whom are drawn from the Scheduled Castes. The Panthers are also clear about who their 'friends'—all true leftists who are dedicated to the task of destroy-ing the caste and class system—and 'enemies'—landlords, capitalists, money-lenders and communalists—are.

The Dalit Panthers should be credited with an appropriate diag-nosis of the problems confronting the Dalits. Similarly, their including the poor and oppressed from the non-Scheduled Castes in the Dalit category provides an adequate base for collective mobilization and action of the deprived. And yet their appeals remain unheeded and no collective action worth the name has been piloted by them so far. The reason for this non-performance should be located in the structure of deprivation in Indian society. As I have noted at the very beginning, the Dalits (as I have defined the term) are subjected to cumulative domination and are victims of multiple deprivations. Their experiential reality is not authentic to and shared by others who are simply economically poor. Small wonder, then, that the clean-caste poor do not share their 'fraternity' with the Dalit poor.

Our analysis reveals that neither the activities of the reformist Republican Party of India nor the radical verbiage of the Dalit Panthers can deliver the goods for the Dalits. Even if the argument that the Dalit Panther have the potential to trigger off a universal protest enveloping all the Dalits of India (as the Panthers define them) is accepted, they are nowhere near the achievement of this target; even the ideological appeal of the Panthers remains a sectarian enterprise confined to certain *jatis* in specific regions. On the other hand, governmental intervention through the policy of protective discrimination remains equally ineffective. In spite of the representation of the Dalits from the national Parliament to local *panchayats,* their participation in the decision-making process remains peripheral and perfunctory. Even their free and unfettered participation in routine elections does not take place with ease; they are physically assaulted, politically intimidated, socially humiliated and economically threatened in the exercise of the constitutionally guaranteed universal adult franchise. It is necessary to understand the reasons for this predicament, which brings us to the next point, namely the economic identity of the Dalits and the nature of their class consciousness.

IV

In the formal legal sense the Dalits are no more subjects but citizens. But the official guarantee does not automatically lead to the authentic exercise of their political rights as I have noted in the foregoing. The most important constraining factor in this context is the incongruence between their official political status (citizens) and actual economic predicament (slaves). It is common knowledge that the vast majority of the Dalits live in India's vast countryside enmeshed in traditional master-slave relations: they are not yet a free-floating proletariat.

In order to situate the Dalits in the economy of India, it is necessary to understand the source of their livelihood. Broadly, we can categorize the sources of livelihood into three. First, those who depend on the investment of their wealth and assessts— the capitalists, rentiers and landlords. There are, if any, only a handful of the Scheduled Castes in this category. Second, those who invest capital and expertise/skill simultaneously—the private practitioners in professions, small traders and entrepreneurs and owner-cultivators.

There is a small sub-stratum of the Scheduled Castes in this category. Third, those who are exclusively dependent on their expertise or labour-power for their livelihood; the majority of the Dalits belong to this category. However, there are at least three broad sub-categories of this last category. (*a*) Those who are in the top professions (medicine, law, engineering, university teaching) and in the upper echelons of the civilian bureaucracy and the defence services. Understandably a few Scheduled Castes are in these occupations due to the policy of reservation. (*b*) Those who are in the middle-level occupations (school teachers, nurses, clerks, army *jawans*). An increasing proportion of the Scheduled Castes find placement in this category due to the government policy of protective discrimination. But their representation on these services remains much smaller than is warranted by their size in the general population. (*c*) Those who are in the lowest rung of the occupational ladder earning their livelihood by selling their unskilled labour-power. The overwhelming majority of the Dalits belong to this category. Even here, their preponderance is in the disadvantaged sectors—agricultural workers in the rural areas, labourers in the unorganized, informal, underpaid urban sector. It is clear then that the Dalits are economically the most disadvantaged and they are located predominantly in the rural and unorganized urban work force.

I must briefly comment here on the economic content of state policy for the uplift of the Dalits. First, all the five-year plans have set aside specific amounts to be expended exclusively on the welfare of the Scheduled Castes. (In the First Plan the expenditure on this count was Rs 7 crores and by the Fifth Plan it rose to Rs 150 crores.) Second, admissions to educational institutions on a preferential basis have been guaranteed in proportion to their population assuming that this will facilitate upward occupational mobility and economic betterment. Third, special provisions have been made to finance the education of Scheduled Caste students through scholarships and to make available to them infrastructural facilities such as hostels, equipment and books, either free of cost or on a subsidized basis. Fourth, a certain percentage of government jobs have been reserved for the Scheduled Castes at all levels. Fifth, issuing licenses for and financing of industrial enterprises initiated by the Scheduled Castes. Sixth, distribution of land and the subsidized distribution of agricultural inputs to the Scheduled Caste peasantry and the landless. Seventh, the development of institutions and infrastructural facilities, such as cooperatives, keeping in mind the specific needs and resources of the Scheduled Castes.

While it cannot be denied that a small section of the Scheduled Castes, particularly those from the dominant groups among them (the typical examples are the Chamars, the Mahars and the Pulayas), have experienced upward mobility in the secular context through state measures mentioned earlier, the following unanticipated consequences should be noted. (*a*) The acceleration of class polarization among the Scheduled Castes and the emergence of a bourgeoisie among them. (*b*) Crystallization of enmity and envy towards the well-off sections among the Scheduled Castes on the part of the clean castes, particularly the poor among the latter. (*c*) The alienation of the Scheduled Caste elite, particularly the urban elite, from their antecedent social base. At the same time they do not easily get absorbed into the clean caste groups leading to an identity crisis. (*d*) The emergence of a leadership from the well-off Scheduled Castes who often act as political brokers and spokesmen of the Dalits with the top leadership in their respective contexts, but use their leadership roles as a political resource to further their career interests and material prospects, in the process endangering the wider interests of their less fortunate Dalit brethren (see Oommen 1975d: 486–93).

Although slavery was formally abolished in India a century ago, its current incarnations with minor modifications abound in contemporary India: forced labour, bonded labour, the patron-client system. Again, legally these practices have been abolished but the utter economic dependence of the Dalits on their rural employers, who are drawn from the upper or intermediate castes, renders it difficult for them to move out of their substantive slavery. The non-Dalit agricultural workers do not suffer from this socio-cultural disability. This makes the organization of the rural poor on a common platform nearly impossible. The Indian agrarian proletariat has not yet emerged; they are fractionated caste-wise, and since caste operates in a regional-cultural context, there is scarcely any possibility of mobilizing the Dalits on an all-India basis. This is evident from the fact that while in certain pockets of India Dalit revolts and protests are apparent, and even virulent, in the adjacent region there may not be any overt manifestation of mobilization, that is conflict with their oppressors.

Even in those areas where Dalit consciousness has crystallized on class lines, the political parties have muted the prospects of their mobilization. While one should accord the credit to the Communist Parties of India for being in the forefront to mobilize peasants and workers in a few regions, their efforts have not met with requisite success. And this for several reasons. First, an inappropriate conceptualization of peasantry in India. Following the maxim propounded in the All India Congress Committee, Faizpur, resolution of 1937, the 'leftists' have organized struggles to transfer 'land to the tiller', the peasant. But the 'peasant' of this description in India was, and is, scarcely a tiller of the land. Drawn from the intermediary castes who are below the twice-born varna categories but above the pollution line (that is above the Dalits), the 'peasant' castes of India were tenants, sharecroppers and marginal farmers who usually supervised farm operations. They are the primary beneficiaries of peasant movements and land reform legislation, and the actual tillers of land, the Dalits, were for long left out from the purview of mobilization even by the Communist Parties of India. A.K. Gopalan, the veteran CPI(M) leader, remarked in 1968: 'We have to make them [the landless labourers] the hub of our activities. Reluctance to take up their specific demands, fearing that this will drive the rich and middle peasants away from us, will have to be given up' (Gopalan 1968: 5). This meant the agrarian proletariat constituted mainly by the Dalits was not the focus of 'peasant' movements in India.

Second, the proliferation of Communist Parties and factions, each of them claiming to follow the most appropriate ideology and strategy, has substantially damaged the prospects of a unified movement of the agrarian poor, even in those regions where the potential existed. Third, those Communist Parties of India CPI and CPI(M) which are caught in the vortex of electoral politics, have to pander to the caste sentiments of the Dalits to gain electoral support contrary to their doctrine that caste consciousness is 'false' and the only authentic consciousness is class-based.

Finally, unlike the Backward Class movements (see Section II) which had a psychic location among the Dalits, the belated attempts by the Communist Parties to mobilize the agrarian proletariat are essentially a phenomenon external to the Dalits, at least in most cases. The leaders of the communist sponsored agrarian mobilizations are drawn predominantly from the clean castes, if not entirely from the twice-born varna categories, who cannot easily build an empathy with the targets of their mobilization, the lowly placed Dalits.

In those areas where communists succeeded in their efforts to
successfully mobilize the agrarian proletariat, a cultural revolt
preceded or at least paralleled their attempts. True, latterly one
witnesses an increasing recongnition of the hiatus that exists between
the leadership and the participants involved in agrarian mobilizations and the required amends are made by inducting leaders with
a Dalit background into the movement. Even this is not an un-
mixed blessing: one often sees that the political brokers drawn
from the Dalits and induced into leadership positions are under-
going a process of embourgeoisement. As I see it, this is the consequence of the fact that such Dalit leaders are not the initiators of
protest, but simply the agents who carry out the protest activity on
behalf of the parties/organizations which 'employ' them for the
purpose.

V

As I have noted at the very outset, an understanding of social
development implies important dimensions: the point of departure,
the desired point of destination, and the mechanism through which
this process of displacement is brought about. We propose to
evaluate the consequences of change experienced by the Dalits
through this frame.

I have summarized in Table 9.2 the changes that have occurred
among the Dalits of India in the last two centuries. It is my contention that the Dalits suffered from multiple deprivations and were
the victims of cumulative domination. Therefore, any effort to
bring about changes in one of the dimensions to the exclusion of
the others will not result in the authentic social development of the
Dalits. However, there are two crucial aspects in accomplishing
this task. First, recognizing a hierarchy in the structure of deprivations as perceived by the Dalits. Second, the signal importance of
Dalit participation in bringing about this development. But available evidence suggests that the initiators of change drawn from
among the non-Dalits invariably ignored these aspects in working
their strategy of change. Even the Dalit initiators of change were
not always successful, either because their efforts were confined to
specific *jatis* and regions, or because they gradually turned into
political brokers/agents, between their constituency and the establishment—the government and political parties. The net result has

Table 9.2

Social Transformation among Dalits and the Consequences for their Future Development

Identities at the Point of Departure	Identities at the Point of Desired Destination	The Process of Displacement: Mechanisms of Change	Observed Consequences
1. Untouchable	Equality (Socio-cultural)	A. Movement initiated by non-Dalits	Limited change and improvement of status; emergence of Dalit consciousness
		B. Protests piloted by the Dalits	Crystallization of confidence and self-respect; emergence of 'dominant castes' among the Dalits
2. Subject	Citizenship (Political)	A. Legislative measures	Emergence of a political elite from the 'dominant castes' among the Dalits
		B. Political mobilization organized by Dalit parties and organizations	Acquisition of political clout by the 'dominant castes' among the Dalits
3. Slave	Free Worker (Economic)	A. State initiated development measures	Emergence of a 'Dalit' bourgeoisie
		B. Mobilization by non-Dalit political parties and organizations	Differentiation between those who are 'successful'—drawn from Dalit 'dominant castes' —the political elite and the bourgeoisie—and the Dalit masses

been the fractionation of Dalits into 'dominant' and 'dominated' *jatis,* on the one hand, and a small privileged bougeoisie and a mass of underprivileged Dalits, on the other, rendering the prospects of their universal mobilization an impossibility. This 'vivisection' of the Dalits has eroded their revolutionary potential and robbed them of their protest orientation. The way out seems to be by transcending the caste orientation, and aligning with the deprived from all sections of society; the prerequisite to this is cultural revolt, as already noted in Chapter 8.

10

The Interactionist Paradigm and the Study of Social Movements

Particular theoretical traditions in sociology conventionally concentrate on specific substantive themes. The interactionists by and large focus on small-scale, face-to-face interactions—episodes, encounters, situations. This is in tune with the conception they hold of society, as an on-going process of interaction in which actors constantly adjust to one another and continuously interpret the social world they inhabit. Interpretation of the life-world is an act of assigning meanings to objects and events. And, meanings are rarely fixed, but invariably created, evolved, modified, developed and changed within interaction situations. Given this orientation it is not surprising that the interactionist paradigm is rarely invoked to study large-scale collective actions and historical events such as social movements and revolutions.

Here I propose to ask and answer a few questions which are typically of the interactionist orientation with reference to social movements. In doing this, I hope to demonstrate that the interactionist framework can be profitably extended to a substantive area to which it is scarcely applied. Understandably, the present focus is on the internal milieu of social movements. More specifically, I propose to concentrate on the following questions: how do leaders of movements project and present themselves to actual and potential followers? To what extent are the content and style of communication modified to suit different conditions and types of clients? How are the boundaries of social movements defined and what are the mechanisms invoked to maintain them? How are new identities and commitments created, nurtured and maintained among participants? Does interaction between leaders and followers and among followers of movements result in a new self-definition?

Let me also specify the analytical strategy that I have adopted here. I have not tried to apply the interactionist paradigm to the analysis of a particular social movement. This would have called for a fresh empirical enquiry. As far as I know this task is yet to be attempted in India. Therefore, I have scanned through a large number of studies on social movements and identified a few which provide the relevant data to undertake the present analysis. But the authors from whom I draw the data for the analysis do not invoke the interactionist paradigm. Understandably, I had to improvise by shuttling back and forth from one author to another depending upon the specific type of data I was looking for. Admittedly, this is not an enviable position and I am acutely aware of the limitations of such an effort.

EMERGENCE OF LEADERS

I have argued elsewhere (Oommen 1972a) that to cope with a crisis situation one of three alternatives may emerge: (*a*) appearance of a charismatic leader who promises to lead the people to a new utopia, (*b*) emergence of a new ideology which champions the cause of the deprived, and (*c*) establishing a new organization to deal with the problem at hand. These developments in turn may give rise to the crystallization of three distinct types of movements—charismatic, ideological and organizational. While ideology, organization and leadership are essential dimensions of all movements, a charismatic movement is essentially a leader-centred one. Therefore, the manner in which a charismatic leader presents himself to the wider world and how he is perceived by others, is of pivotal significance to the destiny of the movement. Presently, I will describe the emergence and crystallization of two movements—the Bhoodan-Gramdan[1] movement and the Ramakrishna Mission[2] movement—both of which

[1] As mentioned earlier. *Bhoodan* literally means land-in-gift, and *gramdan* village-in-gift. The ideology of the movement is based on *sarvodaya* (upliftment of all) propounded by Mohandas Karamchand Gandhi. The movement was initiated in the early 1950s by Vinoba Bhave who was hailed as the greatest living disciple of Gandhi. Although it began as an effort to collect land from the landed and distribute it to the landless, the movement soon widened its scope so as to establish communitarian settlements in *gramdan* villages.

[2] The Ramakrishna Mission movement started as a Hindu reform movement based on the ideas of Ramakrishna Paramahamsa. The movement spread far and wide, particularly in the fourth quarter of the 19th century, under the leadership of Swami Vivekananda. Gradually it crystallized into an organization with an order of monks undertaking numerous welfare activities. Latterly, it is argued by the Mission that it is not a Hindu organization and should be treated as a religious minority under the provisions of the Indian Constitution.

can be labelled charismatic movements, although, of course, their leadership differs in terms of their styles of activities.

The Bhoodan movement emerged in 1951 quite by accident. Vinoba Bhave, who led the movement, was walking from place to place (*padayatra*) in the Telengana region of Andhra Pradesh after attending a Sarvodaya conference. Telengana was gradually emerging out of the terror and insecurity which prevailed there from 1948-50, as a result of a violent peasant struggle led by the Communist Party of India. When he was present at an informal gathering in one of the villages, the Untouchable labourers told him that they remained landless in spite of the peasant struggle. On hearing this Vinoba enquired whether there were landowners among those present and if so why they did not share their land with the landless. After a few minutes of silence came the first land donation or *bhoodan* of hundred acres of land. From then on Vinoba walked through the length and breadth of India collecting land and villages in donation.

Vinoba firmly believes that the movement was inspired by God. According to him, 'On that day [the day of the first land donation] God gave me a sign. I meditated on it the whole of the following night and ended up by finding out what I had to do... without this hint on His part I should never have made up my mind to bhoodan (quoted in Del Vasto 1956:85). Vinoba's conviction continued. He said in May 1959, 'My reliance is solely on God. Only His will is fulfilled. Nothing moves but His will' (quoted in Rambhai 1962:276). The belief that God was using him as an instrument to bring about socio-economic change had moulded the ideology, programmes and the mode of functioning of the movement.

Although the immediate aim of the movement was material—collection and distribution of land—Vinoba projected himself and the people perceived him as a 'saint'. This in turn rendered the movement more acceptable to the rural masses. Saints wielded tremendous respect and influence in the Indian tradition as they had no vested interests and ulterior motives. Moreover, not only did they renounce material comforts but they also abjured political power. To reinforce the saintly image, Vinoba moved from village to village on foot, dressed only in a loin cloth, lived on five cups of milk a day, and when he ate, he ate frugally and on a banana leaf. He rose at 4 AM everyday, worked on the *charkha* (hand-operated spinning wheel), regularly prayed in the morning and evening. He spent time in meditation, thus leading the most simple and disciplined life (see Oommen 1972a:34). Vinoba's appearance, behaviour and conduct created awe and respect among the people and he was regarded as a holy man.

In contrast to the spontaneity in the emergence and spread of the Bhoodan movement was the manipulation of symbols and self-publicity involved in the spread of the Ramakrishna Mission movement. Having gone to the United States of America to attend the World Parliament of Religions in 1893, Vivekananda, the chief interpreter of the movement, found himself being vehemently criticized and his credentials questioned. To assert his position Vivekananda had to fall back on the manipulation of his followers. As one commentator observes:

> His technique was simple, if not quite saintly. He asked his disciples in Madras to convene big meetings, arrange crowds, get influential names associated with their conventions, pass resolutions praising his work, and send this publicity material to important men and newspapers in America... Vivekananda himself supplied details of some of these meetings to his important contacts in America, often suggesting, quite falsely, the spontaneous character of this recognition (K.P. Gupta 1974: 31).

If the leader of a movement presents himself as a saint or a charismatic hero, irrespective of whether it is genuine or manipulated, he has to live up to the expectations of the people. In so doing he wears a mask and in this process becomes a new person using a new language, adopting a new style of life, developing new perceptions of self and others, of events, acts and objects. '... and the transformation of perception is irreversible; once having changed there is no going back. One can look back, but he can evaluate only from his new status' (Strauss 1959: 92).

Communication Patterns

The style and content of communication would vary depending upon the character of the constituency being addressed. The Bhoodan movement was exclusively Indian at its incipient stage (later it spread to other countries, particularly to Sri Lanka) and given its nature had to be dependent on the good-will of the rich. Therefore, notwithstanding its equalitarian value orientation, the

Bhoodan movement had to couch its communication in class colla-
borative terms rather than in a confrontationist vein. Vinoba averred,
'If I can be the agent of both the rich and poor I shall be glad. For
the poor I am striving to win rights. For the rich I am striving to
win moral development' (quoted in Tennyson 1955: 59).

Further, Vinoba disapproved of class conflict and violence. He
told the communists that under the changed circumstances violence
had become redundant.

> I want to make it clear to the Communists that it is not necessary
> for them to murder the rich, for the era of democracy has been
> ushered in. As a matter of fact the rich can be killed without a
> pistol, for every adult has now acquired the right to vote.... I
> request the Communists to come out openly and work. If the
> Communists abandon their practice of violence, all good and
> moral people will cooperate with them (quoted in Rambhai
> 1962: 58).

Vivekananda was functioning in a cross-cultural context and he
had to interpret the same set of doctrines differently. He presented
vedanta in diametrically different ways to his American and Indian
audiences.

> In America, Vivekananda drew a portrait of Krishna the divine
> object of surrender, who was immersed in his *lila* (divine play)
> with the *gopis* (milk-maids). In India, this image was changed to
> project a fighting Krishna, the charioteer of Arjuna, who was
> vigorously pleading for an activist affirmation.... In America, he
> ..ld his audiences to practise *yoga* and renunciation, instead of
> supporting missionary humanitarian work. In India, he exhorted
> his followers to practise a little *bhoga* (indulgence), inculcate
> some *rajas* (materialism), and engage wholeheartedly in altruistic
> services. In America he criticized the machine culture because,
> instead of solving the problem of poverty, it created only new
> wants. In India, he not only upheld the necessity of material
> civilization but even thought of organizing monks for industrial
> purposes (K.P. Gupta 1974: 37-38).

It is clear that both Vinoba and Vivekananda were manipulating
their audiences, moulding the content of communication following
the dictum: each according to one's need. In so doing they were

trying to weld together collectivities of differing backgrounds and orientations—rich and poor, communists and democrats, Indians and Americans—so as to create a *new collectivity* sharing a common identity based on their sense of belonging to the same movement. However, this brings in new issues and problems, those of defining and maintaining the boundaries of movements.

Recruitment and Socialization

One of the problems faced by all social movements is demarcating their boundaries. Even when this problem is settled one faces the issue of distinguishing between a wide variety of participants. However, overlooking several differences one may distinguish between those at the core from those at the periphery as they have different roles and obligations within the movement as I have noted in Chapter I. But even in this context the variations across movements are substantial. For example, in the case of the Bhoodan movement the core participants were constituted by *jeevandanis* (those who dedicate their entire life for the work of the movement) and *shantisainiks* (peace brigades). They together constitute *loka-sevaks* (servants of humanity). A *loka-sevak* is expected to serve everybody irrespective of caste, class or creed. He should not participate in party politics but should devote himself to the service of humanity through truth and non-violence. Every *loka-sevak* is expected to sign the following pledge before he/she is admitted to that status within the movement.

(1) I believe in truth, non-violence and non-possession and I will endeavour to the best of my ability to live up to them.
(2) I believe that real freedom can be realized by the awakening of the *loka-niti* [the universal law of humanity]. Therefore, I will not associate myself with any kind of politics in any form.
(3) I will always serve with a spirit of devotion and self-sacrifice without expecting anything in return.
(4) I pledge myself to work for the abolition of all differences of caste, class and creed.
(5) I will devote most of my time and thought for the realization of the *sarvodaya* ideal through non-violent revolution based on *bhoodan* and supported by village industries (quoted in Rambhai 1962: 511).

The pledge provides the ideological framework and value system which every *loka-sevak* is expected to internalize and within which to function. Should a *loka-sevak* adhere to these prescriptions he/she is likely to be subjected to the process of self-mortification, although of a different type, that which Goffman (1968) conceptualized *vis-a-vis* the inmates of total institutions. The Ramakrishna Mission *ashrams* (monasteries) share several features of total institutions and the core participants in the movement, namely, the monks, are expected to stay there. And yet the Mission monks are said to be given substantial flexibility of action.

> ...the participating individuals move back and forth between sacred *jnana* (wisdom) and secular *karma* (action) but there is no attempt ever to create a vedantic society.... From the earliest period, the mission activities have alternated between the religious and the philanthropic. The choice has been dependent upon the *swabhavik* (natural) inclinations of the participating monk. The mission has merely helped each individual to choose a course of action most appropriate for his spiritual stage of development. There has never been an attempt to completely re-orient the direction of the total movement (K.P. Gupta 1974:40).

If this assertion is correct and accepted it could be argued that self-mortification leading to the breakdown of an inmate's former self-concept need not occur in all total institutions. On the other hand, self-mortification can and may occur in other situations as in the case of the *loka-sevaks* of the Bhoodan movement as I have tried to indicate. If so, we need to explore more carefully the social conditions and societal situations which would lead to the breakdown of the old and emergence of the new self-concept. For example, it could be argued that such a situation may prevail in a whole nation-society insofar as it is a highly regimented one.

The styles of recruitment and socialization of ordinary participants, that is, followers, would also vary depending on the nature of movements. Those movements which are oriented to achieve specific individual goals, although through and in an environment conditioned by collective presence, differ radically from the mass movements which are geared to grapple with collective deprivations. For example, in order to achieve *sadhana* (self-realization) participants in *guru-centred* movements have to undergo very regular, disciplined and prolonged activities such as meditation. Admittedly, prolonged individual attention needs to be paid to each new recruit and only a limited number of participants can be socialized at any given point in time. In fact the recruits undergo a period of pre-entry socialization so that they can finally decide whether they want to be recruited. Once the aspiring participant makes up his/her mind an initiation ceremony is invariably prescribed. The following account by an American disciple of his initiation into a *guru*-centred movement[3] in Banaras illustrates this.

> Sita Ram [the *guru*] then invited me into his rooftop *sadhana* room and instructed me in the techniques of the first stage. This was a most pleasant time and what I experienced there gave me a new feeling of closeness to Sita Ram, if for no other reason than that he took the time to explain what he knew to me so clearly and so sincerely. Even more enjoyable was the time spent meditating together although it was over much before I wanted it to be. We were soon embracing out on the roof again and I felt much like a child as I skipped down the stairs behind my new guruji to meet the brothers waiting below (Kellom and Kellom 1979:69).

After nine days the disciple's wife was also initiated.

> In the days that followed we experienced a new closeness with members of the organization that continued to grow during our stay in Banaras. While we had originally been the center of attention whenever we came to Sigra, as time passed we were allowed to fade into the comfortable background of the brotherhood.... We became more and more a part of the Sangha and were included in many social activities of the group (Kellom and Kellom 1979 : 69-70).

Such a movement needs to keep a delicate balance between individual freedom on the one hand and collective experience and identity on the other. As the *guru* put it:

[3] The movement under reference is Akhand Mahayoga Sangha founded by Sita Ram Pandey, the adopted son of Pandit Shri Gopinath Kaviraj, an internationally known philosopher and Tantrik. It is typical of the numerous *guru*-centred movements to establish an organization into which disciples are inducted after the prescribed initiation ceremony. Sita Ram functions from his home in Sigra, Banaras.

.... When the god's grace comes, when the divine light comes we will get it, but why shouldn't I prepare myself also, so if the divine light comes in my lifetime I will be ready to hold it. In the same way, all those who will be in my contact, I should prepare the same base for them also.... That is why I have added the word *'Sangha'* to *Akhanda Mahayoga. Because all of us together under the shadow of the Divine Mother are preparing ourselves for god's grace* (Kellom and Kellom 1979: 63, emphasis added).

In this yogic *Sadhana* one's profession or any occupation will in no way be any hindrance. The two essential requisites are steadfastness of conduct and faith in the intrinsic truth of the path. Apart from this one is free to lead one's life as one wishes (Kellom and Kellom 1979 :73).

In contrast to the individualized movements, the recruitment to mass movements which are geared to deal with collective deprivations do not, and perhaps cannot, insist on any rigorous recruitment procedure. However, the new recruits are often expected to sign a pledge or take a set of vows which should regulate their conduct. For example, Satyashodhak Samaj,[4] a movement which mobilized Shudras (ritually clean, lower castes) of Maharashtra, laid down 28 rules to be followed by its members/followers. The ninth rule prescribed the vows that all members of society were required to take on joining it. These were:

(1) I will not worship anything except our Creator. (2) I will not bring into discredit the pure rights that have been given by our Creator by countenancing either those who, through the arrogant assumptions on their books, behave as though others were inferior, or those who accept such inferiority. (3) I will stop being party to the killing of animals, and will give up alcohol, as far as I can. (4) I will hold firmly to my pride in the truth, will help the old, the lame, and the very young in our society, and will strive to give enough education to all our children that they may understand their rights (Quoted in O'Hanlon 1985:231).

It is clear from the vows prescribed that the *samaj* wanted to

[4] The Satyashodhak Samaj (the truth-seeking organization) was established by Mahatma Jotirao Phule in 1873 mainly to provide a collective identity to the Shudra castes of Maharashtra so as to fight against upper caste, particularly Brahmin, dominance.

bring about changes in those habits, attitudes and behaviour among the lower castes which were perceived to be detrimental to their progress. By taking and adhering to these vows a new sense of pride and identity was being imparted to the *samaj* members. The norms prescribed by Ad Dharm[5], the reform movement of the Untouchables of Punjab, were similar in that these were intended to be correctives to the loose style of life in which they were indulging at that time. The Ad Dharm prescribed:

Ad Dharmis should abstain from theft, fraud, lies, dishonesty, looking at someone else's wife with bad intentions, using anything which brings intoxication, gambling, and usurping other's property or belongings. All of these things, which are against the law of nature, are against the law of Ad Dharm (quoted in Juergensmeyer 1982:121).

Clearly Ad Dharm prescribed a new life-style for Untouchables and through that a new social order. But the procedure of recruitment to the movement would vary depending upon the purpose for which it was done. The Naxalite movement[6] which also wanted to establish a new social order, although of a different type, wanted to constitute squads to physically liquidate those persons identified as class enemies by applying a prescribed set of norms. Given the fact that the act of murder would necessarily invite severe punishment from the state, those who are recruited for the purpose need to be protected. Further, only those who are highly motivated can

[5] Ad Dharm literally means ancient or original moral order or religion. The 'Untouchables' of India believe that they were the original settlers of the country and following Aryan invasion they were subjugated and assimilated with a low status into Hinduism. Ad Dharm declares that they are not Hindus and their religion is pre-Aryan. The movement emerged in 1925 in Punjab under the leadership of Swami Shudranand.

[6] The Naxalite movement derives its name from the place where it began, Naxalbari in West Bengal. Disillusioned with the slow pace of rural social transformation that was taking place in Bengal's countryside in spite of the fact that the Communist party in India (Marxist) was in power, a section of party radicals rejected the democratic parliamentary road to social revolution. They launched a violent peasant struggle to forcefully capture land from feudal landlords to be distributed to the peasantry and landless agricultural workers. The movement started in 1967 and its most important leader was Charu Mazumdar. Subsequently, a new political party, the Communist Party of India (Marxist-Leninist) was formed and the movement continued under its guidance.

be assigned the task. Therefore, Charu Mazumdar, the theorist of the movement prescribed:

> The method of forming a guerilla unit was to be wholly conspiratorial. No inkling of such a conspiracy should be given out even in the meetings of political units of the party. The conspiracy should be between individuals and on a person-to-person basis. The petty bourgeois intellectual comrade must take the initiative in this respect as far as possible. He should approach the poor peasant who, in his opinion, has the most revolutionary potentiality, and whisper in his ears, 'don't you think it is a good thing to finish off such and such *jotedar* (landlord)'? This is how the guerillas have to be selected and recruited singly and in secret, and organized into a unit (quoted in Dasgupta 1974:44).

CREATING A NEW IDENTITY

Given the fact that most movements by definition ought to be ever-expanding, they have to keep their boundaries open. And yet, boundary maintenance is necessary particularly when a movement competes for clients with other movements and all of them draw their recruits from the same social base. This is exemplified in the case of the Arya Samaj.[7] The Arya Samaj had to compete for identity with orthodox Hinduism from which it was breaking away, as well as with other Hindu protest movements, particularly the Brahmo Sàmaj, which was too modern, and Sikhism, which had not clearly established a specific social identity at the time.

To establish its distinctiveness the Arya Samaj rejected the traditional and obscurantist Hindu practices of idolatry, polytheism, child marriage, caste system, Brahmanical claims to superiority, pilgrimage, horoscope, ban against widow remarriage, and restriction on foreign travel. Further, the Arya Samaj created its own forms of worship, dietary and marriage practices, in short, a new style of life (see Jones 1976). On the other hand, it was particularly

---

[7] The Arya Samaj, a modernized version of Hinduism, was initiated as a movement by Swami Dayanand Saraswati, a Gujarati Brahmin. The publication of his *Satyarth Prakash* (Light of Truth) in 1875 may be considered to be the beginning of the movement. In fact in the same year the Arya Samaj was founded in Bombay to propagate his ideas. However, Punjab was the most hospitable of all regions to his ideas and movement.

important for the Arya Samajists to distance themselves from the Brahmos because they had gone too far and surrendered to the English. As one devout Arya Samajist put it:

> ...I beg permission of my Brahmo friends to warn them against a most denationalizing course which they seem to be pursuing. As members of the Indian nation it is their duty to reform the evils which have crept into our institution by the tyranny and ignorance of ages, but not to uproot them unless they are found to have been pernicious even in their original states (quoted in Jones 1976:113).

While Arya Samajists did show fraternal overtones to Sikhism they found it wanting: 'Nanakji [the founder of Sikhism] had noble aims, but he had no knowledge of vedic scriptures or sanskrta'. Further, although the Sikhs do not worship idols '... they worship *Granth Sahib* which is as good as idolatry'. Not only that, 'The superstitious Sikhs do believe him [Nanak] to be an incarnation of the Deity and would be uncommonly wrath if anybody dared to hint *Granth Sahib* is not absolutely true'. Finally, 'All we can say about him is that he made less mistakes than could be expected from a man who had received no education worth the name and who had entirely to depend on the resources of his own uncultivated mind' (quoted in Jones 1976: 135-37).

The problem of creating and retaining a new identity is also faced by a collectivity which is the object of assimilation or conversion from several quarters. This was the predicament of the Ad-Dharmis. The Christians, the Hindus, the Sikhs and the Arya Samajists tried to convert and/or claim them. As one Ad Dharmi remarked:

> Christians sent Bibles to the homes of our people and tried to lure us with education: the Arya Samaj wanted to 'purify' us; and the Sikhs attempted *amrit prachar* (preaching Sikh baptism). The Hindu *qaum* tried to get back at us, the Arya Samaj spread their messages through our neighbourhoods. ...Sikhs started teaching us Gurumukhi. The upper castes too woo us and because they were afraid of the rise of Ad Dharm, suddenly started drinking water from our hands, and opened their schools to us (quoted in Juergensmeyer 1982: 67).

In such a situation the movement has to distance itself from all the competing collectivities, particularly the ones with which it is identified in the popular mind. In the case of the Ad Dharmis, Hinduism posed the problem and therefore the founder of the movement invariably used to close his speeches with the following lines: 'what is your religion: Truth. Who is your *guru*? Ravi Das, Rishi Valmiki. Who are the Hindus? The Aryans from outside. We are not Hindus' (quoted in Juergensmeyer 1982: 112)

SACRALIZATION AND DEMONIZATION

Creating a new identity in the case of social movements invariably involves the twin processes of sacralization and demonisation (see Oommen 1985). As Juergensmeyer observes:

> The events of the Ad Dharm rallies were moments in which the affairs and concerns of the participants' ordinary lives were elevated to a level of spiritual validity, humane concern, and social power. But these events also managed to create elements of sacred place and sacred community. The fields near the villages on which the rallies were held were sometimes compared to the fields of Kurukshetra, the Battlefields of the Bhagvad Gita (1982: 113).

The process of sacralization may often call for the performance of certain rituals, particularly if the new recruits to the movement are drawn from a different and stigmatized social background. The Arya Samaj wanted to reclaim those who converted to Christianity and Islam. But like Hinduism, Arya Samaj, the modernized version, too did not have any mechanism of conversion. Consequently, the Arya Samaj had to invent a new ritual, that of *shuddh'* (purification), in order to reconvert Muslims and Christians. Purification was doubly necessary because the majority of those converted were originally Untouchables. Reconversion provided the Arya Samaj with a new weapon of defence against Islam and Christianity. And its official publication, *Arya Patrika,* said:

> Is it not strange that *karors* [tens of millions] of Hindus were made Mahomedans by force and yet those who remained behind took no steps to open the door and re-admit them in their society

when the age of terror was gone. Millions of our brethren, in whose veins runs the same blood as in ours... have turned into deadly foes....Thanks to the all-preserving God that in this stage when different religions were eating away the remnant of the Hindu society some steps are being taken to save what can be saved (quoted in Jones 1976:132).

While sacralization as a process is a necessary and an often sufficient strategy to carve out a new identity (for the participants in the movement) from the proximate collectivities, demonization is invariably needed to distance the more hated and resourceful enemy. At the time when Arya Samaj was virulent in its activities in colonial India, Christianity which indulged in large-scale proselytization was its greatest threat. Consequently, it was necessary to demonize Christianity. Dayanand attacked Christianity at two levels; for its belief and practice of customs which were particularly repugnant to Hindus, and for its 'irrational' and 'superstitious' theology.

Referring to the practice of animal sacrifice in the Old Testament Dayanand exclaimed: 'How wild and savage-like it is for God to receive the sacrifice of oxen, and sprinkle blood on the alter'. Commenting on the story of the Israelites in Egypt Dayanand reacted: 'Horrible. This God of the Christians goes at mid-night like a robber and mercilessly kills children, old men and even cattle; shows no kindness; there is great bewailing in Egypt, but his cruelty knows no abatement'. Dayanand found the Holy Communion of Christians abominable. 'No civilized man will do such things except an uneducated and wild savage—to tell his disciples that their bread is his body and their drink is his blood. And this thing the Christians of these days call "Lord's Supper"... how awful' (quoted in Jones 1976:139-40).

Dayanand even questioned the philosophical notions such as original sin and characterized Christianity as a religion full of superstitions, irrationality and illogicality thereby demonizing it '... is it not horrible to say that all men from their birth are sinners; that the sin of the father produces a sin in and gives a punishment to his poor son? When shall reason and experience guide all the world and bias be universally relinquished?' Dayanand questioned (quoted in Jones 1976:141). And, the Christians were accused of the familiar fraudulent proselytization. '...it is an open secret that

the Christian Missionaries of India have taken advantage of the
famine to swell the number of their converts by taking over the
children of the famine-stricken Hindus and Muhammadans', con-
tended Lala Lajpat Rai, another leading light of the Arya Samaj
(quoted in Jones 1976:237).

The processes of sacralization and demonization independently
and/or in unison give birth to a new collective identity to movement
participants. But the character of this identity would necessarily
vary depending upon the background of the collectivity. Thus, the
new identity of an erstwhile dominant collectivity will be qualitatively
different from that of an oppressed and stigmatized group. Once the
disabilities for which a collectivity has fought are at least partly overcome its confidence increases, which in turn gives them a new self-
identity. The following statements of the Ad Dharmis exemplify this:

> Before, we were only interested in removing untouchability. We
> have that now, and the government gives us much. We have our
> people in the government, but they are still treated like slaves.
> They fear their superiors and the high caste people.... We have to
> organize our people within the government, and organize our
> political interests (quoted in Juergensmeyer 1982:258).

> During the British rule, we were twice slaves: slaves of the British
> and slaves of the Hindus. We have gotten rid of the British, now we
> have to assert our own right against the upper castes.... Hinduism
> is a fraud to us. Ad Dharm is our only true religion (ibid.:262).

FISSION AND FUSION

However, in the process of transformation the collectivity under
question may undergo a process of fission or fusion. Thus, Ad
Dharm produced both radicals and moderates thereby giving birth to
new movements and collective identities. The Dalit Panthers, a
radical splinter group from the Ad Dharmis, say, 'We're not like the
Ad Dharm. Our movement is not religious, but revolutionary. For
religion, let them go to Ravi Das' (quoted in Juergensmeyer
1982:265). And the moderate faction of the Dalits think their object
is to '...fight the atrocities against lower castes, spread Ambedkarism
and the cultural heritage of our own *gurus*, and protect the reservations
for lower caste positions in government jobs' (ibid.:266).

It seems then that there is a close connection between destig-matization and emergence of new collective identities. If an erstwhile group of slaves or Untouchables are successful in emancipating themselves from ritual or social stigma they would be emboldened to pursue new goals, usually instrumental ones (see Chapter 9). In this process, the collectivity may get divided on the basis of new goals that the different factions may come to pursue, thereby lead-ing to fission and crystallization of new collective identities. But the reverse process, namely, the failure to achieve the goal and hence a fusion to consolidate different factions and splinters, cannot be ruled out. What happened to the Arya Samaj proximated this.

As noted earlier, the mission of Arya Samaj was to modernize Hinduism. To achieve its goal it had to denigrate 'conservative' Hindus, 'over-modernized' Brahmos and 'ignorant' Sikhs. But once the Hindu consciousness crystallized into a political expression it was necessary to ignore the differences among all varieties of Hindus so as to encapsulate them into a united Hindu nation, which was the new acutely-felt collective need. And, Lala Lal Chand, an articulate Arya Samajist put it thus:

An attempt at unification has failed and failed miserably. Instead of the growth of one united nation, a sharp line of demarcation has been drawn and sanctioned by authority. In making their attempt the Hindus have lost ground and their interests have been pushed backward. There is surely time yet to turn round and try to recover lost ground. And this can only be achieved by asserting purely Hindu interest, and not by Indian propaganda. The consciousness must arise in the mind of each Hindu that he is a Hindu, and not merely an Indian, and when it does arise the newly awakened force is bound to bring its results (quoted in Jones 1976:280).

Not only should the new identity embrace *every* Hindu but it should also be totalistic. As Lal Chand advocated:

...the substitution of Hindu Sabhas for Congress committees, of a Hindu press for the Congress press, organization of a Hindu Defence Fund with regular office and machinery for collecting information and seeking redress by self-help, self-ameliorations and petitions and memorials supplemented by agitation in the

press and advocacy through trusted leaders in matters both special
and common but do. ....ed primarily by regard for Hindu
interests (Jones 1976: 280-87).

Lal Chand was clear in his advocacy of the nature of the new identity.
'The point I wish to urge is that patriotism ought to be communal
and not merely geographical' (ibid.: 287). It is clear that these
remarks indicate the moving away from the sectarian Arya Dharm
to a consolidated Hindu consciousness. But the effort to provide
the patriotism of Hindus with communal content may also be seen
as a reaction to invest Muslim patriotism with Islamic communalism,
eventually leading to the creation of two polities—India and Pakistan.
Once this process sets in, other religious collectivities which
would equate patriotism and communalism would also insist on an
independent or separate 'political roof'. And this is precisely what
Khushwant Singh (1966: 305) articulated. 'The only chance of survival
of the Sikhs as a separate community is to create a state in which
they form a compact group, where the teaching of Gurmukhi and
the Sikh religion is compulsory, and where there is an atmosphere
of respect for the traditions of their Khalsa forefathers'. Needless
to say the bases invoked by one collectivity for creating an identity
determines whether or not collective identities coalesce or multiply.
The emergence of a collective self-identity may manifest in
various ways. One possible clue to understand this is the devotion,
commitment and enthusiasm with which the participants in the movement undertake the tasks assigned to them and the satisfaction they
derive out of it. As noted earlier, the aim of the Naxalite movement
was to bring about a revolution in India through the liquidation of
the most critical class enemy, namely feudal landlords. To achieve
this goal small murder squads were constituted. The following
extracts from *liberation*, the official organ of the Communist Party
of India (Marxist- Leninist), which piloted the movement, clearly
indicate how the squad members rejoiced in accomplishing the
assigned tasks.

'Not satisfied with his death, the peasants painted slogans with
his blood. This demonstrates the intensity of the wrath of the
masses against this notorious feudal lord' (June 1969).
'People expressed their hatred for this class enemy by painting
slogans with his blood' (August 1969).

'I hit the agent on the head and killed him with one stroke' (September 1969)

'After this [i.e.,killing] we then severed his head and hung it in front of his house, and wrote with his blood slogans like "Long Live Chairman Mao" (December 1969).

'The class hatred of the guerillas against the class enemy was so intense that they hung his severed head outside the door of his house' (March 1970) (Reproduced from Dasgupta 1974: 46).

Only those who completely identify themselves with the movement and have a new self-definition of themselves could have indulged in and rejoiced over these violent activities. Indeed it is an adequate demonstration of successful socialization, identity formation and self-mortification.

CONCLUDING OBSERVATIONS

I want to suggest the following general points based on this discussion. First, each movement differs with regard to the specific details of its emergence and this in turn affects the manner in which the leadership presents itself to the wider world. However, irrespective of the variations in the styles of leadership, these should gain legitimacy among the immediate and potential clients. Second, the styles of communication, both verbal and non-verbal, are to be suitably moulded so as to fit the contexts — intra-societal, multi-class, cross-cultural, interpersonal and the like. And yet, the mode of communication should be such that it should be appealing to a sufficiently critical number (which would vary from case to case) so that it leads to the formation of a movement. Third, the message (ideology) of the movement need be differentially presented so that the recruits to the movement with differing backgrounds should perceive it as meaningful to their specific situations, needs and interests. But if the ideology is too narrow, sectarian and parochial it would affect the potentiality of the movement's growth and spread. Fourth, all movements need to accept a hierarchy among its participants in terms of their status, roles, motivations and interests. However, in spite of these differences, the community spirit among the totality of participants needs to be emphasized and maintained. Fifth, in the case of movement participants, particularly for the ordinary ones, there may not be any prescribed symbols of identification—dress, badge or insignia. All the same, they may be expected to undergo some prescribed initiation ceremony—signing a pledge, taking a vow, filling a membership form, participating in some prescribed non-verbal acts—which marks their formal entry and acceptance into the movement. Sixth, creating a new identity often entails establishing a new style of life exclusive to the movement participants. Pursuantly, if a movement faces a threat from several sources simultaneously, it has to distance itself from all of them. In this process, it has to discern the hierarchy of threat involved so as to evolve an appropriate strategy. Seventh, the process of creating a new identity invariably leads to the process of sacralization of persons, events and objects crucial to the movement. Further, it may call for the creation of a new set of *rites de passage* which can adequately cope with similar practices of competing movements. Eighth, an aggressive identity assertion would necessitate not only sacralization of one's movement but also demonization of the enemy. Demonization may be attempted not only with regard to the macro-dimensions such as ideology and top leadership, but also *vis-à-vis* micro aspects such as the strategy and procedure the enemy pursues in specific contexts and localities. Ninth, collective identity formation through participation in a movement entails the possibility of fission and/or fusion of the collectivity. Fission usually occurs when factions within a movement define and perceive that the goals they should pursue are different. Fusion is the inevitable result of the need for consolidation of different shades of opinions so as to meet an overarching enemy, usually perceived as alien and/or political. Finally, successful socialization will produce a band of committed participants who will come to identify themselves totally with the goals of the movement. These participants do develop a new self-definition of themselves and are invariably willing to be martyrs of their faith.

References

Ahmad, Imtiaz. 1971. Caste Mobility Movements in North India. *Indian Economic and Social History Review* 8(2).

———. 1981. *Ritual and Religion among Muslims in India.* New Delhi: Manohar.

Aiyappan, A. 1965. *Social Revolution in a Kerala Village.* London: Asia Publishing House.

Alavi, Hamza. 1965. Peasants and Revolution. *Socialist Register.* London: The Merlin Press.

———. 1973. Peasant Class and Primordial Loyalties. *Journal of Peasant Studies* 1(1).

Alberoni, Francesco. 1984. *Movements and Institutions.* New York: Columbia University Press.

Alexander, K.C. 1972. Neo-Christians in Kerala, in J. Michael Mahar (ed.), *The Untouchables in Contemporary India.* Tuscon: The University of Arizona Press.

———. 1975. Emerging Farmer-Labour Relations in Kuttanad. *Economic and Political Weekly* 8(34).

———. 1979. *Rural Organizations in South India.* Ithaca: Cornell University Press.

All India Congress Committee. 1959. *AICC Economic Review* 10(19).

Altbach, Philip G. 1966. The Transformation of the Indian Student Movement. *Asian Survey* 6(8).

———. (ed.). 1968. *Turmoil and Transition: Higher Education and Student Politics in India.* Bombay: Lalvani.

———. 1971. *The Student Revolution: A Global Analysis.* Bombay: Lalvani.

Asthana, Pratima. 1974. *Women's Movement in India.* Delhi: Vikas.

Babb, Lawrence A. 1972. Satnamis—Political Involvement of a Religious Movement, in Michael Mahar (ed.), *The Untouchables in Contemporary India.* Tuscon: University of Arizona Press.

Badrinath, C. 1977. Dissent, Protest and Social Reform: The Historical Context, in S.C. Malik (ed.), *Dissent, Protest and Reform in Indian Civilization.* Simla: Indian Institute of Advanced Study.

Bali, Arun, P. 1979. Organization of Virasaiva Movement: An Analysis in the Sect-Church Framework, in M.S.A. Rao (ed.), *Social Movements in India,* vol. 2. Delhi: Manohar.

Balram, N.E. 1973. *Communist Movement in Kerala.* Trivandrum: Prabhatham Printing and Publishing Company (Malayalam).

Barton. Allen, H. 1955. The Concept of Property-Space in Social Research, in P.F. Lazersfeld and Morris Rosenberg, *The Language of Social Research.* Glencoe: The Free Press.

Basu, Aparna. 1976. Role of Women in the Indian Struggle for Freedom, in B.R. Nanda (ed.), *Indian Women From Purdah to Modernity.* New Delhi: Vikas.

Beteille, Andre.1970. Peasant Associations and Agrarian Class Structure. *Contributions to Indian Sociology* 4 (new series).

Bhadra, Ranajit K. 1977. Revitalization Movements among the Gonds of Madhya Pradesh. *Eastern Anthropologist* 30(2).

Bharadwaj, Gopal.1977. Socio-Political Movements among the Tribes of India, in S.C. Dube (ed.), *Tribal Heritage of India*, vol. 1. New Delhi: Vikas.

Bhat, Chandrashekhar. 1978. Reform Movements among the Waddars of Karnatak, in M.S.A. Rao (ed.), *Social Movements in India* , vol. 1. Delhi: Manohar.

Bhatt, V. 1973. Ideological and Socio-Historical Role of Elites in the Brahmo Samaj and Arya Samaj Movements, in K.S. Mathur et al. (eds.), *Studies in Social Change*, Lucknow: Ethnographic and Folk Culture Society.

Bhoite, Uttam and **Anuradha Bhoite.**1977. The Dalit Sahitya Movement in Maharashtra: A Sociological Analysis. *Sociological Bulletin* 26(1).

Bose, N.K.1941. The Hindu Method of Tribal Absorption. *Science and Culture* 7(2).

————. 1967. *Culture and Society in India.*Bombay: Asia Publishing House.

Brass, R. and **M.F. Franda.**1973. *The Communist Movement in India.* Cambridge (Mass.): MIT Press.

Brodkin, E.I.1972. The Struggle for Succession: Rebels and Loyalists in the Indian Mutiny of 1857. *Modern Asian Studies* 6(3).

Brown, D.M.1961. *The Nationalist Movement: Indian Political Thought from Ranade to Bhave.*Berkeley: California University Press.

Chakraborty, Aparajita. 1981. Tenancy and Mode of Production. *Economic and Political Weekly* (Review of Agriculture), March.

Chandra, Bipan. 1979. Peasantry and National Integration in Contemporary India, in B. Chandra (ed.), *Nationalism and Colonialism in Modern India.* New Delhi: Orient Longman.

Chandra, Pratap. 1977. Study of Ideological Discord in Ancient India: Search for a Suitable Model, in S.C. Malik (ed.), *Dissent, Protest and Reform in Indian Civilization.*Simla: Indian Institute of Advanced Study.

Chatterjee, Bankim Chandra. 1882. *Anand Math.* Calcutta: Bangadarsha (Bengali).

Chattopadhyaya, Kamaladevi. 1975. The Women's Movement: Then and Now, in Devaki Jain (ed.), *Indian Women.* New Delhi: Publication Division.

Chaube, S.C. 1973. *Hill Politics in North-East India.* New Delhi: Orient Longman.

Church, Richard. 1978. Vinoba Bhave, Jayaprakash Narayan and Indian Democracy. Paper presented at the annual meeting of the Canadian Society for Asian Studies, University of Guelph, 23–26 May (mimeo.).

Choudhary, S. 1971. *Peasant and Workers Movement in India 1905–1929.* New Delhi: Peoples Publishing House.

————. 1977. *Moplah Uprising, 1921–23.* New Delhi: Agam Prakashan.

Chowdhary, S.R. 1977. *Leftist Movements in India 1917–1947.* Calcutta: Minerva Associates.

Conlon, E.F. 1974. Caste by Association: The Gauda Sarasvata Brahmana Unification Movement. *Journal of Asian Studies* 33(3).

Copland, Ian. 1973. The Maharaja of Kolhapur and the Non-Brahmin Movement, 1902-10. *Modern Asian Studies* 7(2).

Cormack, Margaret L. 1972. University Students: Today's Militant Minority, in L.M. Singhvi (ed.), *Youth Unrest: Conflict of Generations.* Delhi: National Publishing House.

Crawley, W.F. 1971. Kisan Sabhas and Agrarian Revolt in the United Provinces 1920–21. *Modern Asian Studies* 5(2).

Dale, Stephen F. 1975. The Mappila Outbreak: Ideology and Social Conflict in 19th Century Kerala. *Journal of Asian Studies* 35(1).

————. 1976. The Mappilas during Mysorean Rule: Agrarian Conflict in 18th Century Malabar. *South Asia* 6.

Damle, Y.B. 1977. Protest, Dissent and Social Reform: A Conceptual Note, in S.C. Malik (ed.), *Dissent, Protest and Reform in Indian Civilization*: Simla: Indian Institute of Advanced Study.

Dasgupta, Biplab. 1974. *The Naxalite Movement*. New Delhi: Allied.

Del Vasto, Lanze. 1956. *Gandhi to Vinoba*. London: Rider and Co.

Desai, A.R. 1954. *The Social Background of Indian Nationalism*. Bombay: Popular Prakashan.

————. (ed.). 1979. *Peasant Struggles in India*. Bombay: Oxford University Press.

Desai. I.P. 1977. The Vedachni Movement, in I.P. Desai and Banwarilal Chaudhary (eds.), *History of Rural Development in Modern India*, vol. 2. Delhi: Impex India.

Devahuti. 1977. Asoka's Dissent from the Hindu and the Buddhist Goals and Methods of Chakravarti, the Great Conqueror, in S.C. Malik (ed.), *Dissent, Protest and Reform in Indian Civilization*. Simla: Indian Institute of Advanced Study.

Devanandan, P.D. 1970. *The Dravida Kazagham: A Revolt Against Brahminism*. Bangalore: Christian Institute for Study in Religion and Society.

Dhan, R.O. 1977. Tribal Movements in Chottanagpur, in S.C. Malik (ed.), *Dissent, Protest and Reform in Indian Civilization*. Simla: Indian Institute of Advanced Study.

Dhanagare, D.N. 1974. Social Origins of the Peasant Insurrection in Telengana, 1946–51. *Contributions to Indian Sociology* 8 (new series).

————. 1975a. The Politics of Survival: Peasant Organization and Left-Wing in India. *Sociological Bulletin* 25(1).

————. 1975b. *Agrarian Movements and Gandhian Politics*. Agra University.

————. 1975c. Congress and Agrarian Agitation in Oudh, 1920-22 and 1930–32. *South Asia* 5.

————. 1976. Peasant Protest and Politics: The Tebhaga Movement in Bengal (India), 1946–47. *Journal of Peasant Studies* 3(3).

————. 1977. Agrarian Conflict, Religion and Politics: The Moplah Rebellions in Malabar in the 19th and Early 20th Centuries. *Past and Present* 47.

Dommen, A.G. 1967. Separatist Tendencies in Eastern India. *Asian Survey* 7(10).

Eisenstadt, S.N. 1965. *Modernization: Protest and Change*. New Jersey: Prentice Hall.

Ekka, Philip. 1972. Revivalist Movements among the Tribals of Chhottanagpur, in K.S. Singh (ed.), *Tribal Situation in India*. Simla: Indian Institute of Advanced Study.

Elliott, C.M. 1974. Decline of a Patrimonial Regime: The Telengana Rebellion in India, 1946–51. *Journal of Asian Studies* 94(1).

Farquhar, J.N. 1924. *Modern Religious Movements in India*. New York: Macmillan (Reprinted in 1967).

Fic, Victor M. 1969. *Peaceful Transition of Communism in India: Strategy of the Communist Party*. Bombay: Nachiketa.

————. 1970. *Kerala, Yenan of India. Rise of Communist Power, 1957–1969*. Bombay: Nachiketa.

Fiske, Adele, 1972. Scheduled Caste Buddhist Organizations, in Michael Mahar (ed.), *The Untouchables in Contemporary India*. Tuscon: The University of Arizona Press.

Forbes, G.H. 1979. Women's Movement in India: Traditional Symbols and New Roles, in M.S.A. Rao (ed.), *Social Movements in India*, vol. 2. Delhi: Manohar.

Forrester, D.B. 1977. The Depressed Classes and Conversion to Christianity, 1860-1960, in G.A. Oddie (ed.),*Religion in South Asia*. Delhi: Manohar.

Fuchs, Stephen. 1965. *Rebellious Prophets: Indian Religions*. Bombay: Asia.

Galtung, Johan. 1986. The Green Movement: A Socio-Historical Exploration. *International Sociology* 1(1).

Gandhi, M.K. 1938. *Hind Swaraj or Indian Home Rule*. Ahmedabad: Navjeevan Publishing House.

Garlington, W. 1977. The Bahai Faith in Malwa, in G.A. Oddie (ed.), *Religion in South Asia*. Delhi: Manohar.

George, K.M. 1977. Protest Voices of Creative Writers of Kerala, in S.C. Malik (ed.), *Dissent, Protest and Reform in Indian Civilization*. Simla: Indian Institute of Advanced Study.

Ghose, S. 1969. *The Renaissance to Militant Nationalism in India*. Bombay: Asia.

Goffman, Erwing. 1968. *Asylums*. Harmondsworth: Penguin Books.

Gopalan, A.K. 1968. Strengthen the Kisan Sabha (Presidential address at the 19th Session of the All-India Kisan Sabha). *People's Democracy* 4(6).

Gough, Kathleen, 1969. Peasant Resistance and Revolt in South India. *Pacific Affairs* 41(4).

————. 1974. Indian Peasant Uprising. *Economic and Political Weekly* 11(32–34), special number.

Government of India. 1955. *Report of the State Reorganization Commission*. New Delhi: Publications Division.

————. 1964. *Gramdan Movement*. New Delhi: Planning Commission.

Guha, Amalendu. 1979. Great Nationalism, Little Nationalism and Problem of Integration: A Tentative View. *Economic and Political Weekly* 14(7–8), annual number.

————. 1982. The Indian National Question: A Conceptual Frame. *Economic and Political Weekly* 17(31).

Gupta, Dipankar. 1977. The Causes and Constraints of an Urban Social Movement. *Contributions to Indian Sociology* 11(1).

Gupta, K.P. 1974. Religious Evolution and Social Change in India: A study of the Ramakrishna Mission Movement. *Contributions to Indian Sociology* 8.

Gusfield, Joseph R. 1970. *Protest, Reform and Revolt: A Reader in Social Movements*. New York: John Wiley & Sons.

Halappa, G.S. 1964. *History of Freedom Movement in Karnataka*, 2 vols. Bangalore: Government of Mysore.

Harcourt, M.V. 1977. Kisan Populism and North Indian Politics: The Context of the 1942 Rebellion in Bihar and Eastern UP, in D.A. Low (ed.), *Congress and the Raj*. Delhi: Arnold Heinemann.

Hardgrave, R.L. 1965. *The Dravidian Movement*. Bombay: Popular Prakashan.

————. 1969. *The Nadars of Tamilnad: The Political Culture of a Community in Change*. Berkeley: University of California Press.

————. 1977. The Mappila Rebellion, 1921: Peasant Revolt in Malabar. *Modern Asian Studies* 11(1).

Hardiman, David. 1976. Politicisation and Agitation among Dominant Peasants in Early 20th Century India: Some Notes. *Economic and Political Weekly* 11(9).

Harper, Edward B. 1968. Social Consequences of an 'Unsuccessful' Low Caste Movement, in James Silverberg (ed.), *Social Mobility in the Caste System in India: An Interdisciplinary Symposium*. The Hague: Mouton.

Heberle, R. 1951. *Social Movements: An Introduction to Political Sociology*. New York: Appleton-Century-Crofts.

Heimsath, C. 1964. *Indian Nationalism and Hindu Social Reform*. Princeton: Princeton University Press.

Hobsbawm, Eric J. 1959. *Primitive Rebels*. Manchester: Manchester University Press.

Hoffman, Daniel P. 1961. *India's Social Miracle*. California: Naturegraph Co.

Irschick, Eugene F. 1969. *Politics and Social Conflict in South India*: The Non-Brahmin Movement and Tamil Separation 1916-1929. Bombay: Oxford University Press.

Jay, Edward. 1962. Revitalization Movements in Tribal India, in L.P. Vidyarthi (ed.), *Aspects of Religion in Indian Society*. Meerut: Kedarnath and Ramnath.

Jeffrey, Robin. 1974. The Social Origins of a Caste Association, 1874-1905: The Founding of the SNDP Yogam. *South Asia* 4.

————. 1976. Temple Entry Movement in Travancore, 1860-1940. *Social Scientist* 4(8).

Jodha, N.S. 1981. Agricultural Tenancy: Fresh Evidence from Dryland Areas in India. *Economic and Political Weekly* (Review of Agriculture) 16(52).

Johnson, G. 1973. *Provincial Politics and Indian Nationalism*, South Asian Studies No. 14. Cambridge Universtiy Press.

Jones, Kenneth W. 1968. Communalism in the Punjab: The Arya Samaj Contribution. *Journal of Asian Studies* 28(1).

————. 1976. *Arya Dharm: Hindu Consciousness in the 19th Century Punjab*. Delhi: Manohar.

Jordens, J.T.F. 1977. Reconversion to Hinduism, the Shuddhi of the Arya Samaj, in G.A. Oddie (ed.), *Religion in South Asia: Religious Conversion and Revival Movements in South Asia in Medieval and Modern Times*. Delhi: Manohar.

Joshi, Ram. 1970. Shiva Sena: A Movement in Search of Legitimacy. *Asian Survey* 10(11).

Juergensmeyer, Mark. 1982. *Religion as Social Vision: The Movement against Untouchability in 20th Century Punjab*. Berkeley: University of California Press.

Katzenstein, M.F. 1976. Origins of Nativism: The Emergence of Siva Sena in Bombay, in Donald B. Rosenthal (ed.), *City in Indian Politics*. New Delhi: Thompson Press.

Kellom, Kolleen and **Gar Kellom.** 1979. *A Guru-Centred Movement in the Making: Akhand Mahayoga Sangha of Varanasi*, in M.S.A. Rao (ed.), *Social Movements in India* vol. 2. Delhi: Manohar.

Khare, R.S. 1970. *The Changing Brahmins: Associations and Elites Among the Kanya Kubjas of Northern India.* Chicago: Universtiy of Chicago Press.

Khubchandani, Lachman M. 1983. *Plural Languages, Plural Cultures: Communication, Identity and Socio-Political Change in Contemporary India.* Honolulu: University of Hawaii Press.

Kothari, Rajni and **Rushikesh Maru.** 1965. Caste and Secularism in India: Case Study of a Caste Federation. *Journal of Asian Studies* 25(1).

Kotovsky, G. 1964. *Agrarian Reform in India.* New Delhi: People's Publishing House.

Laushey, David M. 1975. *Bengal Terrorism and Marxists.* Calcutta: Firma K.L. Mukhopadhyay.

Leonard, L.G. 1967. Political and Social Change in South India: A Study of the Andhra Movement. *Journal of Commonwealth Political Studies.*

Lipset, S.M., Martin Trow and James Coleman. 1956. *Union Democracy.* Illinois The Free Press.

Low, D.A. (ed.), 1977. *Congress and the Raj: Facets of the Indian Struggle 1917-47.* New Delhi: Arnold-Heinemann.

Lynch, Owen. 1969. *The Politics of Untouchability: Social Mobility and Social Change in a City of India.* Columbia: Columbia University Press.

Mahapatra, L.K. 1968. Social Movements Among Tribes of Eastern India. *Sociologue* 18(1).

──────. 1972. Social Movements among Tribes in India, in K.S. Singh (ed.), *Tribal Situation in India.* Simla: Indian Institute of Advanced Study.

Majumdar, R.C. 1963. *History of Freedom Movement in India*, 3 vols. Calcutta: Firma K.L. Mukhopadhyay.

Majumdar, Veena. 1976. The Social Reform Movement in India from Ranade to Nehru, in B.R. Nanda (ed.), *Indian Women from Purdah to Modernity.* Delhi: Vikas.

Malik, S.C.(ed.). 1977. *Dissent, Protest and Reform in Indian Civilization.* Simla: Institute of Advanced Study.

Manmohan Kaur, 1968. *Role of Women in the Freedom Movement.* New Delhi: Sterling.

Marwah, I.S. 1979. Tabligh Movement among the Meos of Mewat, in M.S.A. Rao (ed.), *Social Movements in India,* vol. 2. New Delhi: Manohar.

Mathew, George. 1982. Politicisation of Religion: Conversions to Islam in Tamil Nadu. *Economic and Political Weekly* 17(25).

Mathur, A.S. and **J.S. Mathur.** *Trade Union Movement in India.* Allahabad: Chaitanya.

Mathur, J.S. 1964. *Indian Working Class Movement.* Allahabad: Central Book Depot.

Mathur, Y.B. 1972. *Muslims and Changing India.* Delhi: Trimurthi Publications.

McCormack, William. 1963. Lingayats as a Sect. *Journal of the Royal Anthropological Institute of Great Britain and Ireland* 93 (part I).

Means, G.P. and **I.N. Means.** 1966–67. Nagaland: The Agony of Ending a Guerrilla War. *Pacific Affairs* 39(3 & 4).

Menon, P.K.K. (ed.) 1972. *The History of Freedom Movement in Kerala,* 2 vols. Trivandrum: Government of Kerala Press.

Metcalf, T.R. 1965. *The Aftermath of Revolt in India, 1857-1870.* Princeton: Princeton University Press.

Mies, Maria. 1976. Peasant Movement in Maharashtra: Its Development and its Perspective. *Journal of Contemporary Asia 6(2).*

Mills, C.W. 1959. *The Sociological Imagination.* New York: Oxford University Press.

Mishra, Girish. 1968. The Socio-Economic Background of Gandhi's Champaran Movement. *Indian Economic and Social History Review* 4(3).

Misra, Udayon. 1978. The Naga National Question. *Economic and Political Weekly 13(14).*

Mohan Ram. 1971. *Maoism in India.* Delhi: Vikas.

Mohanty, Manoranjan. 1977. *Revolutionary Violence: A Study of the Maoist Movement in India.* New Delhi: Sterling.

Moore, Barrington. 1966. *Social Origins of Dictatorship and Democracy.* Harmondsworth: Penguin Books.

Mukherji, Partha N. 1966. Gramdan in Village Berain: Sociological Analysis. *Human Organization* 25(1).

———. 1977. Social Movement and Social Change: Towards a Conceptual Clarification and Theoretical Framework. *Sociological Bulletin* 26(1).

———. 1978. Naxalbari Movement and the Peasant Revolt in North Bengal, in M.S.A. Rao (ed.), *Social Movements in India.* Vol. 1. Delhi: Manohar.

———. 1982. Sarvodaya after Gandhi: Contradiction and Change. Paper presented at a seminar on 'Gandhi and Our Times'. New Delhi: Centre for the Study of Developing Societies (Mimeo.).

Mukhia, Harbans 1979. Was there Feudalism in Indian History? Presidential Address, Section II, Indian History Congress, 40th Session. Waltair: Andhra University.

Nagesh, H.V. 1981. Forms of Unfree Labour in Indian Agriculture. *Economic and Political Weekly* (Review of Agriculture) 16(39).

Nair, C. Gopalan. 1921. *The Moplah Rebellion.* Calcutta.

Nandi, R.N. 1975. Origins of Virasaiva Movements. *Indian Historical Review* 2(1).

Narayana Rao, K.V. 1973. *The Emergence of Andhra Pradesh.* Bombay: Popular Prakashan.

Narendra Dev, Acharya. 1946. *Socialism and the National Revolution.* Bombay: Padma Publications.

Nargolker, V. 1975. *J.P.'s Crusade for Revolution.* Delhi: S. Chand & Co.

Natarajan, L. 1953. *Peasant Uprising in India: 1850-1900.* Bombay: People's Publishing House.

Natarajan, S. 1959. *A Century of Social Reforms in India.* Bombay: Asia Publishing House.

Nayyar, Baldev Raj. 1966. *Minority Politics in the Punjab.* Princeton: Princeton University Press.

Oddie, G.A. 1975. Christian Conversion in the Telugu Country, 1860–1900: A Case Study of One Protestant Movement in the Godavery-Krishna Delta. *Indian Economic and Social History Review* 12(1).

———. 1977a. Christian Conversion among Non-Brahmans in Andhra Pradesh with Special Reference to Anglican Missions and the Dornakal Diocese, 1900-1936, in G.A. Oddie (ed.), *Religion in South Asia.* New Delhi: Manohar.

———. (ed.). 1977b. *Religion in South Asia.* New Delhi: Manohar.

Ogle, M.B., L. Schneider and **J.V. Wiley.** 1954. *Power, Order and the Economy.* New York: Harper and Bros.

O'Hanlon, Rosalind. 1985. *Caste Conflict and Ideology.* Cambridge: Cambridge University Press.

Omvedt, Gail. 1975. Rural Origins of Women in Liberation in India. *Social Scientist* 4(4–5).

———. 1976. *Cultural Revolt in a Colonial Society: The Non-Brahmin Movement in Western India, 1873–1930.* Bombay: Scientific Socialist Education Trust.

———. 1981a. Capitalist Agriculture and Rural Classes in India. *Economic and Political Weekly* (Review of Agriculture) 16(52).

———. 1981b. Rasta Ruko, Kulaks and the Left. *Economic and Political Weekly* 16(48).

Oommen, T.K. 1966. Myth and Reality in India's Communitarian Villages. *Journal of Commonwealth Political Studies* 4(2).

———. 1967. Charisma, Social Struture and Social Change. *Comparative Studies in Society and History* 10(1).

———. 1970a. Non-violent Approach to Land Reforms: The Case of an Agrarian Movement in India. *Zeitschrift fur Auslandische Landwirtschaft* 9(10).

———. 1970b. Rural Community Power Structure in India. *Social Forces* 49(2).

———. 1971a. Agrarian Tension in a Kerala District: An Analysis. *Indian Journal of Industrial Relations* 7(2).

———. 1971b. *Student Unions in India: An Introduction.* New Delhi: Vishwa Yuvak Kendra.

———. 1971c. Green Revolution and Agrarian Conflict. *Economic and Political Weekly* 6(26).

———. 1972a. *Charisma, Stability and Change: An Analysis of Bhoodan Gramdan Movement in India.* Delhi: Thompson Press.

———. 1972b. Politicisation of Caste. *Indian Journal of Sociology* 3(1 & 2).

———. 1974. Student Politics in India: The Case of Delhi University. *Asian Survey* 14(9).

———. 1975a. Agrarian Legislations and Movements as Sources of Social Change. *Economic and Political Weekly* 10(40).

———. 1975b. Student Power in India: A Political Analysis. *Political Science Review* 14(1–2).

———. 1975c. Impact of Green Revolution on Weaker Sections, in *Changing Agrarian Relations in India.* Hyderabad: National Institute of Community Development.

———. 1975d. Scheduled Castes: Then and Now, in B.N. Pande (ed.), *The Spirit of India.* Bombay: Asia Publishing House.

———. 1976. Problems of Building Agrarian Organizations in Kerala. *Sociologia Ruralis* 16(2).

———. 1977a. Scheduled Castes and Scheduled Tribes, in S.C. Dube (ed.), *India Since Independence.* Delhi: Vikas

———. 1977b. From Mobilization to Institutionalization: The Life Cycle of an Agrarian Labour Movement in Kerala, in S.C. Malik (ed.), *Dissent, Protest and Reform in Indian Civilization.* Simla: Indian Institute of Advanced Study.

———. 1977c. Sociological Issues in the Analysis of Social Movements in Independent India. *Sociological Bulletin* 27(1).

Oommen, T.K. 1979. Where is the Sociological Framework. *Indian Book Chronicle* 4(18).

————. 1980. Mobilization of Primordial Collectives and Social Development: The Indian Situation. *Kerala Sociologist* 8.

————. 1982. Foreigners, Refugees and Outsiders in the Indian Context. *Sociological Bulletin* 31(1), March.

————. 1983a. Towards Reconciling Traditional and Modern Values: The Indian Experiment, in Joachim Deppert (ed.), *India and the West*. New Delhi: Manohar.

————. 1983b. Religious Pluralism in India: A Sociological Appraisal, in Ram Singh (ed.), *Christian Perspectives on Contemporary Indian Issues*. Madras: Institute for Development Education.

————. 1985. *From Mobilisation to Institutionalisation: The Dynamics of Agrarian Movement in 20th Century Kerala*. Bombay: Popular Prakashan.

————. 1986. Insiders and Outsiders in India: Primordial Collectivism and Cultural Pluralism in Nation Building. *International Sociology* 1(1), March.

Ostergard, G. and **M. Currell.** 1971. *The Gentle Anarchists: A Study of the Leaders of the Sarvodaya Movement for Non-violent Revolution in India*. Oxford: Oxford University Press.

Overstreet, G.D. and **M. Windmiller.** 1959. *Communism in India*. Berkeley: The University of California Press.

Pandey, S.M. 1966. Indian Labour Movement: Growth and Character. *Indian Journal of Labour Economics* 9(1).

————. 1968. Ideological Conflict in the Kanpur Trade Union Movement. *Indian Journal of Industrial Relations* 3(3).

————. 1971. The Emergence of Peasant Movements in India: An Area Study. *Indian Journal of Industrial Relations* 7(1).

Pannickar, K.N. 1979. Peasant Revolts in Malabar in the 19th and 20th Centuries, in A.R. Desai (ed.), *Peasant Struggles in India*. Bombay: Oxford University Press.

Parganika, B.L. 1967. The Satnami Movement. *Journal of Social Research* 10(1).

Parvathamma, C. 1972. *Sociological Essays on Veerasaivism*. Bombay: Popular Prakashan.

————. 1977. Veerasaivism: A Saivite Sectarian Movement of Protest in Karnataka, in S.C. Malik (ed.), *Dissent, Protest and Reform in Indian Civilization*. Simla: Indian Institute of Advanced Study.

Patwardhan, S. 1973. *Change among India's Harijans*. Delhi: Orient Longman.

Pavier, Barry. 1974. The Telengana Armed Struggle. *Economic and Political Weekly* 9 (32, 33 & 34).

Pouchepadass, J. 1974. Local Leaders and Intelligentsia in the Champaran Satyagraha (1917): A Study in Peasant Mobilization. *Contributions to Indian Sociology* 8 (new series).

————. 1980. Peasant Classes in Twentieth Century Agrarian Movement in India, in Eric Hobsbawn et al. (eds.), *Peasants in History*. Delhi: Oxford University Press.

Punekar, S.D. 1970. Trade Union Movement in India, in V.B. Singh (ed.), *Labour Research in India*. Bombay: Popular Prakashan.

Rambhai, Suresh K. 1962. *Vinoba and his Mission*. Kashi: Akhil Sarva Seva Sangh.

————. 1958. *Progress of a Pilgrimage*. Kashi: Akhil Sarva Seva Sangh.

Ramasubban, Radhika. 1978. The Naga Impasse in India. *Eastern Anthropologist* 31(4).

Ranga Rao, K. 1978. Peasant Movement in Telangana, in M.S.A. Rao (ed.), *Social Movements in India*, vol.1 Delhi: Manohar.

Rangasami, Amrita. 1978. Mizoram: Tragedy of Our Own Making. *Economic and Political Weekly* 13(14).

Rao, M.S.A. 1977. Themes in the Ideology of Protest Movements, in S.C. Malik (ed.), *Dissent, Protest and Reform in Indian Civilization. Simla: Indian Institute of Advanced Study.*

————. 1978a. Conceptual Problems in the Study of Social Movements, in M.S.A. Rao (ed.), *Social Movements in India*, vol. 1. Delhi: Manohar.

————. 1978b. *Social Movements and Social Transformation in India: A Study of two Backward Classes Movements.* New Delhi: Macmillan.

Reddy, Muni, 1947. *The Student Movement in India.* Lucknow: KSR Acharya.

Revri, Chamanlal. 1972. *The Indian Trade Union Movement.* New Delhi: Orient Longman.

Rex, John. 1974. *Sociology and Demystification of the Modern World.* London: Routledge and Kegan Paul.

Rizvi, S.A.A. 1965. *Muslim Revivalist Movements in Northern India in the 16th and 17th Centuries.* Agra: Agra University.

————. 1977. Islamic Proselytisation (Seventh to Sixteenth Centuries), in G.A. Oddie (ed.), *Religion in South Asia.* Delhi: Manohar.

Ross, A.D. 1969. *Student Unrest in India: A Comparative Approach.* Montreal: McGill Queens University Press.

Rowe, William L. 1968. The New Chauhans: A Caste Mobility Movement in North India, in James Silverberg (ed.), *Social Mobility in the Caste System in India: An Interdisciplinary Symposium.* The Hague: Mouton.

Roy, Ajit. 1967. Some Aspects of the National Question in India. *Marxist Review,* October.

Roy, Ashish K. 1975. *The Spring Thunder and After.* Calcutta: Minerva Associates.

————. 1977. Indian Communist Movement and the Preasantry: An Overview. *China Report* 13(6).

Roy, Amarendra Nath. 1967. *Students Fight for Freedom.* Calcutta: Ananda Bazar Patrika.

Roy Burman, B.K. 1971. National Movements among Tribes. *Secular Democracy* 4 (3 & 4).

————. 1979. Challenges and Responses in Tribal India, in M.S.A. Rao (ed.), *Social Movements in India,* vol. 2. Delhi: Manohar.

Rudolph, L.I. and **S.H. Rudolph.** 1960. The Political Role of India's Caste Association. *Pacific Affairs* 35(1)

Rudra, Ashok. 1981. Against Feudalism. *Economic and Political Weekly* 16(52).

Rush, Gary R. and **Serge Denisoff.** 1971. *Social and Political Movements.* New York: Meredith Corporation.

Saha, C.P.1978. *History of the Working Class Movement in Bengal.* New Delhi: People's Publishing House.

Sanjeevi, N. 1977. Literary and Cultural background of DK/DMK, in S.C. Malik (ed.), *Dissent, Protest and Reform in Indian Civilization.* Simla: Indian Institute of Advanced Study.

Saraswati, Baidyanath. 1977. Notes on Kabir: A Non-literate Intellectual, in S.C. Malik (ed.), *Dissent, Protest and Reform in Indian Civilization.* Simla: Indian Institute of Advanced Study.

Sarkar, Krishnakant. 1979. Kakdwip Tebhaga Movement, in A.R. Desai (ed.), *Peasant Struggles in India.* Bombay: Oxford University Press.

Sarkar, Sumit. 1973. *The Swadeshi Movement in Bengal, 1903–1908.* New Delhi: People's Publishing House.

Seal, Anil. 1968. *The Emergence of Indian Nationalism: Competition and Collaboration in the Later 19th Century.* Cambridge: Cambridge University Press.

Sekhar, M.C. 1968. *Social Change in India: First Decade of Planning.* Poona: Deccan College Postgraduate and Research Institute.

Selznick, Philip. 1951. Institutional Vulnerability in Mass Society. *American Journal of Sociology* LVI (2).

Sen, Jyoti. 1972. The Jharkhand Movement, in K.S. Singh (ed.), *Tribal Situation in India.* Simla: Indian Institute of Advanced Study.

Sen, Sunil. 1972. Agrarian Struggle in Bengal, 1946–47. New Delhi: People's Publishing House.

Seshadri, K. 1970. The Telugu Agitation and the Politics of Andhra Pradesh. *Indian Journal of Political Science* 31(1).

Shah, Ghanshyam. 1974. Traditional Society and Political Mobilization: The Experience of Bardoli Satyagraha (1920–28). *Contributions to Indian Sociology* 8 (new series).

———. 1977a. *Caste Association and Political Process.* Bombay: Popular Prakashan.

———. 1977b. *Protest Movements in Two Indian States.* Delhi: Ajanta Publications.

———. 1980. Anti-Untouchability Movements. Paper presented at the seminar on Removal of Untouchability. Ahmedabad, October.

Sharma, G.K. 1971. *Labour Movement in India: Its Past and Present.* New Delhi: Sterling.

Sharma, K.L. 1976. Jharkhand Movement in Bihar. *Economic and Political Weekly* 11(1–2).

Shils, Edward. 1957. Primordial, Personal, Sacred and Civil Ties. *British Journal of Sociology* 8.

Siddiqui, M.H. 1978. *Agrarian Unrest in North India.* Delhi: Vikas.

Sills, David. 1957. *The Volunteers.* Illinois: The Free Press.

Silverberg, James (ed.). 1968. *Social Mobility in the Caste System in India: An Interdisciplinary Symposium.* The Hague: Mouton Publishers.

Singh, Khushwant. 1966. *History of the Sikhs,* vol. 2. Princeton: Princeton University Press.

Singh, K.S. 1966. *Dust Storm and Changing Mist: Story of Birsa Munda and his Movement in Chhottanagpur.* Calcutta: Firma K.L. Mukhopadhyay.

———. 1977. From Ethnicity to Regionalism: A Study of Tribal Politics and Movements in Chotanagpur from 1900 to 1975, in S.C. Malik (ed.), *Dissent, Protest and Reform in Indian Civilization.* Simla: Indian Institute of Advanced Study.

Singh, Rajendra. 1974. Agrarian Social Structure and Peasant Unrest: A study of Land Grab Movement in District Basti, East UP. *Sociological Bulletin* 23(1).

———. 1978. Peasant Movements in Uttar Pradesh, in M.S.A. Rao (ed.), *Social Movements in India,* vol. 1. New Delhi: Manohar.

Singh, Y. 1973. *Modernization of Indian Tradition.* Delhi: Thompson Press.

Sinha, Surajit. 1959. Bhumji—Kshatriya Social Movement in South Manbhum. *Bulletin of the Department of Anthropology* 8(2).

———. 1968. Study in Tribal Solidarity Movements—General Propositions, in S. Sinha (ed.), *Research Programme in Cultural Anthropology and Related Disciplines.* Calcutta: Anthropological Survey of India.

———. 1972. Tribal Solidarity Movements in India: A Review, in K.S. Singh (ed.), *Tribal Situation in India.* Simla: Indian Institute of Advanced Study.

Smelser, N.J. 1962. *The Theory of Collective Behaviour.* London: Routledge and Kegan Paul.

Spencer, Lavan. 1974. *The Ahmadiya Movement.* Delhi: Manohar.

Srinivas, M.N. 1962. *Caste in Modern India and Other Essays.* London: Asia Publishing House.

Stark, W. 1963. *Fundamental Forms of Social Thought.* New York: Fordham University Press.

Stokes, Eric. 1970. Traditional Resistance Movement and Afro-Asian Nationalism: The Context of the 1857 Mutiny Rebellion in India. *Past and Present* 48.

Strauss, A.L. 1959. *Mirrors and Masks.* Glencoe, Illinois: The Free Press.

Suntharalingam, R. 1974. *Politics and Nationalist Awakening in South India 1852–1891.* Tuscon: Arizona State University Press.

Suri, Pushpa. 1977. Arya Samaj Movement with special Reference to Punjab, in S.C. Malik (ed.), *Dissent, Protest and Reform in India Civilization.* Simla: Indian Institute of Advanced Study.

Tara Chand. 1983. *History of Freedom Movement in India,* vols. 3 & 4. New Delhi: Publications Division.

Tennyson, Hallam. 1955. *Saint on March.* London: Victor Gollancz.

Thapar, Romila. 1977. Ethics, Religion and Social Protest in the First Millennium B.C. in Northern India, in S.C. Malik (ed.), *Dissent, Protest and Reform in Indian Civilization.* Simla: Indian Institute of Advanced Study.

Thorner, Alice. 1982. Semi-feudalism or Capitalism: Contemporary Debate on Classes and Modes of Production in India. *Economic and Political Weekly* 17 (49, 50, 51).

Tottenham, G.F.K. 1922. *The Mappilla Rebellion, 1921–22.* Madras: Government Press.

Toynbee, Arnold and **Daiseku Ikeda.** 1976. *Choose Life: A Dialogue* (R.L. Gage, ed.). London: Oxford University Press.

Troise, Joseph. 1979. Social Movements among the Santals, in M.S.A. Rao (ed.), *Social Movements in India,* vol. 2. Delhi: Manohar.

Vashishta, V.K. 1977. Arya Samaj Movement in Rajasthan during the 19th Century, in S.C. Malik (ed.), *Dissent, Protest and Reform in Indian Civilization.* Simla: Indian Institute of Advanced Study.

Venkatarangaiya, H. (ed.) 1965. *Freedom Struggle in Andhra Pradesh.* Hyderabad: Government of Andhra Pradesh.

Venugopal, C.N. 1977. Factor of Anti-Pollution in the Ideology of Lingayat Movement. *Sociological Bulletin* 26(2).

Vishwa Yuvak Kendra. 1973. *Dynamics of Student Agitation.* Bombay: Somaiya.

Weiner, Myron. 1963. *Politics of Scarcity: Public Pressure and Political Response in India.* Bombay: Asia.

Wilkinson, Paul. 1971. *Social Movement.* London: Macmillan.

Wilkinson, T.S. and **M.M. Thomas** (eds.). 1972. *Ambedkar and the Neo-Buddhist Movement.* Madras: The Christian Literature Society

Wolf, Eric. 1971. Peasant Wars of the Twentieth Century. London: Faber and Faber.

Wood, Conrad. 1974. Historical Background of the Moplah Rebellion. *Social Scientist 3(1).*

————. 1976a. The Moplah Rebellions between 1800–02 and 1921–22. *Indian Economic and Social History Review* 13(1).

————. 1976b. The First Moplah Rebellion Against British Rule in Malabar. *Modern Asian Studies* 10(4).

Wood, J.R. 1975. Extra Parlimentary Opposition in India: An Analysis of Populist Movement in Gujarat and Bihar. *Pacific Affairs* 48 (3).

Worsley, Peter. 1964. *The Third World.* London: Weidenfeld and Nicholson.

Yang, Anand A. 1976. Agrarian Reform and Peasant Dissidence: The Continuing Crisis in India. *Journal of Peasant Studies* 5(3).

Yinger, Miltion (ed.). 1957. *Religion, Society and the Individual.* New York: Macmillan.

Zelliott, E. 1970. Mahar and Non-Brahmin Movements in Maharashtra. *Indian Economic and Social History Review* 7(3).

————. 1977. The Psychological Dimension of the Buddhist Movement in India, in G.A. Oddie (ed.), *Religion in South Asia.* Delhi: Manohar.

Index